QUALITY AND CONTROL

Quality and Control

AN ACCOUNTING PERSPECTIVE

Ahmed Riahi-Belkaoui

Q

QUORUM BOOKS
Westport, Connecticut • London

Library of Congress Cataloging-in-Publication Data

Riahi-Belkaoui, Ahmed
    Quality and control : an accounting perspective / Ahmed Riahi-Belkaoui.
      p.   cm.
    Includes index.
    ISBN 0–89930–767–1 (alk. paper)
    1. Quality control–Costs–Accounting. 2. Quality of products–Cost
effectiveness.   I. Title.
    HF5686.C8R457   1993
    657'.42–dc20   92–34942

British Library Cataloguing in Publication Data is available.

Library of Congress Catalog Card Number: 92–34942
ISBN: 0–89930–767–1

First published in 1993

Quorum Books, 88 Post Road West, Westport, CT 06881
An imprint of Greenwood Publishing Group, Inc.

Printed in the United States of America

The paper used in this book complies with the
Permanent Paper Standard issued by the National
Information Standards Organization (Z39.48-1984).

10 9 8 7 6 5 4 3 2 1

To the Riahi-Belkaouis

CONTENTS

EXHIBITS

PREFACE

Quality is becoming one of the most important managerial objectives. It is vital for survival in the fierce competitive environment of the global economy. It is demanded by consumers and by society as a legitimate ground for a viable relationship. Firms have begun to respond to the new environment and put a greater focus on planning and controlling for quality. This book is aimed at describing these processes of planning and controlling for quality and providing a guide for implementation. In six chapters, quality is first explained, then shown to be implementable by a process of accounting and control: accounting for quality costs and control of direct costs, overhead costs, and mix and yield factors. Chapters 4, 5, and 6 include appendixes representing interesting research articles that complement the content of the chapters.

The book should be of interest to a variety of reader groups, including researchers in the management accounting area, accounting practitioners interested in the design of a quality control system, executives involved in the management of quality, and accounting students from typical undergraduate or graduate courses in management accounting.

Many people helped in the development of this book. Eric Valentine and Katie Chase of Greenwood Press are true professionals. They have my best gratitude. I wish also to thank my research assistants at the University of Illinois at Chicago—Catherine Sierra and Latonja L. Brown—for their cheerful and intelligent assistance. Finally to Hédi and Janice, thanks for everything.

1

THE QUALITY CONCEPT

INTRODUCTION

Managers all over the world know that they have to improve the quality of their product because consumers demand it. Firms are responding to these consumer demands by implementing quality programs in their companies. This response is also triggered by the urgent need to be competitive not only on the price dimension but also on the quality dimension. It is now a reality that quality and profitability are positively correlated. A quality product generates better demand and yields better profitability. Given this concern with quality, this chapter explicates the meaning of quality, the nature of quality planning, control and reporting, the performance of U.S. firms in the quality dimension, and the relationship between cost and quality.

MEANING OF QUALITY

Approaches to the Definition of Quality

Quality can be easily defined as meeting the customer requirements that would include availability, delivery, reliability, maintainability, and cost effectiveness among other features.[1] Customer satisfaction is the ultimate goal of quality control. It can be expressed as the following ratio:[2]

$$\text{Customer satisfaction} = \frac{\text{Perceived Quality}}{\text{Needs, Wants, and Expectations}}$$

Customer satisfaction depends therefore on the perceived quality of the products, and on the existence of a corporate-wide quality control. Quality can be product-based with a focus on increased quantities of an element or attribute of the product, user-based with a focus on customer preferences, operations-based with a focus on conformance to requirements, or value-based with a focus on pricing.[3] One fallacy is that productivity and quality are in fundamental conflict: "Higher quality could only be achieved through more inspection, more processing, or tighter tolerances—all of which lowered productivity."[4]

There is, however, multiple evidence in both U.S. and Japanese manufacturing concerns of situations where high-performance organizations are capable of producing high quality and high productivity in tandem, with one reinforcing the other.[5]

The definitions of quality differ depending on the discipline interested in the concept and in the ultimate beneficiary. Five approaches to defining quality have been identified: transcendent, product-based, user-based, manufacturing-based, and value-based. Each of these approaches is explicated here:[6]

1. According to the transcendent view, quality is equivalent to "innate excellence."[7] It can't be defined with precision but can be recognized with experience and through some of its appealing characteristics.

2. According to the product-based approach, quality is associated with the presence of some ingredient or attribute possessed by the product.[8] Quality can be objectively assessed by the presence or absence of these measurable attributes. The approach is not without limitations:

> A one-to-one correspondence between product attributes and quality does not always exist. Sometimes high-quality products are simply different; instead of possessing more of a particular attribute, they are based on entirely different concepts. When quality is a matter of aesthetics, the product-based approach is also lacking, for it fails to accommodate differences in taste.[9]

3. According to the user-based approach, quality is tied to customer satisfaction. This approach is evident in (a) the marketing notion of "ideal points": price combinations of product attributes that generate the greatest satisfaction to a given consumer;[10] (b) the economic notion of quality differences reflected in shifts in a product's demand curve;[11] and (c) in the operational management concept of "fitness for use."[12]

4. According to the manufacturing-based approach, quality is tied to meeting engineering and manufacturing requirements and control. A "conformance to requirements" leads to a quality product.[13]

5. According to the value-based approach, quality is tied to performance at an acceptable price and conformance at an acceptable cost. One limitation is stated as follows: "Despite its obvious importance, this approach is difficult to apply in practice. It blends two related but distinct concepts: excellence and worth. The result is a hybrid—'affordable excellence' that lacks well-defined limits and is often highly subjective."[14]

Experts and Quality

Four experts are generally associated with the concept of quality: W. Edwards Deming, Joseph M. Juran, Genichi Taguchi, and Philip B. Crosby.

W. Edwards Deming is considered to be the man who discovered quality, taught it to the Japanese, then brought it to America.[15] Six principles define his philosophy:

1. Quality is defined by the customer.
2. Understanding and reducing variation in every process is a must.
3. All significant, long-lasting quality improvements must emanate from top management's commitment to improvement, as well as its understanding of the means by which systematic change is to be achieved.
4. Change and improvement must be continuous and all-encompassing. It must involve every member in an organization, including outside suppliers.
5. The ongoing education and training of all the employees in a company is a prerequisite for achieving the sort of analysis that is needed for constant improvement.
6. Performance ratings that seek to measure the contributions of individual employees are usually destructive.

He proposed 14 steps that management should follow to direct the company toward the quality goal:[16]

1. Continually improve products and services in order to further the firm's competitive position.
2. Adopt the new philosophy; don't accept delays and mistakes.
3. Don't rely on mass inspection to detect defects; use statistical controls to assure that quality is built into the product.
4. Discontinue the practice of selecting suppliers based on price; reduce the supply base and establish long-term, trusting, single-source partnerships where both buyer and seller can pursue quality improvements.
5. Find problems—whether caused by faulty systems or by production workers—and correct them.
6. Use modern methods of on-the-job training.
7. Improve and modernize methods of supervision.
8. Drive out fear, so that everyone can work productively for the firm.
9. Open up communications between departments.
10. Stop using numerical goals, posters, and slogans as a way to motivate workers without giving them the methods to achieve these goals.
11. Don't depend on work standards that assign numerical goals.
12. Remove barriers that deprive employees of their pride of workmanship.
13. Establish a dynamic program of education and training.

14. Create an executive management structure that will emphasize the above 13 points each day.

Joseph M. Juran was also instrumental in helping the Japanese with their drive for quality. He, however, commented:

> A segment of the Western press has come up with the conclusion that the Japanese miracle was not Japanese at all. Instead it was due to the Americans, Deming and Juran, who lectured to the Japanese soon after World War II. Deming will have to speak for himself. As for Juran, I am agreeably flattered but I regard the conclusion as ludicrous. I did indeed lecture in Japan as reported and I did bring something new to them—a structural approach to quality. I also did the same thing for a great many other countries, yet none of these attained the results achieved by the Japanese. So who performed the miracle?[17]

Juran devised a "quality trilogy" based on planning, control, and improvement. The planning phase involves the following five steps:

1. A decision of who the customers are.
2. The establishment of customers' needs.
3. The design of product features that meet customer desires.
4. The design of the processes that will manufacture these features.
5. The operationalization of the product and process designs.[18]

The control phase is a typical feedback loop involving an evaluation of the operational results, a comparison of the actual results with budgeted results, and taking action to correct the variance.

The improvement phase involves reaching higher quality levels than those already achieved. It is a continuation of efforts towards higher and better goals.

Genichi Taguchi is a Japanese quality engineer who proposed the idea of a "loss formation" that measures the losses a product imposes in society from the time it is shipped. He defines quality as the "loss a product causes to society after being shipped, other than any losses caused by its intrinsic functions."[19] These losses include warranty costs, dissatisfied customers, and general discontent. The quality of a product is defined by a target or ideal state that can satisfy the customer and by tolerances around the stated value. Quality is therefore either conformance to specifications or conformance with the degree of variability around the ideal state. Variables that lead the product to deviate from the target value are either controllable variables that can be adjusted easily or uncontrollable variables (noise factors) that are difficult and expensive to regulate. The noise factors can be described as follows:

> Noise factors can be divided into three types: outer noise, inner noise, and between product noise. Outer noise consists of variables external to the product's design,

components, and manufacturing processes, which provoke deterioration in a quality characteristic's performance when the product is used by a consumer. Inner noise is brought about by the decay of a product's parts and materials, only harder to pinpoint because it shows up as variation among product units or processes where uniformity is supposed to prevail.[20]

Dimensions of Quality

David Garvin identifies eight dimensions or categories of quality that can be identified as a framework for analysis: performance, features, reliability, conformance, durability, serviceability, aesthetics, and perceived quality.[21]

1. *Performance* refers to the operating characteristic of a product. It is a dimension of quality when the preferences of customers focus on it.
2. *Features* refers to the secondary characteristics that supplement the product's basic functioning.[22] They are also dependent on the customer's preferences to quality as quality dimensions.
3. *Reliability* refers to the probability of a product's failing to perform within a specified period of time.
4. *Conformance* refers to the degree to which a product's operating characteristics meet preestablished standards.[23]
5. *Durability* refers to the amount of use a customer gets from using the product before it deteriorates.[24]
6. *Serviceability* refers to the elapsed time before a product is repaired and service is restored.[25]
7. *Aesthetics* refers to how a product looks, feels, sounds, or smells.[26]
8. *Perceived quality* refers to how customers perceive the product on the basis of incomplete information available to them.

A corporation can elect to meet all or none of these dimensions of quality. It is a matter of finding their own quality niche.

WORKING TOWARD QUALITY

Quality Policy

The efficient implementation of quality in a firm starts logically by the official stating of a quality policy that will answer fundamental questions about the firm's commitment to questions. Examples of such questions include:

1. Should our product be the best in the industry, or should it merely be competitive? Where, in fact, do we want it to be? (Each of these positions demands a certain price that individual companies must recognize.)

2. Are quality practices and techniques to extend to design and service, or do we want to confine quality assurance to manufacturing?

3. To which management level should quality assurance report?

4. What level of costs are acceptable in achieving the quality program?

5. How will customer quality needs be satisfied in after-sales service? How flexible should the company be in setting customer claims for substandard quality?

6. What degree of control should be exercised over vendors?[27]

An example of a quality policy for a capital goods manufacturer is shown in Exhibit 1.1. It clearly and simply declares the firm's commitment to the delivery of a quality product that will satisfy the customers. Thereby the quality program can be easily evaluated by customer surveys and high level of customer satisfaction.

Quality Plan

The quality policy states the commitment to quality. The quality plan operationalizes the commitment by a statement of the specific quantifiable goals needed to achieve the quality policy. The plan states how the quality policy is to be achieved, the responsibility for every action, and the time frame required. The end product is a quantitative statement of the standards of performance required for all departments toward the achievement of their quality objectives. Exhibit 1.2 shows a page from the quality plan of a capital-goods manufacturer.

Quality Department

For quality to become part of the corporate culture, a quality department may have to be created. Its responsibility may be twofold: "First, it should audit the quality activities of the other departments and report upon them to the department managers and to general management. Second, it has direct responsibilities of its own."[28]

The first responsibility includes an audit and reporting of the quality performance of other departments in a way to monitor the quality problem and motivate the department to act in a manner compatible with a total quality philosophy. This first role of the quality department should cover all the departments of a firm, from those directly associated in the manufacturing process to all the others associated either in forwarding essential services to the manufacturing function or associated with the distribution and sale of the final product. The final goal is not just a product that conforms to the technical requirements, but also a customer satisfied with the product.

The second responsibility involves the continuous inspection and testing of the activities of the firm to insure compliance with the quality requirements set for each department, quality planning, defect-prevention activities (quality engineering), and quality training.[29]

Exhibit 1.1
Quality Policy Statement

QUALITY GOODS, INC.

QUALITY POLICY

Policy statement

1. It is the policy of Quality Goods, Inc. to deliver products whose performance quality is judged by our customers to be among the leaders in the industry.

2. Our goal is to provide the proper environment in which product quality meets or exceeds contractual obligations with our customers, and which gives the necessary service level to customers to fulfill the intended function of our products for a period of time to satisfy customer requirements. Customer claims for defective workmanship will be evaluated and settled within the time limits expressed in individual contracts.

3. It will be the responsibility of company general managers, in cooperation with their respective quality assurance managers, to establish an effective quality function which achieves the company's quality program.

4. To assure effectiveness of the quality program in the most objective manner possible, each quality assurance manager will report directly to the general manager of the operating unit and be placed at the same organizational level of manufacturing, engineering, materials and marketing.

5. Final product acceptance decisions, based on company quality requirements and specifications, are the sole responsibility of each unit's general manager.

6. Quality programs are intended for application to all functional areas (marketing, engineering, materials, and manufacturing) involved with shipping and servicing specified quality products for customers.

7. Quality programs will be achieved within specified quality cost budgets established by unit general managers which have been approved by the company president.

Reference Procedures

QA 202	Quality Board Responsibilities
QA 203	The Company Quality Plan
QA 300	Cost of Quality Reporting
QA 315	Vendor Quality
QA 402	Design Quality and Reliability
QA 403	Pre-Production Quality
QA 500	Product and Process Quality
QA 600	Quality Information Systems
QA 703	Field Service Quality
QA 805	Quality Measurement Systems
QA 830	Quality Surveys
QA 900	Quality Training

Source: Martin Smith, "Management Communication," in L. Walsh, R. Wurster, and R. J. Kimber, eds., *Quality Management Handbook* (New York: Marcel Dekker, 1986), p. 57. Reprinted courtesy of Marcel Dekker, Inc.

Exhibit 1.2
Portion of a Quality Plan

QUALITY GOODS, INC.

QUALITY PLAN

1983-1985

Section #6: Engineering Quality Systems

Problem/Opportunity	Plan of Action	Person(s) Assigned	. Time Frame
There is no pre-produc-tion quality planning resulting in excess scrap/rework and warranty problems.	Develop a procedure which includes design review, reliability predic-tions, life-cycle testing, etc.	Director of Engineering, Manager of Quality Engineering	10/83
Quality characteristics are not specified on engineering drawings which creates confusion in manufacturing as to which characteristics are most important.	Identify quality characteristics by critical - major - minor categories on engineering drawings.	Manager Design Engineering, Quality Manufacturing	1/84
There are constant errors made in manu-facturing due to specification of wrong parts.	Define bill-of-materials system.	Director of Engineering, Manager Manu-facturing Engineering, Manager Quality	3/84

Source: Martin Smith, "Management Communication" in L. Walsh, R. Wurster, and R. J. Kimber, eds., *Quality Management Handbook* (New York: Marcel Dekker, 1986), p. 59. Reprinted courtesy of Marcel Dekker, Inc.

Organizations need to implement a quality function as an inseparable part of every employee's performance and responsibility.[30] A quality manager and staff need to be concerned with the following:

• encouraging and facilitating quality improvement;
• monitoring and evaluating the process of quality improvement;
• promoting the "partnership" in quality, in relations with customer and suppliers;
• planning, managing, auditing, and reviewing quality systems;
• planning and providing quality training and counseling or consultancy;
• giving advice to management in the establishment of quality systems and process control, relevant statutory/legislative requirements with respect to quality, quality improvement programming necessary, and inclusion of quality elements in all job instructions and procedures.[31]

To be effective, the quality department should be clearly independent of the manufacturing, engineering, and distribution departments and should be a separate department reporting either to the controller's department or directly to the chief executive officer. The independence factor is extremely important for the efficient conduct of the quality management. As stated by J. M. Groocock,

the need for the quality department to be independent of the manufacturing and engineering departments is not a reflection of the importance of the quality department. The quality responsibilities of the company as a whole cannot be over-emphasized, but the quality department as such bears only a part of those responsibilities. It can be argued that the quality department is not as important as the manufacturing department or the engineering department, so why should it report at the same level? Equal claims for importance can be made for the purchasing section or production control and these are part of manufacturing. The quality department has to be independent in order to do its job, and views about its importance compared to other groups within the company are largely irrelevant to this point.[32]

Quality Assurance

Quality assurance precedes quality control. Quality assurance refers to the process of ensuring the correctness of the final product or service. It comprises both quality control engineering and quality control inspection functions. Quality control includes all the physical actions that are taken to create assurance. Quality assurance is needed to avoid problems of lack of quality, which arises in any one of the following circumstances:

1. A product may, on receipt, be defective, therefore requiring repair or replacement or else can only be used less efficiently (i.e. its performance is downgraded).
2. A product may be delivered late because the supplier had to carry out unanticipated repair and rework.

3. A product may fail in service because its inadequateness was not apparent when originally supplied.[33]

Quality assurance requires the development of quality system standards. Various quality standards systems define matters such as "responsibilities, which activities need to be controlled, when written procedures or instructions are required, the need for calibration of inspection equipment, the need for systematic reporting and analysis of defects and non-conformances and the need for systematic quality audits."[34] The engineering standards include areas of materials, construction, and inspection.

To ensure the desired quality standards, a quality assurance system is needed, which could include the following ten subsystems:

1. Management of the quality system
2. Product quality and reliability development
3. Product and process quality planning
4. Supplier quality assurance
5. Product and process quality evaluation and control
6. Special quality studies
7. Quality information feedback
8. Quality measurement equipment
9. Quality training and manpower development
10. Field quality evaluation and control[35]

Each of the subsystems can be rated. The sum of all the ratings can give a total quality rating.[36]

Quality Cost Reporting

Quality cost reporting is an essential part of management control. Its purposes are

1. to enable the unit's managers to know the size of their quality-cost problem so that they can apply appropriate resources to its solutions;
2. to show broadly where the problem is, e.g. inspection or in warranty, so that unit management can concentrate effort effectively;
3. to enable unit management to set targets for quality-cost reductions and to plan actions to meet the targets;
4. to enable progress toward meeting the targets to be measured;
5. to enable company management to motivate unit management to set ambitious targets and to provide help to unit management for their achievement.[37]

Exhibit 1.3
Quality Cost Report

QUALITY COST REPORT
FOR THE MONTH ENDING _____

(In Thousands of U.S. Dollars)

DESCRIPTION	CURRENT MONTH			YEAR TO DATE		
	QUALITY COSTS	AS A PERCENT OF		QUALITY COSTS	AS A PERCENT OF	
		SALES	OTHER		SALES	OTHER
1 PREVENTION COSTS						
1.1 Product Design						
1.2 Purchasing						
1.3 Quality Planning						
1.4 Quality Administration						
1.5 Quality Training						
1.6 Quality Audits						
TOTAL PREVENTION COSTS						
PREVENTION TARGETS						
2 APPRAISAL COSTS						
2.1 Product Qualification Tests						
2.2 Supplier Product Inspection and Test						
2.3 In Process and Final Inspection and Test						
2.4 Maintenance and Calibration						
TOTAL APPRAISAL COSTS						
APPRAISAL TARGETS						
3 FAILURE COSTS						
3.1 Design Failure Costs						
3.2 Supplier Product Rejects						
3.3 Material Review and Corrective Action						
3.4 Rework						
3.5 Scrap						
3.6 External Failure Costs						
TOTAL FAILURE COSTS						
FAILURE TARGETS						
TOTAL QUALITY COSTS						
TOTAL QUALITY TARGETS						

MEMO DATA	CURRENT MONTH		YEAR TO DATE		FULL YEAR	
	BUDGET	ACTUAL	BUDGET	ACTUAL	BUDGET	ACTUAL
Net Sales						
Other Base (Specify)						

Source: L. Walsh, R. Wurster, and R. J. Kimber, eds., *Quality Management Handbook* (New York: Marcel Dekker, 1986), p. 104. Reprinted courtesy of Marcel Dekker, Inc.

The reporting could consist of reporting the variances between the budgeted quality costs and the actual quality costs if the firm had earlier budgeted for the quality problem; reporting only the actual quality costs if no budgeting for quality existed; reporting either the variance or the actual quality costs as a ratio to some financial measure of a segment's level of activity or performance. Examples of activity or performance levels include profit, sales, size, value added, and so on. Sales is generally favored as a means of a segment's level of activity.[38] An example of a quality cost report is shown in Exhibit 1.3.

QUALITY IN THE UNITED STATES

Comparison with the Japanese

Quality efforts in the United States are now part of the manufacturing scene. They can work to generate healthier profits; but in some cases the story is different. Witness the following quotation:

> In most companies it doesn't work that way. There are quality efforts but something is missing. Pronouncements from the executive suite fall flat. Skeptical workers pay little heed. Managers resist to be caught up in deadlines and turf battles. Or a program does catch on—then dies in a few years.[39]

One way of implementing quality schemes is through employee empowerment. "This involves cutting out layers of management and pushing decision making down in the ranks. The aim is to improve morale and productivity by making workers' jobs more meaningful while eliminating costly supervisors and inspection staff."[40]

The concern with quality in the United States is best evident by the Malcolm Baldrige National Quality Award, which requires firms to increase employee involvement, compare themselves to leaders, and shorten the time it takes to design and introduce products. The trophy is considered very prestigious and companies strive to achieve the criteria set by the Baldrige examiners. It is intended to compete with Japan's Deming prize, named after U.S. quality expert W. Edwards Deming. What the Baldrige examiners are looking for is best exemplified by the following six statements:

1. Top executives incorporate quality valuation in day-to-day management.

2. Its products are as good as or better than those of its competitors.

3. It is working with suppliers to improve the quality of their products or services.

4. Customers' needs and wants are being met—and customer satisfaction ratings are as good or better than competitors'.

5. The company trains workers in quality techniques and has systems in place to ensure that products are high quality.

6. The quality system yields concrete results, such as gains in market share and reduction in product-cycle time.[41]

It is very easy to claim that the success of Japanese companies is based on government help, low wages, and special cultural advantages, but that is far from the truth. Their successes are due to the realization that mass-production techniques are inefficient. The Japanese have shifted from the mass-production techniques to a system of "recrafting," whereby a worker's knowledge, skill, and experience far outweigh his or her performance in structured tasks and obedience, and an "Ohio" system that allows the formation of cooperative networks among manufacturers, suppliers, and customers. This is especially crucial at a time when a GM plant in the United States takes 31 hours to build a car with a defect rate of 130 per hundred cars and when a Toyota plant in Japan takes 16 hours to build a car with an average of 45 defects per hundred.

In a speech given on April 27, 1990, John A. Saxton, vice-president, Noxell (Procter & Gamble), highlighted the following differences between the Japanese companies and the typical U.S. companies:[42]

Best Japanese Companies	*Typical U.S. Companies*
Emphasis on customer satisfaction	Emphasis on profit
Supply demand/Market-in	Create demand/Product-out
Management by means/systems	Management by objectives
Total approach	Sequestered/fragmented approach
Patience	Impatience
Incremental improvements	Breakthrough improvements
Teams	Individuals
Teaching by leaders	Teaching by staff/consultants
Investment in continuous education	Expenditures in sporadic training
Technical background possessed by top management	Finance or marketing background possessed by top management
Contact between top management and plant/customers	Minimum contact between top management and plant/customers
Homogeneity characterized by conformity	Diversity characterized by individuality
Problems are sought	Problems are sign of weakness
Communication by visual techniques	Communication by verbal techniques
Sequential phases of corporate direction	Independent corporate programs not sustained
Standardization is essential	Standardization is constraining
Focus is clear to everyone	Everything is important
Improvement is everyone's responsibility	Others are responsible for improvement
Top people working in TQ	TQ is handled by staff

Methodical/relentless	Hit and run
Make commitments	Make promises
Engineers/development in plants	Engineers/development away from plants
Management span of support	Management span of control
Continuity	Frequent assignment changes
Crisis mentality	Complacency

Comparisons of quality differences between U.S. and Japanese companies abound. The general result is a more enlightened concern with quality in the Japanese companies. For example, a study by D. Gavin of eleven U.S. and seven Japanese companies that assemble air-conditioning units reported the following median results on the quality of four variables:

1. The percentage of incoming parts and materials failing to meet specifications was 3.30 percent for the U.S. and 0.15 percent for the Japanese firms.
2. The coil leaks per 100 units in the fabrication department were 4.4 percent for the U.S. companies and 0.1 percent for the Japanese firms.
3. The defects per 100 units in the assembly line were 63.5 percent for the U.S. and 0.9 percent for the Japanese firms.
4. The service-call rate per 100 units under first-year warranty coverage was 10.5 percent for the U.S. and 0.6 percent for Japanese firms.[43]

Performance of U.S. Firms

Each year for the past nine years, *Fortune* magazine has surveyed some 8,000 senior executives, outside directors, and financial analysts with respect to over 300 companies in more than 30 industry groups. Companies include those with sales of at least $500 million in their particular industry group. Those participating in the survey are asked to rank each company, within the industry they are familiar with, on eight key attributes utilizing a scale of 0 (poor) to 10 (excellent). *Fortune* then publishes individual rankings of companies from averages obtained.

The eight key attributes utilized in the survey consist of quality of management; quality of products/services offered; innovativeness; value as a long-term investment; soundness of financial position; ability to attract, develop, and keep talented people; responsibility to the community and environment; and wise use of corporate assets. The attributes represent a multidimensional model of organizational effectiveness, in that multiple goals are assessed. They also reflect a multiple constituency view of the firm as having many stakeholders. These include not only investors interested in investment value, financial position, and use of assets, but also customers interested in quality, employees interested in meaningful employment, and the global community with their concerns over the environment.

With regard to the individual importance of each of the above attributes, historically "80 percent of the respondents to Fortune's survey pick quality of management as paramount." The second most important criterion appears to be quality of products or services. Over the past years, a marked increase in the number of respondents citing responsibility to the community and environment as paramount to a corporate reputation has been observed. Interestingly, *Fortune* · also notes that spectacular profits do not necessarily guarantee spectacular reputation rankings.

Exhibit 1.4 contains the average rankings by industry for the period 1987–91 afforded companies on the variable of quality of management. In four out of the past five years Merck (Pharmaceuticals) has appeared in the *Fortune* list of overall best performers with regard to quality of management. Merck has also dominated its own industry group in each of the last five years. Other firms that also appeared in the overall best and ranked first in their respective industry groups for the period 1987–91 included Liz Claiborne (Apparel), Rubbermaid (Rubber Products), 3M (Scientific and Photographic Equipment), and J. P. Morgan (Commercial Banking). While the *Fortune* survey does not rank the following companies in the overall best category for quality of management, each has garnered that honor within their own industry group for the past five years: Dow Chemical (Chemicals), Boeing (Aerospace), Procter and Gamble (Soaps and Cosmetics), Northwestern Life (Life Insurance Companies), and UPS (Transportation).

While leading their industry group for four years, Sara Lee (Food) was overtaken by Conagra in 1991, which had last ranked first in 1987. U.S. Tobacco (Tobacco) ranked first in its industry grouping for 1991, which had been dominated on quality of management by Phillip Morris (now Food) for the period 1988–90. The following companies ranked first on quality of management for four of the past five years in their respective industries: Herman Miller (Furniture), Kimberly-Clark (Forest Products), Shell Oil (Petroleum Refining), Illinois Tool (Metal Products), General Electric (Electronics), Ford Motor (Motor Vehicles and Parts), Pepsico (Beverages), Wal-Mart (Retailing), and Bellsouth (Utilities). Wal-Mart has also been ranked in the top three companies on an overall basis for the past three years on quality of management.

Those companies receiving the lowest ranking for quality of management during the past four to five years within their industry include McGraw-Hill (Publishing), Texaco (Petroleum Refining), Manville (Building), and Equitable Life (Life Insurance Companies). It is interesting to note that companies receiving overall worst rankings in quality of management during the past five years were predominantly found in such industries as commercial banking, savings institutions, and life insurance.

Companies that fell from favor include James River (Forest Products), which ranked first by industry on quality of management in 1987 but whose rankings have declined ever since; Chrysler (Motor Vehicles); and Cummins Engineering (Industrial and Farm Equipment), which was ranked first in 1987 and last in

Exhibit 1.4
Corporate Reputation Scores: Quality of Management

MINING, CRUDE OIL PRODUCTION

	1991	1990	1989	1988	1987
AMAX	—	—	—	5.67	4.58
ASARCO	6.03	—	—	—	—
BURLINGTON RES.	—	7.00	—	—	—
CYPRUS MINERALS	—	6.72	6.31	6.51	—
FREEPORT-MCMORAN	7.03	—	7.24	6.95	6.49
INSPIRATION RES.	—	—	5.29	5.65	5.12
INTERNATIONAL MIN.	—	—	—	—	6.08
LOUISIANA LAND & EX	6.48	6.68	6.25	6.39	5.64
MAXUS ENERGY	6.65	6.26	6.06	—	—
MITCHELL ENERGY	—	6.62	6.44	6.78	6.41
NERCO	6.56	6.30	6.02	6.04	—
NEWMONT MINING	6.10	—	—	—	—
OCCIDENTAL PET.	—	—	—	—	5.50
ORYX ENERGY	7.27	—	—	—	—
STANDARD OIL	—	—	—	—	6.57
UNION TEXAS	6.65	6.95	6.46	6.01	—
VULCAN MATERIALS	6.36	6.59	7.27	6.70	6.63
WESTMORELAND COAL	6.12	5.96	5.60	5.98	5.78

FOOD

	1991	1990	1989	1988	1987
ARCHER DANIELS	6.84	6.97	6.69	6.81	6.68
BEATRICE	—	5.44	5.28	—	—
BORDEN	6.24	6.48	6.78	6.93	6.38
CONAGRA	7.82	7.54	7.57	7.49	7.74
CPC INTERNAT'L	—	—	—	6.01	5.87
GENERAL MILLS	7.51	7.42	7.25	7.49	7.24
H.J. HEINZ	7.76	—	—	—	—
IC INDUSTRIES	—	—	—	—	6.12
KRAFT	—	—	7.10	6.70	6.85
OCCIDENTAL	4.92	5.23	4.99	5.57	—
PHILIP MORRIS	7.68	—	—	—	—
PILLSBURY	—	—	4.35	6.69	7.51
QUAKER OATS	—	7.41	—	—	—
RALSTON PURINA	6.62	6.83	6.99	7.20	7.57
RJR NABISCO	5.96	5.91	—	—	—
SARA LEE	7.54	7.97	7.97	7.91	7.74

TOBACCO

	1991	1990	1989	1988	1987
AMERICAN BRANDS	7.26	7.13	6.21	6.55	5.86
DIBRELL BROS.	6.65	6.69	—	—	—
LORILLARD	6.76	6.85	—	—	—

16

Exhibit 1.4 (Continued)

TOBACCO

	1991	1990	1989	1988	1987
PHILIP MORRIS	—	9.57	8.65	8.41	7.89
RJR NABISCO	—	—	7.80	8.06	8.08
STANDARD COMM.	5.60	6.33	—	—	—
UNIVERSAL	6.89	7.31	6.65	—	—
U.S. TOBACCO	7.70	7.78	6.48	6.40	6.09

TEXTILES

	1991	1990	1989	1988	1987
AMOSKEAG	3.12	—	—	—	—
ARMSTRONG WORLD	6.27	7.15	7.19	7.53	7.45
BURLINGTON	5.77	6.15	5.49	5.00	5.64
COLLINS & AIKMAN	—	—	—	7.08	8.36
CONE MILLS	7.02	—	—	—	—
DIXIE YARNS	—	6.92	7.28	—	—
DWG	4.92	5.33	5.54	5.44	6.06
FIELDCREST CANNON	—	5.21	5.06	6.38	6.45
GUILFORD MILLS	—	6.99	7.27	—	—
J.P. STEVENS	4.73	—	—	6.07	5.83
SHAW INDUSTRIES	8.08	8.11	7.76	8.20	7.65
SPRINGS INDUST.	7.53	7.65	7.56	—	7.22
UNITED MERCHANTS	—	4.23	4.49	5.05	4.97
WEST POINT PEPP.	4.70	5.72	7.47	7.44	8.05
WICKES	4.84	—	—	—	—

APPAREL

	1991	1990	1989	1988	1987
CLAIBORNE	8.60	8.42	8.46	9.14	8.98
CRYSTAL BRANDS	6.56	—	—	—	—
FARLEY NORTHWEST	—	—	—	5.41	—
FRUIT OF THE LOOM	6.23	6.20	6.34	—	—
HARTMARX	4.57	5.93	6.78	6.24	6.82
INTERCO	—	—	6.45	6.16	6.35
KELLWOOD	5.82	7.03	7.25	6.33	6.42
LESLIE FAY	6.73	6.40	6.30	5.59	—
LEVI STRAUSS	8.37	—	—	—	—
MANHATTAN	—	—	—	—	4.08
OXFORD INDUSTRIES	—	5.91	6.05	5.80	6.36
PHILLIPS-VAN HEUSEN	6.60	6.33	6.26	5.10	5.89
RUSSEL	7.72	—	—	—	—
VF	6.68	7.97	8.22	8.13	8.43
WARNACO	—	5.32	5.83	5.30	—

(continued)

Exhibit 1.4 (Continued)

FURNITURE

	1991	1990	1989	1988	1987
BASSETT	6.89	—	6.35	6.12	—
HON INDUSTRIES	—	6.85	6.67	6.57	7.42
INTERCO	4.65	5.27	—	—	—
JOHNSON CONTROLS	6.74	—	—	—	—
KIMBALL	6.44	6.43	6.75	—	—
LA-Z-BOY CHAIR	6.75	—	—	—	—
LEAR SEATING	6.40	—	—	—	—
LEGGETT & PLATT	7.58	7.29	7.54	7.45	8.25
MASCO	—	7.44	8.43	—	—
HERMAN MILLER	7.87	7.62	8.61	8.03	7.89
MOHASCO	—	5.64	6.79	6.13	6.32
OHIO MATERIALS	—	6.13	7.63	—	—
SEALY HOLDINGS	6.38	—	—	—	—

FOREST PRODUCTS

	1991	1990	1989	1988	1987
BOISE CASCADE	5.47	6.17	6.56	6.50	6.26
CHAMPION INTER.	4.66	5.24	5.81	5.82	5.29
GEORGIA PACIFIC	7.13	7.24	6.44	6.71	6.39
GREAT NORTHERN	—	—	—	—	6.26
I PAPER	6.81	6.24	5.28	4.72	4.31
JAMES RIVER CORP.	6.19	7.06	7.17	7.38	8.02
KIMBERLY-CLARK	7.86	7.55	7.65	7.85	7.92
MEAD	6.18	6.64	6.83	6.48	6.27
SCOTT	7.05	7.43	7.15	7.21	6.73
STONE CONTAINER	5.60	6.80	6.89	—	—
UNION	—	—	—	7.16	—
WEYERHAEUSER	4.70	5.16	5.89	5.82	5.27

PUBLISHING, PRINTING

	1991	1990	1989	1988	1987
BERKSHIRE HATHAWAY	8.55	8.47	—	—	—
R.R. DONNELLEY	7.44	7.34	6.77	7.29	7.33
DOW JONES	—	7.12	7.65	8.49	8.22
GANNETT	7.30	7.44	7.41	7.80	7.70
KNIGHT-RIDDER	6.98	6.74	6.80	6.95	7.33
MCGRAW-HILL	5.24	5.29	5.07	5.82	6.22
NEW YORK TIMES	6.93	7.16	7.29	7.93	8.04
READERS DIGEST	7.02	—	—	—	—
TIME WARNER	6.43	6.49	6.74	6.94	6.37
TIMES MIRROR	6.50	6.60	6.78	7.16	6.89
TRIBUNE	6.96	7.08	7.02	6.75	6.62
WASHINGTON POST	—	—	7.33	6.99	6.92

Exhibit 1.4 (Continued)

CHEMICALS

	1991	1990	1989	1988	1987
AMERICAN CYANAMID	—	—	6.13	6.36	6.12
BASF	6.37	6.43	6.57	6.21	6.13
BAYER	6.46	6.74	6.78	6.38	—
DOW CHEMICAL	8.09	8.30	8.43	8.08	7.63
E.I. DU PONT	7.91	7.94	7.70	7.82	7.61
FMC	—	—	—	5.83	5.82
W.R. GRACE	5.08	5.00	4.49	4.87	4.79
HANSON INDUSTRIES	5.28	5.54	5.74	—	—
HERCULES	—	—	—	—	6.45
HOECHST CELANESE	6.23	6.51	6.42	6.19	6.75
MONSANTO	6.96	7.09	6.16	6.25	6.51
PPG INDUSTRIES	6.81	7.11	—	—	—
UNION CARBIDE	5.05	5.23	4.62	4.82	4.35

PETROLEUM REFINING

	1991	1990	1989	1988	1987
AMOCO	7.99	7.99	7.73	7.78	7.98
ARCO	8.05	7.85	7.34	7.13	6.36
BP AMERICA	—	—	6.67	—	—
CHEVRON	6.49	6.66	6.59	6.59	6.95
EXXON	6.05	6.19	8.22	7.91	8.26
MOBIL	6.83	6.75	6.76	6.53	6.26
PHILLIPS	6.62	6.49	—	5.13	5.13
SHELL	8.15	8.10	8.21	8.34	8.42
TENNECO	—	—	5.04	5.48	6.05
TEXACO	6.35	5.40	3.92	4.12	4.71
UNOCAL	6.11	6.00	—	—	—
USX	5.32	5.55	5.42	5.10	4.82

RUBBER PRODUCTS

	1991	1990	1989	1988	1987
ARMSTRONG	—	—	—	—	6.51
ARMTEK	—	—	6.43	6.52	—
CARLISLE	6.76	6.18	6.29	—	6.54
CONSTAR	—	5.80	—	—	—
COOPER	7.86	7.66	7.71	7.77	6.73
DAYCO	—	—	—	5.15	5.36
DORSEY	—	—	—	5.88	5.61
ENVIRODYNE	—	—	6.00	—	—
FERRO	—	6.67	—	—	—
FIRESTONE	—	—	—	6.04	5.63
GENCORP	—	—	6.67	7.20	6.86

(continued)

Exhibit 1.4 (Continued)

RUBBER PRODUCTS

	1991	1990	1989	1988	1987
B.F. GOODRICH	—	—	—	6.04	5.51
GOODYEAR	6.48	6.99	7.49	7.67	7.80
JOHNSON	—	7.44	—	—	—
KNOLL	—	—	5.00	—	—
MILLIPORE	—	7.18	—	—	—
PREMARK	6.53	6.98	7.17	6.85	—
RAYCHEM	6.17	—	—	—	—
RUBBERMAID	9.14	8.95	8.98	8.91	8.49
A. SCHULMAN	7.91	—	—	—	—
STANDARD PRODUCTS	6.93	7.12	7.36	—	—
TREDEGAR	6.52	—	—	—	—

BUILDING

	1991	1990	1989	1988	1987
AMERICAN STANDARD	6.15	6.64	—	—	—
CERTAINTEED	5.73	—	—	6.16	—
CORNING GLASS WORKS	7.68	7.79	7.42	7.14	7.04
HILLSBOROUGH	—	5.98	—	—	—
LAFARGE	6.20	6.07	5.98	—	—
MANVILLE	5.43	5.28	5.28	4.94	4.20
NATIONAL GYPSUM	5.38	—	5.49	6.36	6.01
NORTEK	—	5.29	—	—	—
NORTON	6.23	6.49	6.32	6.15	5.86
OWENS-CORNING	7.02	7.20	6.68	6.56	6.03
OWENS-ILLINOIS	6.59	6.48	6.44	6.65	6.66
PPG	—	—	7.49	7.46	6.94
TRINOVA	—	—	—	—	6.06
USG	5.86	5.74	5.77	6.55	6.62
JIM WALTER	—	—	5.96	6.38	6.22

METALS

	1991	1990	1989	1988	1987
ALUMAX	—	—	—	6.25	—
ALUMINUM OF AMER.	7.23	7.50	7.06	6.48	6.63
AMAX	6.29	6.57	6.25	—	—
ARMCO	4.98	5.62	5.88	5.40	5.45
ASARCO	—	5.92	—	—	—
BETHLEHEM STEEL	4.97	5.08	5.57	3.97	4.12
CYCLOPS	—	—	—	5.42	—
FARLEY/NWEST	—	—	—	—	5.94
INLAND STEEL	5.96	6.56	6.83	5.91	5.84
KAISER	—	—	4.36	4.32	5.02
LTV	4.33	4.26	4.51	3.60	3.55
MARMON GROUP	—	—	—	—	6.61

Exhibit 1.4 (Continued)

METALS

	1991	1990	1989	1988	1987
MAXXAM	4.85	—	—	—	—
NATIONAL STEEL	4.11	3.99	—	—	—
PENN CENTRAL	—	—	5.26	5.95	6.25
PHELPS DODGE	6.84	6.90	6.64	—	—
REYNOLDS METALS	7.21	7.17	7.21	7.08	6.78

METAL PRODUCTS

	1991	1990	1989	1988	1987
AMERICAN CAN	—	—	—	—	6.64
BALL	6.68	7.07	6.98	6.98	—
CBI INDUSTRIES	—	—	—	—	6.05
COMBUSTION ENG.	—	5.82	—	6.33	—
CROWN CORK & SEAL	6.93	7.14	6.33	6.88	6.60
EMHART	—	—	6.62	6.88	6.63
GILLETTE	7.05	6.89	6.57	6.83	7.26
HARSCO	6.06	6.12	5.98	—	6.06
HILLENBRAND	6.99	7.13	—	—	—
HOUSEHOLD MANU.	—	—	—	5.96	—
ILLINOIS TOOL	8.00	7.85	7.63	8.00	—
MASCO	7.50	—	7.33	7.95	7.18
MCDERMOTT	6.03	—	—	—	—
NEWELL	6.97	7.45	—	—	—
PARKER HANNIFIN	—	—	—	—	6.84
STANLEY WORKS	7.09	7.50	7.11	7.39	7.31
TRIANGLE	—	—	5.74	6.57	6.24
TYCO	—	—	6.32	—	—
TYLER	—	6.11	—	—	—

ELECTRONICS

	1991	1990	1989	1988	1987
AT&T	—	—	6.19	6.24	5.82
EMERSON	7.67	7.72	7.84	7.85	7.92
GENERAL ELECTRIC	8.39	8.22	7.80	8.47	8.23
HONEYWELL	5.96	5.31	5.86	6.11	—
ITT	—	—	5.39	5.61	4.84
LITTON INDUSTRIES	—	—	—	—	5.34
MOTOROLA	8.01	7.47	7.04	7.09	7.03
N. AMERICAN PHILLIPS	5.49	5.86	—	—	—
RAYTHEON	6.50	6.58	6.79	6.86	6.44
TEXAS INSTRUMENTS	6.24	6.55	6.63	6.61	5.59
TRW	6.20	6.38	6.33	6.68	6.69
WESTINGHOUSE	6.81	6.81	6.36	6.58	6.17
WHIRLPOOL	6.33	6.50	—	—	—

(continued)

Exhibit 1.4 (Continued)

TRANSPORTATION EQUIPMENT

	1991	1990	1989	1988	1987
AVONDALE INDUSTRIES	6.04	6.25	—	—	—
BRUNSWICK	6.05	6.40	—	—	—
FLEETWOOD	—	7.24	7.50	7.63	8.00
HARLEY DAVIDSON	8.00	—	8.22	—	—
HARSCO	—	—	—	7.17	—
INTERNATIONAL CNTLS.	—	—	5.56	6.00	—
MINISTAR	—	6.26	6.43	—	—
OGDEN	—	—	—	—	6.56
OUTBOARD MARINE	6.34	6.83	—	—	—
TODD SHIPYARDS	—	—	—	—	6.31
TRINITY	6.43	7.42	—	7.86	—
WINNEBAGO	—	—	—	—	6.42

SCIENTIFIC AND PHOTOGRAPHIC EQUIPMENT

	1991	1990	1989	1988	1987
BAUSCH & LOMB	6.46	—	—	—	—
BAXTER	6.29	6.68	—	—	—
BECTON DICKINSON	6.63	6.57	6.23	6.50	6.50
EASTMAN KODAK	5.88	6.01	7.06	7.00	6.33
EG&G	6.37	—	7.05	6.71	7.19
FISHER SCIENT. GROUP	—	—	5.75	—	—
GENERAL SIGNAL	—	—	6.03	5.61	5.84
HENLEY GROUP	—	5.65	—	—	—
LEAR SIEGLER	—	—	—	5.39	5.80
LITTON	—	5.82	—	—	—
MINNESOTA MINING	8.39	8.42	8.33	8.28	7.88
PERKIN-ELMER	5.21	5.66	6.07	6.34	6.80
POLAROID	5.27	5.75	5.56	6.02	6.05
TEKTRONIX	5.00	5.31	5.73	6.22	5.87
XEROX	6.21	6.45	7.07	6.75	6.16

MOTOR VEHICLES AND PARTS

	1991	1990	1989	1988	1987
ARVIN INDUSTRIES	—	—	6.02	—	—
AMERICAN MOTORS	—	—	—	3.62	4.09
BORG-WARNER	—	5.83	—	6.21	6.36
CHRYSLER	5.01	6.62	6.86	7.75	7.98
DANA	6.97	7.17	7.31	7.60	7.27
EATON	7.27	7.18	—	—	—
ECHLIN	—	—	6.05	—	—
FLEETWOOD	5.55	—	—	—	—
FORD MOTOR	7.73	8.38	8.27	8.40	7.80
FRUEHAUF	—	—	4.86	4.91	5.13
GENERAL MOTORS	5.65	5.47	4.92	4.85	6.47

Exhibit 1.4 (Continued)

MOTOR VEHICLES AND PARTS

	1991	1990	1989	1988	1987
K-H (FRUEHAUF)	—	4.22	—	—	—
MACK TRUCKS	3.68	4.32	5.30	6.02	5.44
MASCO	6.28	—	—	—	—
NAVISTAR	5.26	5.48	5.92	5.69	5.70
PACCAR	7.06	7.24	6.81	6.94	7.05

AEROSPACE

	1991	1990	1989	1988	1987
ALLIED-SIGNAL	5.88	5.70	5.21	5.73	6.31
BOEING	8.36	8.35	8.32	8.00	8.48
GENERAL DYNAMICS	6.35	6.71	6.15	6.02	5.83
LOCKHEED	5.62	6.38	6.42	6.69	6.78
MARTIN MARIETTA	7.35	7.95	7.56	7.47	7.47
MCDONNELL DOUGLAS	4.59	5.52	6.19	6.58	6.84
NORTHROP	4.00	4.16	4.84	6.33	6.95
ROCKWELL	6.98	6.75	6.69	7.01	7.19
TEXTRON	5.75	5.81	5.60	5.84	6.14
UNITED TECHNOLOGIES	6.70	6.56	5.46	6.15	6.22

PHARMACEUTICALS

	1991	1990	1989	1988	1987
ABBOTT LABS	6.76	7.15	7.80	8.11	7.87
AMERICAN HOMES	6.30	6.40	6.24	6.30	7.11
BAXTER	—	—	6.26	6.69	6.34
BRISTOL-MEYERS	7.70	7.65	7.63	7.67	7.37
JOHNSON & JOHNSON	8.07	7.91	7.88	7.97	8.16
ELI LILLY	7.73	7.20	7.30	7.36	7.10
MERCK	9.07	9.11	9.10	9.34	8.44
PFIZER	6.30	5.71	6.12	6.93	7.28
SCHERING-PLOUGH	7.26	7.01	—	—	—
SMITHKLINE BECKMAN	—	4.36	4.42	5.68	6.01
UPJOHN	6.10	—	—	—	—
WARNER-LAMBERT	6.84	6.49	6.32	6.10	5.76

SOAPS & COSMETICS

	1991	1990	1989	1988	1987
ALBERTO-CULVER	6.26	6.12	—	5.50	—
AVON PRODUCTS	4.96	4.87	4.81	6.78	6.39
CHEMED	5.70	—	—	—	—
CHESEBROUGH-POND'S	—	—	6.28	6.54	6.42
CLOROX	6.43	7.29	6.61	7.38	7.06
COLGATE-PALMOLIVE	7.04	7.22	7.21	7.30	6.71
ECOLAB	—	—	5.40	6.40	6.23

(continued)

23

Exhibit 1.4 (Continued)

SOAPS & COSMETICS

	1991	1990	1989	1988	1987
FABERGE	—	—	5.27	—	—
HELENE CURTIS	6.46	—	—	—	—
INTERNAT'L FLAVORS	—	7.48	7.43	7.81	6.61
LEVER BROS.	—	—	7.21	7.10	6.89
NOXELL	—	7.26	—	—	—
PROCTER & GAMBLE	8.79	8.72	8.10	8.29	8.03
REVLON GROUP	5.52	—	5.49	5.57	4.58
STANHOME	6.30	—	—	—	—
UNILEVER U.S.	7.60	7.34	—	—	—

COMPUTERS

	1991	1990	1989	1988	1987
AMDAHL	—	—	6.19	—	—
APPLE COMPUTER	5.79	6.77	7.69	7.41	7.05
BURROUGHS	—	—	—	—	5.71
COMPAQ COMPUTER	7.86	—	—	—	—
CONTROL DATA	4.20	3.45	4.04	4.40	4.09
DIGITAL EQUIPMENT	5.86	6.64	7.39	7.77	8.00
GOULD	—	—	—	4.55	—
HEWLETT-PACKARD	7.46	7.86	7.96	7.52	7.83
HONEYWELL	—	—	—	—	5.40
IBM	7.62	7.22	7.71	7.76	8.33
NCR	6.27	6.31	6.66	6.57	6.65
PITNEY BOWES	5.54	5.77	5.51	5.35	5.87
UNISYS	3.75	4.38	5.88	5.72	—
WANG LABS	3.17	2.72	4.46	4.69	5.52
ZENITH	—	5.01	—	—	—

INDUSTRIAL AND FARM EQUIPMENT

	1991	1990	1989	1988	1987
AMERICAN STANDARD	—	—	5.83	6.16	6.73
BAKER HUGHES	6.58	6.38	6.00	6.23	6.38
BLACK & DECKER	7.00	7.28	7.05	7.07	7.16
BRUNSWICK	—	—	6.42	6.88	—
CATERPILLAR	6.95	7.56	7.33	6.93	7.16
COMBUSTION ENG.	—	—	—	—	6.56
CUMMINS ENGINE	6.02	6.52	6.29	7.15	7.48
DEERE	7.49	7.76	7.23	6.92	7.10
DOVER	6.79	7.02	—	—	—
DRESSER INDUSTRIES	6.46	6.68	6.28	6.26	6.66
INGERSOLL-RAND	6.82	6.78	6.41	6.51	6.76
PARKER HANNIFIN	6.61	6.91	—	—	—
TELEDYNE	—	—	—	7.25	7.45
TENNECO	6.43	6.05	—	—	—
TRINOVA	—	—	5.98	—	—

Exhibit 1.4 (Continued)

TOYS, SPORTING GOODS

	1991	1990	1989	1988	1987
COLECO	—	—	—	4.14	4.65
HASBRO	—	—	—	7.56	7.83
KENNER	—	—	—	6.32	—
MATTEL	—	—	—	5.26	5.60
MINSTAR	—	—	—	5.30	5.35

BEVERAGES

	1991	1990	1989	1988	1987
ANHEUSER BUSCH	7.88	8.04	7.83	7.72	8.24
BROWN FORMAN	6.64	6.66	6.31	6.02	6.12
COCA-COLA	8.11	8.06	7.75	7.53	7.74
COCA-COLA ENTERPR.	6.00	6.20	6.28	—	—
ADOLPH COORS	6.31	5.96	6.04	5.67	5.90
GENERAL CINEMA	—	—	6.54	6.12	6.81
DR PEPPER/SEVEN UP	—	5.99	—	—	—
G. HEILEMAN	—	—	—	5.78	6.07
PEPSICO	8.65	8.40	8.29	8.13	7.92
J.E. SEAGRAM	6.45	6.57	6.23	5.57	6.02

DIVERSIFIED SERVICE COMPANIES

	1991	1990	1989	1988	1987
ARA HOLDING	—	—	6.07	—	—
ALCO STANDARD	—	—	—	6.29	—
AMERICAN FINANCIAL	5.90	5.77	—	—	—
AT&T	7.17	7.24	—	—	—
CAPITAL CITIES	—	—	7.32	—	—
CBS	—	—	—	5.68	4.37
ELECTRONIC DATA SYS	—	—	7.20	7.44	—
FLEMING COMPANIES	6.44	6.09	6.14	6.21	6.47
FLUOR	—	6.27	5.97	5.88	5.87
HALLIBURTON	—	6.48	—	—	6.14
HOSPITAL CORP.	—	—	6.07	5.99	6.52
ENRON	6.62	—	—	—	6.15
MARRIOTT	7.53	—	—	—	—
MCI COMMUNICATIONS	—	7.60	—	—	—
MCKESSON	6.94	6.35	6.65	6.83	6.53
NATIONAL INTERGROUP	—	—	5.16	5.53	—
PACIFIC ENTERPRISES	6.00	—	—	—	—
PRIMERICA	—	—	—	7.32	—
RYDER SYSTEM	—	5.89	—	—	—
SALOMON INC.	—	—	—	—	7.79
SUPER VALU STORES	6.98	6.72	6.41	6.81	6.92
SYSCO	7.28	—	—	—	—
UNITED TELECOM	6.60	6.89	—	—	—
UNION PACIFIC	—	—	—	—	6.54

(continued)

Exhibit 1.4 (Continued)

DIVERSIFIED FINANCIAL COMPANIES

	1991	1990	1989	1988	1987
AETNA LIFE	5.73	6.24	6.11	6.20	6.29
AMERICAN EXPRESS	6.08	7.67	7.99	7.63	7.48
AMERICAN INTERNAT'L	7.79	8.01	7.41	—	—
BEAR STEARNS	—	—	—	6.95	6.85
CIGNA	5.31	5.77	5.64	5.55	5.25
FEDERAL NAT'L MORTG.	6.85	6.70	6.42	5.65	5.64
FIRST BOSTON	—	—	6.48	7.38	7.75
ITT	6.14	6.21	—	—	—
E.F. HUTTON	—	—	—	—	4.51
LOEWS	—	—	—	—	7.34
MERRILL LYNCH	4.98	5.97	5.43	5.62	6.19
MORGAN STANLEY	7.55	8.01	8.00	7.77	—
SALOMON	5.81	6.01	6.06	6.98	—
TRAVELERS	4.95	5.51	5.38	6.12	6.11

COMMERCIAL BANKING COMPANIES

	1991	1990	1989	1988	1987
BANK OF NEW YORK	—	6.36	—	—	—
BANKAMERICA	6.77	5.89	3.76	2.72	2.15
BANKERS TRUST N.Y.	7.44	7.74	7.60	7.78	7.63
CHASE MANHATTAN	3.88	5.56	5.35	5.36	5.63
CHEMICAL BANK	4.28	5.45	5.35	5.50	6.18
CITICORP	6.23	7.85	7.66	7.78	7.84
FIRST CHICAGO	—	—	5.58	—	5.10
FIRST INTERSTATE	3.88	4.57	5.21	6.02	6.28
MANUFACTURERS HANOV.	4.25	4.32	4.04	4.58	5.27
J.P. MORGAN	8.23	8.31	8.63	9.04	8.90
NCNB CORP.	7.21	—	—	—	—
SECURITY PACIFIC	6.65	7.37	7.09	7.22	7.28
WELLS FARGO	—	—	—	7.75	—

LIFE INSURANCE COMPANIES

	1991	1990	1989	1988	1987
AETNA LIFE	6.21	6.20	6.53	6.55	6.41
CONNECTICUT LIFE	5.76	6.00	5.99	6.07	6.24
EQUITABLE LIFE	4.34	4.65	3.54	5.65	5.61
JOHN HANCOCK	5.66	5.61	5.60	5.76	5.86
METROPOLITAN LIFE	6.47	6.27	6.02	6.29	6.05
NEW YORK LIFE	6.23	5.86	5.87	5.60	5.79
NORTHWESTERN LIFE	7.85	7.85	7.61	7.39	7.56
PRUDENTIAL	7.33	7.23	7.41	6.67	6.76
TEACHERS INSURANCE	6.18	5.97	6.06	5.72	6.20
TRAVELERS	4.44	5.05	4.99	6.12	6.28

Exhibit 1.4 (Continued)

RETAILING COMPANIES

	1991	1990	1989	1988	1987
AMERICAN STORES	5.97	5.84	5.57	5.89	6.41
DAYTON HUDSON	7.36	7.18	6.59	—	7.83
FEDERATED DEPT.	—	—	4.70	5.57	6.22
GREAT ATLANTIC	6.19	6.58	—	—	—
K MART	5.40	5.87	6.71	6.51	6.70
KROGER	6.34	6.24	5.78	6.35	6.77
LUCKY STORES	—	—	—	—	5.63
MAY DEPT. STORES	7.13	7.18	6.98	6.96	—
J.C. PENNEY	6.81	6.92	6.67	6.69	6.66
SAFEWAY	6.04	5.92	5.19	5.11	—
SEARS ROEBUCK	3.91	4.76	5.37	5.96	6.63
SOUTHLAND	—	—	—	5.52	6.34
WAL-MART	9.21	9.17	9.08	8.86	—

UTILITIES

	1991	1990	1989	1988	1987
AMERICAN INFO. TECH	7.03	7.26	7.43	7.57	7.43
BELL ATLANTIC	7.28	7.50	7.66	7.61	7.42
BELLSOUTH	7.57	7.96	7.70	7.54	7.44
GTE	6.66	6.53	6.41	5.95	6.07
NYNEX	5.04	6.01	6.89	7.17	6.80
PACIFIC GAS	6.92	6.65	6.61	6.49	6.73
PACIFIC TELESIS	7.47	7.45	7.37	7.09	7.10
SOUTHERN	5.80	6.14	6.32	6.40	6.42
SOUTHWEST BELL	6.64	6.80	6.65	6.60	6.26
US WEST	6.20	6.67	6.52	6.57	6.49

TRANSPORTATION COMPANIES

	1991	1990	1989	1988	1987
AMR	7.93	8.01	7.79	7.80	8.00
BURLINGTON NORTHERN	—	6.66	6.67	6.53	6.75
CONTINENTAL	3.51	—	—	—	—
CSX	5.62	5.43	5.93	6.07	6.48
DELTA	7.77	7.39	7.46	6.85	7.42
FEDERAL EXPRESS	7.44	—	—	—	—
NORFOLK SOUTHERN	—	—	—	6.84	7.18
NWA	5.45	—	5.60	—	—
PAN AM	—	—	—	—	3.96
SANTA FE	—	5.26	5.22	5.08	5.90
TEXAS AIR	—	4.08	3.98	4.87	—
TWA	—	—	—	—	4.56
UAL	5.45	6.63	6.76	4.27	6.76

(continued)

Exhibit 1.4 (Continued)

TRANSPORTATION COMPANIES

	1991	1990	1989	1988	1987
UNION PACIFIC	6.67	6.79	6.72	6.87	—
UPS	7.96	8.19	8.22	8.04	8.02
USAIR	5.24	6.76	—	—	—

SAVINGS INSTITUTIONS

	1991	1990	1989	1988	1987
H.F. AHMANSON	7.75	7.77	7.68	7.62	7.93
CALFED	5.26	5.24	5.93	5.84	6.40
CROSSLAND SAVINGS	3.25	5.08	—	—	—
FINANCIAL CORP.	—	—	2.36	3.38	4.08
FIRST FED. OF MI.	—	—	—	—	5.71
GIBRALTER	—	1.99	3.36	4.28	5.20
GLENFED	5.09	5.48	6.25	5.75	6.17
GOLDEN WEST FIN.	8.73	8.15	—	7.86	7.89
GOLDOME	3.14	—	4.08	—	—
GREAT AMERICAN	2.87	5.37	5.67	6.15	—
GREAT WESTERN	7.45	8.11	8.12	8.10	7.95
HOME FEDERAL S&L	5.33	7.47	7.29	6.70	7.00
MERITOR	3.71	4.03	3.91	4.38	5.04

1991. Can companies effect a change for the better in their industry ranking on quality of management? BankAmerica (Commercial Banking) appears to have done so. After ranking in the overall worst three companies on this attribute for three years (1987–89), it now ranks fourth in its industry.

The most unstable industries, defined in terms of not having any clear leaders on quality of management over the period 1987–91 appear to be Mining and Crude Oil, Transportation Equipment, Computers, Industrial and Farm Equipment, Diversified Service Companies, and Diversified Financial Companies. Quality of management does appear to have a pervasive influence on overall reputation rankings afforded by the *Fortune* survey. In 1991 alone, seven of the top ten ranked companies overall also ranked first on quality of management within their own industry groupings. The three exceptions were Coca-Cola, which ranked second behind Pepsico (Beverages), which was also in the top ten, and Johnson and Johnson (Pharmaceuticals) and Eli Lily (Pharmaceuticals), ranking second and third, respectively, to Merck.

Exhibit 1.5 contains the average rankings by industry for the period 1987–91 afforded companies on the variable of quality of products/services. In all five years, Merck (Pharmaceuticals) has ranked among the top three companies in the *Fortune* survey on this attribute. Similarly it ranked number one in its industry for the past five years on quality of products/services. Other companies that

Exhibit 1.5
Corporate Reputation Scores: Quality of Products/Services

MINING, CRUDE OIL PRODUCTION

	1991	1990	1989	1988	1987
AMAX	—	—	—	5.91	5.93
ASARCO	6.61	—	—	—	—
BURLINGTON RES.	—	6.76	—	—	—
CYPRUS MINERALS	—	6.30	6.43	6.04	—
FREEPORT-MCMORAN	6.72	—	6.63	6.40	6.22
INSPIRATION RES.	—	—	5.64	5.70	5.30
INTERNATIONAL MIN.	—	—	—	—	6.35
LOUISIANA LAND & EX	6.68	6.45	6.43	6.27	6.23
MAXUS ENERGY	6.56	6.17	6.04	—	—
MITCHELL ENERGY	—	6.51	6.35	6.56	6.30
NERCO	6.63	6.26	6.22	5.65	—
NEWMONT MINING	6.40	—	—	—	—
OCCIDENTAL PET.	—	—	—	—	6.17
ORYX ENERGY	6.84	—	—	—	—
STANDARD OIL	—	—	—	—	6.92
UNION TEXAS	6.58	6.52	6.34	5.95	—
VULCAN MATERIALS	6.21	6.40	6.86	6.22	6.55
WESTMORELAND COAL	6.28	6.29	6.35	6.09	5.95

FOOD

	1991	1990	1989	1988	1987
ARCHER DANIELS	6.59	6.49	6.25	6.53	6.52
BEATRICE	—	6.20	6.36	—	—
BORDEN	6.81	7.06	7.08	7.26	7.15
CONAGRA	7.01	6.86	6.71	6.69	6.74
CPC INTERNAT'L	—	—	—	7.09	7.04
GENERAL MILLS	7.82	7.73	7.80	8.04	7.97
H.J. HEINZ	7.69	—	—	—	—
IC INDUSTRIES	—	—	—	—	6.52
KRAFT	—	—	7.86	7.80	7.87
OCCIDENTAL	5.44	5.83	5.54	5.73	—
PHILIP MORRIS	6.75	—	—	—	—
PILLSBURY	—	—	6.54	7.66	7.92
QUAKER OATS	—	7.68	—	—	—
RALSTON PURINA	6.66	7.07	6.99	7.13	7.52
RJR NABISCO	6.35	6.81	—	—	—
SARA LEE	7.66	7.86	8.03	7.97	7.98

TOBACCO

	1991	1990	1989	1988	1987
AMERICAN BRANDS	7.58	7.37	6.79	7.03	6.58
DIBRELL BROS.	6.91	7.12	—	—	—

(continued)

Exhibit 1.5 (Continued)

TOBACCO

	1991	1990	1989	1988	1987
LORILLARD	7.05	7.22	—	—	—
PHILIP MORRIS	—	8.96	8.37	8.45	8.09
RJR NABISCO	—	—	8.07	8.45	7.92
STANDARD COMM.	6.32	6.76	—	—	—
UNIVERSAL	7.27	7.65	7.45	—	—
U.S. TOBACCO	7.90	7.96	7.30	7.17	6.77

TEXTILES

	1991	1990	1989	1988	1987
AMOSKEAG	6.36	—	—	—	—
ARMSTRONG WORLD	7.31	7.69	7.36	7.78	7.77
BURLINGTON	6.76	6.96	6.69	7.04	7.28
COLLINS & AIKMAN	—	—	—	7.25	8.00
CONE MILLS	7.21	—	—	—	—
DIXIE YARNS	—	7.06	7.28	—	—
DWG	5.51	5.81	6.00	5.22	6.31
FIELDCREST CANNON	—	6.94	6.60	7.62	7.65
GUILFORD MILLS	—	7.26	7.39	—	—
J.P. STEVENS	5.75	—	—	6.56	6.95
SHAW INDUSTRIES	7.52	7.59	7.14	7.25	7.11
SPRINGS INDUST.	7.67	7.48	7.32	7.00	7.37
UNITED MERCHANTS	—	5.03	5.08	5.20	5.55
WEST POINT PEPP.	6.78	7.21	7.37	7.80	7.82
WICKES	5.84	—	—	—	—

APPAREL

	1991	1990	1989	1988	1987
CLAIBORNE	8.24	8.42	8.41	8.26	8.15
CRYSTAL BRANDS	6.79	—	—	—	—
FARLEY NORTHWEST	—	—	—	6.17	—
FRUIT OF THE LOOM	6.87	6.63	6.81	—	—
HARTMARX	6.91	7.69	7.62	7.55	7.74
INTERCO	—	—	6.60	6.56	6.66
KELLWOOD	5.89	6.43	6.42	6.07	5.87
LESLIE FAY	6.95	6.46	6.25	6.00	—
LEVI STRAUSS	8.11	—	—	—	—
MANHATTAN	—	—	—	—	5.54
OXFORD INDUSTRIES	—	6.31	6.03	5.81	6.21
PHILLIPS-VAN HEUSEN	6.31	6.67	6.62	6.60	6.39
RUSSEL	8.09	—	—	—	—
VF	7.13	7.80	7.85	7.93	7.90
WARNACO	—	6.44	6.55	5.96	—

Exhibit 1.5 (Continued)

FURNITURE

	1991	1990	1989	1988	1987
BASSETT	6.46	—	6.13	6.09	—
HON INDUSTRIES	—	6.44	5.83	6.00	7.20
INTERCO	5.75	6.05	—	—	—
JOHNSON CONTROLS	7.18	—	—	—	—
KIMBALL	6.63	6.59	6.90	—	—
LA-Z-BOY CHAIR	7.20	—	—	—	—
LEAR SEATING	6.25	—	—	—	—
LEGGETT & PLATT	7.18	6.98	7.12	7.26	8.04
MASCO	—	7.15	8.33	—	—
HERMAN MILLER	8.15	8.00	8.62	8.29	8.36
MOHASCO	—	5.80	6.25	6.10	6.33
OHIO MATERIALS	—	6.73	7.22	—	—
SEALY HOLDINGS	6.56	—	—	—	—

FOREST PRODUCTS

	1991	1990	1989	1988	1987
BOISE CASCADE	6.10	6.31	6.76	6.43	6.20
CHAMPION INTER.	6.22	6.32	6.69	6.51	6.20
GEORGIA PACIFIC	6.26	6.51	6.55	6.45	6.22
GREAT NORTHERN	—	—	—	—	6.62
I PAPER	6.68	6.63	6.42	6.01	5.97
JAMES RIVER CORP.	6.28	6.61	6.79	6.60	6.75
KIMBERLY-CLARK	7.99	8.07	8.09	8.06	7.94
MEAD	6.67	7.11	7.36	6.78	6.60
SCOTT	7.42	7.70	7.57	7.40	7.25
STONE CONTAINER	5.82	6.28	6.41	—	—
UNION	—	—	—	7.13	—
WEYERHAEUSER	6.28	6.45	6.85	6.56	6.36

PUBLISHING, PRINTING

	1991	1990	1989	1988	1987
BERKSHIRE HATHAWAY	7.12	6.87	—	—	—
R.R. DONNELLEY	7.58	7.64	7.49	7.58	7.86
DOW JONES	—	8.30	8.59	9.08	8.77
GANNETT	6.61	6.44	6.15	6.19	6.56
KNIGHT-RIDDER	7.02	7.06	7.00	7.24	7.30
MCGRAW-HILL	6.85	6.90	6.65	6.94	7.19
NEW YORK TIMES	8.29	8.22	8.42	8.49	8.62
READERS DIGEST	7.28	—	—	—	—
TIME WARNER	7.42	7.71	7.55	7.48	7.52
TIMES MIRROR	7.31	7.28	7.22	7.47	7.28
TRIBUNE	6.95	7.06	6.93	6.72	6.65
WASHINGTON POST	—	—	7.76	7.61	7.42

(continued)

Exhibit 1.5 (Continued)

CHEMICALS

	1991	1990	1989	1988	1987
AMERICAN CYANAMID	—	—	7.13	7.02	6.79
BASF	6.78	7.04	7.00	6.61	6.65
BAYER	7.10	7.38	7.34	6.95	—
DOW CHEMICAL	7.71	7.85	8.05	7.84	7.33
E.I. DU PONT	8.15	8.25	8.37	8.39	8.13
FMC	—	—	—	6.01	5.89
W.R. GRACE	6.01	5.93	5.96	5.92	5.84
HANSON INDUSTRIES	5.31	5.66	5.75	—	—
HERCULES	—	—	—	—	6.72
HOECHST CELANESE	6.55	6.82	6.77	6.33	6.47
MONSANTO	7.36	7.34	7.09	6.92	6.85
PPG INDUSTRIES	7.01	7.22	—	—	—
UNION CARBIDE	6.04	6.19	6.09	6.09	5.76

PETROLEUM REFINING

	1991	1990	1989	1988	1987
AMOCO	8.05	8.08	8.05	7.52	7.92
ARCO	7.60	7.34	7.19	6.84	6.84
BP AMERICA	—	—	6.99	—	—
CHEVRON	7.45	7.45	7.35	7.09	7.38
EXXON	7.54	7.43	8.19	7.70	7.96
MOBIL	7.56	7.59	7.52	7.22	7.15
PHILLIPS	7.00	6.96	—	6.56	6.60
SHELL	8.04	8.04	8.22	7.81	8.01
TENNECO	—	—	5.92	6.17	6.17
TEXACO	7.26	7.03	6.75	6.75	6.76
UNOCAL	6.83	6.89	—	—	—
USX	6.16	6.17	6.09	6.10	5.51

RUBBER PRODUCTS

	1991	1990	1989	1988	1987
ARMSTRONG	—	—	—	—	6.41
ARMTEK	—	—	6.36	6.21	—
CARLISLE	6.91	6.45	6.67	—	6.53
CONSTAR	—	6.12	—	—	—
COOPER	7.52	7.27	7.36	6.71	6.40
DAYCO	—	—	—	6.03	6.11
DORSEY	—	—	—	5.88	5.64
ENVIRODYNE	—	—	6.50	—	—
FERRO	—	7.26	—	—	—
FIRESTONE	—	—	—	6.43	6.32
GENCORP	—	—	6.83	6.70	6.62
B.F. GOODRICH	—	—	—	6.56	6.50
GOODYEAR	7.96	7.93	8.02	8.13	8.08

Exhibit 1.5 (Continued)

RUBBER PRODUCTS

	1991	1990	1989	1988	1987
JOHNSON	—	7.85	—	—	—
KNOLL	—	—	5.50	—	—
MILLIPORE	—	7.48	—	—	—
PREMARK	7.57	7.39	7.63	6.80	—
RAYCHEM	7.39	—	—	—	—
RUBBERMAID	9.03	8.99	9.09	8.89	8.55
A. SCHULMAN	7.56	—	—	—	—
STANDARD PRODUCTS	7.09	7.15	6.96	—	—
TREDEGAR	6.24	—	—	—	—

BUILDING

	1991	1990	1989	1988	1987
AMERICAN STANDARD	7.24	7.46	—	—	—
CERTAINTEED	6.30	—	—	6.43	—
CORNING GLASS WORKS	8.16	8.31	8.09	7.98	7.87
HILLSBOROUGH	—	5.87	—	—	—
LAFARGE	6.30	5.88	5.82	—	—
MANVILLE	6.23	5.99	6.01	6.13	5.70
NATIONAL GYPSUM	6.05	—	5.76	6.65	6.61
NORTEK	—	5.71	—	—	—
NORTON	6.64	6.71	6.79	6.73	6.49
OWENS-CORNING	7.40	7.51	7.27	7.61	7.26
OWENS-ILLINOIS	6.97	7.14	6.67	7.02	6.88
PPG	—	—	7.32	7.48	7.32
TRINOVA	—	—	—	—	6.67
USG	6.71	6.54	6.47	6.82	6.95
JIM WALTER	—	—	5.92	6.55	6.03

METALS

	1991	1990	1989	1988	1987
ALUMAX	—	—	—	6.32	—
ALUMINUM OF AMER.	7.65	7.82	7.83	7.47	7.64
AMAX	6.40	6.68	6.46	—	—
ARMCO	6.00	6.26	6.52	6.16	6.19
ASARCO	—	5.95	—	—	—
BETHLEHEM STEEL	5.93	5.89	6.39	5.49	5.45
CYCLOPS	—	—	—	5.79	—
FARLEY/NWEST	—	—	—	—	5.98
INLAND STEEL	6.49	6.88	7.13	6.32	6.52
KAISER	—	—	5.39	5.52	6.07
LTV	5.81	5.78	6.01	5.47	5.28
MARMON GROUP	—	—	—	—	6.25
MAXXAM	5.46	—	—	—	—

(continued)

Exhibit 1.5 (Continued)

METALS

	1991	1990	1989	1988	1987
NATIONAL STEEL	5.28	5.34	—	—	—
PENN CENTRAL	—	—	5.56	5.64	5.72
PHELPS DODGE	6.76	6.71	6.68	—	—
REYNOLDS METALS	7.33	7.37	7.38	7.24	7.34

METAL PRODUCTS

	1991	1990	1989	1988	1987
AMERICAN CAN	—	—	—	—	6.91
BALL	7.16	7.58	7.13	7.21	—
CBI INDUSTRIES	—	—	—	—	6.49
COMBUSTION ENG.	—	6.78	—	6.91	—
CROWN CORK & SEAL	7.07	7.23	6.82	7.14	6.75
EMHART	—	—	6.87	6.80	6.83
GILLETTE	8.26	8.16	7.94	7.82	7.90
HARSCO	6.36	6.56	6.10	—	6.38
HILLENBRAND	6.88	7.28	—	—	—
HOUSEHOLD MANU.	—	—	—	6.26	—
ILLINOIS TOOL	7.76	7.76	7.48	7.86	—
MASCO	7.45	—	7.36	7.67	7.19
MCDERMOTT	6.59	—	—	—	—
NEWELL	6.75	7.04	—	—	—
PARKER HANNIFIN	—	—	—	—	7.11
STANLEY WORKS	7.84	7.99	7.61	7.63	7.78
TRIANGLE	—	—	5.98	6.49	6.24
TYCO	—	—	6.36	—	—
TYLER	—	6.01	—	—	—

ELECTRONICS

	1991	1990	1989	1988	1987
AT&T	—	—	7.92	8.09	8.09
EMERSON	7.14	7.24	7.29	7.45	7.34
GENERAL ELECTRIC	7.66	7.71	7.62	7.76	7.66
HONEYWELL	6.78	6.59	6.75	6.87	—
ITT	—	—	5.93	5.77	5.60
LITTON INDUSTRIES	—	—	—	—	6.02
MOTOROLA	8.33	7.92	7.37	7.50	7.48
N. AMERICAN PHILLIPS	6.13	6.69	—	—	—
RAYTHEON	6.74	6.94	7.21	7.20	6.94
TEXAS INSTRUMENTS	6.87	7.15	7.28	7.07	6.64
TRW	6.58	6.84	6.89	6.96	6.84
WESTINGHOUSE	6.97	6.96	6.59	6.79	6.41
WHIRLPOOL	7.00	7.13	—	—	—

Exhibit 1.5 (Continued)

TRANSPORTATION EQUIPMENT

	1991	1990	1989	1988	1987
AVONDALE INDUSTRIES	6.39	6.77	—	—	—
BRUNSWICK	7.00	7.37	—	—	—
FLEETWOOD	—	7.24	7.14	7.25	6.94
HARLEY DAVIDSON	8.09	—	8.06	—	—
HARSCO	—	—	—	7.17	—
INTERNATIONAL CNTLS.	—	—	6.00	7.00	—
MINISTAR	—	6.59	7.29	—	—
OGDEN	—	—	—	—	7.38
OUTBOARD MARINE	6.95	7.52	—	—	—
TODD SHIPYARDS	—	—	—	—	7.40
TRINITY	6.87	7.44	—	7.83	—
WINNEBAGO	—	—	—	—	7.58

SCIENTIFIC AND PHOTOGRAPHIC EQUIPMENT

	1991	1990	1989	1988	1987
BAUSCH & LOMB	7.64	—	—	—	—
BAXTER	7.00	7.21	—	—	—
BECTON DICKINSON	7.06	7.26	6.95	7.07	7.23
EASTMAN KODAK	7.94	8.12	8.40	8.32	8.12
EG&G	6.80	—	7.22	6.83	7.14
FISHER SCIENT. GROUP	—	—	6.30	—	—
GENERAL SIGNAL	—	—	6.21	6.18	6.09
HENLEY GROUP	—	5.61	—	—	—
LEAR SIEGLER	—	—	—	5.92	6.02
LITTON	—	6.07	—	—	—
MINNESOTA MINING	8.27	8.51	8.44	8.38	8.12
PERKIN-ELMER	6.64	6.93	7.04	6.71	7.48
POLAROID	6.28	7.03	6.86	7.23	6.88
TEKTRONIX	6.47	6.65	7.02	6.94	6.93
XEROX	7.39	7.53	7.43	7.50	7.22

MOTOR VEHICLES AND PARTS

	1991	1990	1989	1988	1987
ARVIN INDUSTRIES	—	—	6.36	—	—
AMERICAN MOTORS	—	—	—	3.83	4.23
BORG-WARNER	—	6.41	—	6.33	6.66
CHRYSLER	5.13	6.11	6.28	6.43	6.74
DANA	6.91	7.22	7.15	7.34	7.05
EATON	7.37	7.42	—	—	—
ECHLIN	—	—	6.57	—	—
FLEETWOOD	5.75	—	—	—	—
FORD MOTOR	7.20	7.72	7.51	7.87	7.49
FRUEHAUF	—	—	5.99	6.09	6.15

(continued)

Exhibit 1.5 (Continued)

MOTOR VEHICLES AND PARTS

	1991	1990	1989	1988	1987
GENERAL MOTORS	6.17	6.11	5.85	5.35	6.19
K-H (FRUEHAUF)	—	5.55	—	—	—
MACK TRUCKS	5.15	5.91	6.82	6.71	6.64
MASCO	6.57	—	—	—	—
NAVISTAR	5.97	6.02	6.76	6.37	6.10
PACCAR	7.17	7.46	7.44	7.28	7.29

AEROSPACE

	1991	1990	1989	1988	1987
ALLIED-SIGNAL	6.33	6.16	6.09	6.16	6.57
BOEING	8.50	8.45	8.79	8.46	8.73
GENERAL DYNAMICS	6.99	7.42	7.04	7.20	7.18
LOCKHEED	6.51	7.12	7.23	7.30	7.36
MARTIN MARIETTA	7.24	7.77	7.47	7.48	7.52
MCDONNELL DOUGLAS	6.45	6.72	7.13	7.36	7.51
NORTHROP	5.38	5.59	5.79	6.64	7.41
ROCKWELL	7.01	6.78	6.90	7.08	7.25
TEXTRON	6.11	6.18	5.99	6.14	6.39
UNITED TECHNOLOGIES	7.04	7.04	6.39	6.67	6.90

PHARMACEUTICALS

	1991	1990	1989	1988	1987
ABBOTT LABS	7.61	7.75	7.93	8.07	7.81
AMERICAN HOMES	6.54	6.70	6.86	7.02	7.26
BAXTER	—	—	6.85	7.11	7.04
BRISTOL-MEYERS	7.93	7.78	7.83	7.82	7.56
JOHNSON & JOHNSON	8.24	8.27	8.34	8.35	8.16
ELI LILLY	8.03	7.57	8.04	7.95	7.84
MERCK	9.14	9.18	9.10	9.36	8.75
PFIZER	7.24	6.93	7.19	7.56	7.70
SCHERING-PLOUGH	7.30	7.21	—	—	—
SMITHKLINE BECKMAN	—	6.37	6.71	6.76	7.07
UPJOHN	6.79	—	—	—	—
WARNER-LAMBERT	6.95	6.88	6.91	6.65	6.64

SOAPS & COSMETICS

	1991	1990	1989	1988	1987
ALBERTO-CULVER	6.05	6.43	—	6.22	—
AVON PRODUCTS	5.98	6.12	6.55	6.96	6.43
CHEMED	6.00	—	—	—	—
CHESEBROUGH-POND'S	—	—	7.10	7.28	7.00
CLOROX	7.28	7.78	7.55	7.52	7.44
COLGATE-PALMOLIVE	7.33	7.30	7.32	7.38	6.94
ECOLAB	—	—	5.64	6.64	6.31

Exhibit 1.5 (Continued)

SOAPS & COSMETICS

	1991	1990	1989	1988	1987
FABERGE	—	—	5.88	—	—
HELENE CURTIS	6.94	—	—	—	—
INTERNAT'L FLAVORS	—	8.08	7.91	8.08	6.56
LEVER BROS.	—	—	7.55	7.38	7.32
NOXELL	—	7.71	—	—	—
PROCTER & GAMBLE	8.89	8.90	8.48	8.55	8.42
REVLON GROUP	6.54	—	6.54	6.57	6.21
STANHOME	6.07	—	—	—	—
UNILEVER U.S.	7.74	7.58	—	—	—

COMPUTERS

	1991	1990	1989	1988	1987
AMDAHL	—	—	7.08	—	—
APPLE COMPUTER	7.43	8.02	8.04	7.86	7.49
BURROUGHS	—	—	—	—	6.00
COMPAQ COMPUTER	7.95	—	—	—	—
CONTROL DATA	4.75	4.50	4.91	4.81	5.26
DIGITAL EQUIPMENT	7.08	7.25	7.66	7.80	8.44
GOULD	—	—	—	4.99	—
HEWLETT-PACKARD	7.93	8.15	8.13	7.88	8.19
HONEYWELL	—	—	—	—	5.83
IBM	7.63	7.35	7.54	7.26	7.90
NCR	6.27	6.25	6.32	6.50	6.49
PITNEY BOWES	5.96	6.23	5.93	5.94	6.38
UNISYS	4.47	4.80	5.51	5.62	—
WANG LABS	3.99	4.23	5.11	5.34	6.35
ZENITH	—	5.77	—	—	—

INDUSTRIAL AND FARM EQUIPMENT

	1991	1990	1989	1988	1987
AMERICAN STANDARD	—	—	6.99	6.84	7.12
BAKER HUGHES	7.19	7.10	6.84	6.76	6.57
BLACK & DECKER	7.55	7.58	7.47	7.54	7.40
BRUNSWICK	—	—	6.89	6.85	—
CATERPILLAR	8.40	8.67	8.47	8.53	8.46
COMBUSTION ENG.	—	—	—	—	6.72
CUMMINS ENGINE	7.46	7.72	7.60	7.87	8.07
DEERE	8.14	8.40	8.04	7.92	8.00
DOVER	6.72	6.91	—	—	—
DRESSER INDUSTRIES	6.71	6.80	6.42	6.23	6.68
INGERSOLL-RAND	7.16	7.27	6.76	6.81	7.08
PARKER HANNIFIN	7.09	7.20	—	—	—
TELEDYNE	—	—	—	6.75	6.79

(continued)

Exhibit 1.5 (Continued)

INDUSTRIAL AND FARM EQUIPMENT

	1991	1990	1989	1988	1987
TENNECO	6.68	6.43	—	—	—
TRINOVA	—	—	6.41	—	—

TOYS, SPORTING GOODS

	1991	1990	1989	1988	1987
COLECO	—	—	—	5.95	5.98
HASBRO	—	—	—	7.27	7.28
KENNER	—	—	—	6.61	—
MATTEL	—	—	—	6.45	6.68
MINSTAR	—	—	—	5.63	5.96

BEVERAGES

	1991	1990	1989	1988	1987
ANHEUSER BUSCH	8.58	8.72	8.58	8.02	8.37
BROWN FORMAN	7.15	7.49	7.20	6.39	6.81
COCA-COLA	8.74	8.94	8.62	8.08	8.43
COCA-COLA ENTERPR.	7.90	8.26	8.09	—	—
ADOLPH COORS	7.76	7.70	7.62	6.88	7.50
GENERAL CINEMA	—	—	7.30	6.10	6.98
DR PEPPER/SEVEN UP	—	7.13	—	—	—
G. HEILEMAN	—	—	—	5.56	5.79
PEPSICO	8.35	8.38	8.33	8.15	7.89
J.E. SEAGRAM	7.04	7.21	7.43	6.09	6.84

DIVERSIFIED SERVICE COMPANIES

	1991	1990	1989	1988	1987
ARA HOLDING	—	—	6.13	—	—
ALCO STANDARD	—	—	—	6.64	—
AMERICAN FINANCIAL	6.06	5.80	—	—	—
AT&T	8.19	8.04	—	—	—
CAPITAL CITIES	—	—	6.61	—	—
CBS	—	—	—	6.28	6.08
ELECTRONIC DATA SYS	—	—	7.46	7.44	—
FLEMING COMPANIES	6.84	6.34	6.49	6.45	6.49
FLUOR	—	6.51	6.44	6.34	6.66
HALLIBURTON	—	6.75	—	—	6.76
HOSPITAL CORP.	—	—	6.60	6.43	6.95
ENRON	6.81	—	—	—	6.22
MARRIOTT	7.55	—	—	—	—
MCI COMMUNICATIONS	—	7.21	—	—	—
MCKESSON	7.39	7.01	7.10	7.03	6.66
NATIONAL INTERGROUP	—	—	5.42	5.72	—
PACIFIC ENTERPRISES	6.35	—	—	—	—
PRIMERICA	—	—	—	6.72	—

Exhibit 1.5 (Continued)

DIVERSIFIED SERVICE COMPANIES

	1991	1990	1989	1988	1987
RYDER SYSTEM	—	6.37	—	—	—
SALOMON INC.	—	—	—	—	7.58
SUPER VALU STORES	6.78	6.69	6.52	6.72	6.91
SYSCO	7.08	—	—	—	—
UNITED TELECOM	6.79	6.83	—	—	
UNION PACIFIC	—	—	—	—	6.30

DIVERSIFIED FINANCIAL COMPANIES

	1991	1990	1989	1988	1987
AETNA LIFE	6.34	6.47	6.62	6.69	6.53
AMERICAN EXPRESS	7.68	8.20	8.30	8.05	7.70
AMERICAN INTERNAT'L	6.90	7.24	6.46	—	—
BEAR STEARNS	—	—	—	6.61	6.32
CIGNA	5.99	6.20	6.13	6.42	5.89
FEDERAL NAT'L MORTG.	6.94	6.95	6.79	6.26	6.33
FIRST BOSTON	—	—	7.06	7.37	7.57
ITT	6.12	6.31	—	—	—
E.F. HUTTON	—	—	—	—	5.59
LOEWS	—	—	—	—	6.24
MERRILL LYNCH	5.95	6.78	6.54	6.47	6.82
MORGAN STANLEY	7.01	7.55	7.71	7.52	—
SALOMON	6.40	6.85	7.02	7.35	—
TRAVELERS	5.77	6.15	6.21	6.47	6.41

COMMERCIAL BANKING COMPANIES

	1991	1990	1989	1988	1987
BANK OF NEW YORK	—	6.21	—	—	—
BANKAMERICA	6.29	5.96	4.81	4.86	5.12
BANKERS TRUST N.Y.	7.25	7.42	7.17	7.36	7.33
CHASE MANHATTAN	5.30	6.14	5.79	5.97	6.12
CHEMICAL BANK	5.32	5.96	5.63	5.88	6.36
CITICORP	6.95	7.64	7.42	7.32	7.54
FIRST CHICAGO	—	—	5.82	—	5.83
FIRST INTERSTATE	5.21	5.52	5.56	6.16	6.23
MANUFACTURERS HANOV.	5.15	5.37	5.07	5.51	5.72
J.P. MORGAN	7.80	7.85	7.91	8.37	8.20
NCNB CORP.	6.65	—	—	—	—
SECURITY PACIFIC	6.59	6.92	6.79	6.92	6.99
WELLS FARGO	—	—	—	6.88	—

LIFE INSURANCE COMPANIES

	1991	1990	1989	1988	1987
AETNA LIFE	6.32	6.13	6.25	6.50	6.30
CONNECTICUT LIFE	6.00	6.09	6.14	6.39	6.35

(continued)

Exhibit 1.5 (Continued)

LIFE INSURANCE COMPANIES

	1991	1990	1989	1988	1987
EQUITABLE LIFE	5.32	5.68	5.46	6.18	6.18
JOHN HANCOCK	5.93	6.13	5.98	6.03	5.94
METROPOLITAN LIFE	6.50	6.24	6.05	6.20	6.03
NEW YORK LIFE	6.48	6.36	6.28	5.99	6.24
NORTHWESTERN LIFE	8.03	7.99	8.02	7.82	7.90
PRUDENTIAL	6.99	6.81	6.87	6.50	6.42
TEACHERS INSURANCE	6.63	6.37	6.33	6.12	6.88
TRAVELERS	5.41	5.58	5.68	6.13	6.17

RETAILING COMPANIES

	1991	1990	1989	1988	1987
AMERICAN STORES	6.55	6.27	5.90	6.16	6.51
DAYTON HUDSON	7.56	7.28	6.99	—	7.45
FEDERATED DEPT.	—	—	6.58	6.72	7.12
GREAT ATLANTIC	6.05	6.38	—	—	—
K MART	5.32	5.62	6.02	5.52	5.67
KROGER	6.68	6.75	6.65	6.54	6.91
LUCKY STORES	—	—	—	—	5.75
MAY DEPT. STORES	7.10	6.98	6.67	6.67	—
J.C. PENNEY	6.78	6.88	6.59	6.52	6.66
SAFEWAY	6.36	6.31	5.92	5.79	—
SEARS ROEBUCK	5.68	6.12	6.32	6.24	6.66
SOUTHLAND	—	—	—	5.59	6.05
WAL-MART	7.66	7.34	7.28	6.99	—

UTILITIES

	1991	1990	1989	1988	1987
AMERICAN INFO. TECH	7.33	7.34	7.54	7.57	7.49
BELL ATLANTIC	7.61	7.60	7.72	7.72	7.63
BELLSOUTH	7.73	7.74	7.81	7.59	7.66
GTE	6.94	6.68	6.73	6.15	6.43
NYNEX	6.42	6.68	7.30	7.38	7.19
PACIFIC GAS	7.32	7.21	7.38	7.31	7.28
PACIFIC TELESIS	7.48	7.39	7.39	7.22	7.23
SOUTHERN	6.82	6.92	6.94	7.07	7.22
SOUTHWEST BELL	7.33	7.21	7.27	7.19	7.21
US WEST	7.13	7.10	7.13	7.21	7.18

TRANSPORTATION COMPANIES

	1991	1990	1989	1988	1987
AMR	7.46	7.50	7.74	7.10	7.16
BURLINGTON NORTHERN	—	6.37	6.32	6.08	6.35
CONTINENTAL	4.07	—	—	—	—
CSX	5.74	5.70	6.19	5.86	6.47

Exhibit 1.5 (Continued)

TRANSPORTATION COMPANIES

	1991	1990	1989	1988	1987
DELTA	7.74	7.42	7.61	6.99	7.61
FEDERAL EXPRESS	8.48	—	—	—	—
NORFOLK SOUTHERN	—	—	—	6.67	7.01
NWA	5.29	—	4.94	—	—
PAN AM	—	—	—	—	4.69
SANTA FE	—	5.79	5.76	5.42	5.89
TEXAS AIR	—	4.15	3.44	3.15	—
TWA	—	—	—	—	5.12
UAL	6.12	6.39	6.80	5.76	6.70
UNION PACIFIC	6.77	6.53	6.69	6.56	—
UPS	8.27	8.36	8.32	8.07	8.12
USAIR	5.13	6.01	—	—	—

SAVINGS INSTITUTIONS

	1991	1990	1989	1988	1987
H.F. AHMANSON	7.55	7.66	7.10	7.35	7.26
CALFED	6.00	5.95	6.30	6.19	6.59
CROSSLAND SAVINGS	4.65	5.66	—	—	—
FINANCIAL CORP.	—	—	3.51	4.05	4.51
FIRST FED. OF MI.	—	—	—	—	5.59
GIBRALTER	—	3.75	4.67	5.13	5.49
GLENFED	5.90	5.92	6.34	6.28	6.30
GOLDEN WEST FIN.	7.17	7.00	—	6.70	6.14
GOLDOME	4.05	—	4.99	—	—
GREAT AMERICAN	4.54	5.80	6.08	6.27	—
GREAT WESTERN	7.20	7.60	7.40	7.66	7.37
HOME FEDERAL S&L	5.74	7.10	6.99	6.38	6.79
MERITOR	4.22	4.45	4.67	4.90	5.61

appeared in the top three overall and topped their industry for each of the five years include Rubbermaid (Rubber Products), Procter and Gamble (Soaps and Cosmetics), and Boeing (Aerospace). The following companies did not appear in the overall best companies during the past five years on quality of products/services, but did rank first in their respective industries on this attribute for five years straight: Liz Claiborne (Apparel), Herman Miller (Furniture), Kimberly Clark (Forest Products), E. I. DuPont (Chemicals), Corning Glass Works (Building), American Express (Diversified Financial Companies), J. P. Morgan (Commercial Banking Companies), and Northwestern Life (Life Insurance Companies). This list differs and is more extensive than the information provided previously on quality of management, indicating possibly that product quality may be more easily assessed than management quality.

Once again, Philip Morris (formerly Tobacco, now Food) is shown to domi-
nate the Tobacco category until its industry switch, to be replaced in 1991 by
UST (Tobacco) on quality of products/services. Similarly, after leading the industry for four years, Dow Jones's drop from the Publishing and Printing Group
left the New York Times in first place with regard to products/services for 1991.
The Petroleum industry also experienced a change in leadership on this attribute
from Shell (1987–89) to the new leader, Amoco (1990–91). Alcoa led the Metals
group on product quality in four of five years, with Reynolds Metals a leader in
1988. The same phenomenon was observed in the Metal Products industry,
where product quality was dominated by Gillette in every year except 1988,
which belonged to Illinois Tool. After the breakup of AT&T, Motorola (Electronics) emerged as the industry leader on product quality. 3M remained dominant in
the Scientific and Photographic Equipment industry for the past four years, while
Eastman Kodak, which ranked first back in 1987, has experienced a steady
decline in rankings. Ford Motor Company lost a four-year lead on product
quality to Eaton (Motor Vehicles and Parts) in 1991. In the Computer industry,
Compaq, a new entrant to the survey, bumped Hewlett-Packard out of a three-
year lead in 1991. Caterpillar (Industrial and Farm Equipment) regained the top
spot on product quality from Black & Decker, which held that honor in 1990.
Coca-Cola (Beverages) ranked first in its industry on product quality in four of
five years, upset by Pepsico in 1988. In the retailing industry, Wal-Mart has
dominated on this attribute since 1988, overtaking Dayton Hudson. Bellsouth
(Utilities) dominated for four of five years on product quality in that industry. A
major upset by a newcomer to the survey in the Transportation industry for 1991,
Federal Express, was observed; for the first time in the five-year period, UPS
took second. Finally, leadership changed hands regarding quality of prod-
ucts/services in the Savings Institutions industry. Top-ranked Great Western
(1987–89) was a consistent second to H. F. Ahmanson (1990–91).

On an overall basis, transportation companies appeared in the worst three
companies on quality of products/services in the *Fortune* survey over the past
five years. These companies included Continental (also ranked lowest in industry
for 1991), Texas Air (also ranked lowest in 1988–90) and Pan Am (ranked as
industry lowest in 1987). The computer industry was also represented in this
group. In particular, Wang Labs has ranked lowest on product quality in the
industry for 1990–91 and prior to this Control Data (1987–89) held this spot.
Savings Institutions were also represented here, including the defunct Financial
Corp. and Gibraltar. While BankAmerica (Commercial Banking) was also included, and ranked lowest in its industry for 1987–89, a turnaround on quality of
products/services was observed in its industry rankings for 1990–91, similar to
that observed under quality of management.

The industries that appear most ambiguous in rankings on quality of prod-
ucts/services over the past five years include Mining and Crude Oil Production,
Food, Textiles, Transportation Equipment, and Diversified Service Companies.
In 1991 alone, seven of the top ten overall ranked companies also ranked first on

quality of products/services within their own industry groupings. The three exceptions were Pepsico (Beverages), which ranked second to Coca-Cola (Beverages), which was also in the top ten overall; and Johnson & Johnson (Pharmaceuticals) and Eli Lily (Pharmaceuticals) ranking second and third, respectively, by industry to Merck.

RELATIONS BETWEEN COST AND QUALITY

Management quality requires the identification and measurement of the cost of quality. Quality costs are those necessary to the achievement of product quality, involving mainly the conformance to all product requirements. They include *appraisal costs,* or costs of appraising products for conformance to requirements; *failure costs,* or costs incurred by failure to meet product specifications; and *prevention costs,* or costs of preventing product failures. Specific elements of each of these costs are shown in Exhibit 1.6. The traditional relationship between these costs and quality measured as conformance percentage is shown in Exhibit 1.7. Basically as a firm improves its quality, management prevention and appraisal costs will rise exponentially and internal and external failure costs will decrease. According to this traditional framework, the objective is to minimize costs while maximizing quality, and absolute quality performance is not economically practical—in effect, zero defects cost too much.[44] A better framework is where the costs of prevention are no longer infinitely high.[45] The framework includes the hidden costs of quality. As stated by Atkinson et al., "these hidden costs are included to recognize that they are often substantially greater than the traditionally measured failure costs. Companies have used multipliers to capture the relationship between measured failure costs and the total failure costs for the organization."[46]

Similarly, Campanella et al. state that "Westinghouse Electric Corporation, for example, reported that its 'experience indicates that a multiplier effect of at least three or four is directly related to such hidden effects of quality failure.' The bulk of failure costs are 'hidden' below the surface and usually are responsible for 'sinking the ship.' "[47]

Exhibit 1.6
Quality Cost Definitions

1. *Prevention Costs*
    a. *Product design*: Costs incurred in the quality control of new product design developments or major design changes prior to the release of engineering drawings.
        (1) *Design reviews*: The total cost (including planning) of all design reviews conducted prior to the release of design documents for the fabrication of prototypes or pilot models. These reviews should maximize initial conformance to the required characteristics of the design with regard to function, reliability safety, configuration, producibility, serviceability, maintainability, and product cost.
        (2) *Design checking and support*: The cost of engineering drawing checkers, reliability, components, and materials engineers as applicable to the prevention of design deficiencies.
    b. *Purchasing*: Costs incurred in the quality control of vendor-supplied parts, materials, and processes, prior to the finalization of purchase order commitments.
        (1) *Supplier reviews*: The cost of reviewing and evaluating suppliers' capabilities to meet company requirements.
        (2) *Supplier rating*: The cost of developing and maintaining a supplier rating system based on actual performance to established requirements.
        (3) *Purchase order technical data reviews*: The cost for reviews of purchase order technical data (usually by quality personnel) to assure its ability to communicate, clearly and completely, purchased product technical and quality requirements to respective suppliers.
        (4) *Supplier quality planning*: The total cost of planning for the incoming and source inspections and tests necessary to determine acceptance of supplier products. Includes the preparation of necessary documents and development costs for inspection and test equipment.
    c. *Quality planning*: Cost incurred in the evaluation of manufacturing plans and in the development and integration of quality plans.
        (1) *Manufacturing process evaluations*: The cost of activities established for the purpose of evaluating new manufacturing machinery, fabrication equipment, processes, and tools to assure their capability for initially and consistently performing within required limits.
        (2) *Inspection and test planning*: The total cost for development of necessary product inspection and test plans, documentation systems, and workmanship standards. Includes development costs for new or special-quality programs, acceptance gages, and product test equipment.
    d. *Quality administration*: Costs incurred in the overall administration of the quality management function.
        (1) *Administrative labor*: Compensation costs for all quality personnel (e.g., managers and directors, supervisors, and clerical) who are 100% administrative.
        (2) *Administrative expenses*: All other costs and expenses charged to or allocated to the quality management function and not specifically covered elsewhere in this report.
    e. *Quality training*: Costs incurred in the development and implementation of formal training programs for the purpose of preventing errors. Includes the total cost (course preparation, instruction, and necessary materials) of quality improvement programs, new employee quality orientations, and other programs designed to provide:

44

Exhibit 1.6 (Continued)

       (1) Inspector and operator training in new manufacturing methods, processes, or workmanship standards.

       (2) Tester training in new product designs and testing procedures.

       (3) Training required by new or revised company procedures affecting the control of quality.

This item is specifically not intended to include any portion of the the basic apprentice or skill training necessary to be qualified for individual assignments throughout the company.

  f. *Quality audits*: The cost of quality audits specifically performed to measure the effectiveness of quality system performance. Includes audits applied to areas (e.g., handling, order writing, etc.) that are not normally included as part of the appraisal system and product audits over and above the normal appraisal system (e.g., finished goods ready for delivery).

2. *Appraisal costs*

  a. *Product design/qualification tests*: Costs incurred in the qualification testing of new products or major changes to existing products. Includes costs for the inspection and test of qualification units under ambient conditions and the extremes of environmental parameters. Qualification inspections and tests are usually conducted to verify that all design requirements have been met or, when failures occur, to identify clearly where redesign efforts are required. Qualification may be performed on prototype units, pilot runs, or the initial production run of new products.

  b. *Supplier product inspection and test*: Costs incurred in providing appraisal of supplier's products for conformance to requirements.

       (1) *Routine inspections and tests*: Total costs for the normal or routine incoming inspection and test of purchased materials, products, or processes. These costs represent the continuing normal cost of purchased goods inspection and test.

       (2) *Qualification of supplier product*: The cost of additional inspection and test (including environmental tests) required to qualify the release of production quantities of purchased goods. These costs may be repeated periodically. They typically apply to the following situations:

         (a) First article inspection (detailed inspection and key environmental tests) on a sample of the first production buy of new components or material.

         (b) Qualification test or first article inspection for second and third sources of previously qualified end-product components.

         (c) First article inspection of the initial supply of customer furnished parts.

         (d) First article inspection of the initial purchased quantity of goods for resale.

       (3) *Source inspections, tests, and control programs*: All company-incurred costs (including travel) for the conduct of any of the activities described in items (1) and (2) at the vendor's plant or at an independent test laboratory. This item will normally include product acceptance costs associated with direct shipments from vendor to customer or to installation sites.

  c. *In-process and final inspection and test*: Costs incurred for all in-process and final inspection and acceptance tests of manufactured products.

Exhibit 1.6 (Continued)

      (1) *Planned inspections and tests*: The cost of all planned inspections and tests conducted on manufactured product at selected points throughout the manufacturing process, including the total cost of destructive test samples (does not include sorting of rejected lots of material or product).

      (2) *Setup inspections*: The cost of all setup or first-piece inspections utilized to assure that each combination of machine and tool is properly adjusted to produce acceptable products before the start of each production lot.

      (3) *Special tests (production)*: The cost of all nonroutine inspections and tests conducted on manufactured product as a part of the acceptance plan. These costs will normally include periodic sampling of sensitive product for more detailed and extensive inspections and tests to assure continued conformance to critical environmental requirements.

      (4) *Process control measurements*: The cost of all inspections, tests, and measurements conducted on product processing equipment and/or materials (e.g., plating tank temperature and chemical content) to assure their conformance to preestablished standards. Includes adjustments made to maintain continued acceptable results.

      (5) *Laboratory support*: The total cost of any laboratory tests required in support of inspection and test plans.

      (6) *Miscellaneous inspections*: The cost of all inspections not covered elsewhere (e.g., stores, packaging, and shipping activities).

      (7) *Depreciation allowances*: Total depreciation allowances for all capitalized inspection or test equipment.

    d. *Maintenance and calibration*: Costs incurred in the maintenance and calibration of acceptance inspection and test equipment.

      (1) *Maintenance and calibration labor*: The cost of all inspections, calibration, maintenance, and control of measurement equipment, instruments, and gages used for the inspection and test of product and manufacturing processes.

      (2) *Measurement equipment expenses*: The procurement or manufacturing cost of all inspection and test equipment and gages that are not capitalized.

3. *Failure Costs*

    a. *Design failure costs*: Costs incurred due to initial design inadequacies.

      (1) *Engineering corrective action*: After initial release of design to production, the total cost of all problem investigation and redesign efforts (including requalification as necessary) except as directed by and billed to the customer.

      (2) *Rework due to design changes*: The cost of all rework (materials, labor, and burden) specifically required as part of the implementation plan (effectivity) for engineering changes.

      (3) *Scrap due to design changes*: The cost of all scrap (materials, labor, and burden) required as a part of the implementation plan (effectivity) for engineering changes.

    b. *Supplier product rejects*: Cost incurred due to purchased item rejects.

Exhibit 1.6 (Continued)

      (1) *Disposition costs*: The cost to disposition or sort incoming inspection rejects. Includes the cost of reject documentation, review and evaluation, disposition orders, handling, and transportation (except as charged to the supplier).

      (2) *Replacement costs*: The added cost of replacement for all items rejected and returned to the supplier. Includes additional transportation and expediting costs when not paid for by the supplier.

      (3) *Correction action plans*: The cost of company-sponsored failure analyses and investigations into the cause of supplier rejects and determination of necessary corrective actions. Includes the cost of visits to supplier plants for this specific purpose and the cost to provide added inspection protection while the problem is being resolved.

c. *Material review and corrective action*: Costs incurred in the review and disposition of nonconforming manufactured products and the corrective actions necessary to prevent recurrence.

      (1) *Disposition costs*: All costs incurred in the review and disposition of nonconforming manufactured product, in the analysis of quality data to determine significant items for correction action (Pareto principle), and in the investigation of these to determine cause.

      (2) *Failure analysis costs*: The cost of failure analyses conducted or obtained in support of defect cause identification.

      (3) *Investigation support costs*: The additional cost of special runs of product or controlled lots of material (designed experiments) conducted specifically to obtain information useful to the determination of the cause of a particular defect.

      (4) *Manufacturing corrective actions*: The actual cost of manufacturing corrective actions taken to remove or eliminate the causes of nonconformances identified for correction. This item will normally include such activities as rewriting operator instructions, redevelopment of specific manufacturing processes or flow procedures, redesign or modification of tooling, and the development and implementation of specific training needs.

d. *Rework*: The total cost (labor, material, and overhead) of reworking defective product.

      (1) *Manufactured product rework*: The total cost (material, labor, and burden) of all rework or repairs done to manufactured product as required by specific work order, personal assignment, or as a planned part of the standard manufacturing operation. Does not include rework due to design change [see item 3.a(2)].

      (2) *Reinspection and retest*: That portion of inspection and test labor that is incurred because of rejects (includes documentation of rejects, fault finding in test, and inspection and test after rework) and sorting of defective lots.

      (3) *Supplier product rework*: The total cost of supplier product repairs not billed to suppliers. Also includes any added production costs necessitated by the decision to use material that is less than totally conforming.

Exhibit 1.6 (Continued)

e. *Scrap*: The total cost (material, labor, and overhead) of defective product that cannot be reworked to conform to requirements.

  (1) *Product spoilage*: Product spoilage is considered as material or product which, because of irreparability or uneconomical rework cost, is discarded (scrapped). This item includes the total cost (material, labor, and burden) of all such material and product, regardless of whether it is accounted for on scrap tickets, counted as planned or unplanned yield losses, or simply discarded on the manufacturing floor. Does not include scrap due to design change [see item 3.a(3)].

  (2) *Substandard product costs*: Total amount of selling costs and price differential required to sell nonconforming or off-grade products.

  (3) *Material losses*: Scrap is also intended to cover the cost of material or parts shortages due to damage, theft, and other (perhaps unknown) reasons. A measure of these costs may be obtained from a periodic review of inventory adjustments.

  (4) *Labor losses*: When direct productive labor is lost for reasons of product defects, regardless of cause, these losses are the equivalent of scrap, except that there are no concurrent material losses. Typical losses are caused by machine shutdowns and reset-up or line stoppages due to defective material being produced or defective raw material being supplied.

f. *External failure costs*: All costs incurred due to product defects or suspected defects after delivery to customer.

  (1) *Complaint investigations*: The total cost of investigating and resolving individual customer complaints.

  (2) *Returned goods/field service*: The total cost of evaluating and repairing or replacing defective goods after delivery or acceptance by the customer. This includes the full cost of any necessary recall activity. It does not include repairs accomplished as part of a maintenance or modification contract.

  (3) *Retrofit costs*: Costs to correct nonconformance to the required engineering drawing issue (configuration or change level) or to update product to a mandatory new design change level.

  (4) *Warranty claims*: The total cost of additional claims paid to the customer to cover legitimate expenses, such as repair costs to remove the defective hardware from their system.

  (5) *Liability costs*: Company-paid costs due to product liability claims, including the cost of product liability insurance.

  (6) *Penalties*: Cost of penalties due to less than full product performance.

Source: L. Walsh, R. Wurster, and R. J. Kimber, eds., *Quality Management Handbook* (New York: Marcel Dekker, 1986), pp. 99–104. Reprinted courtesy of Marcel Dekker, Inc.

Exhibit 1.7
Traditional Cost of Quality Concept

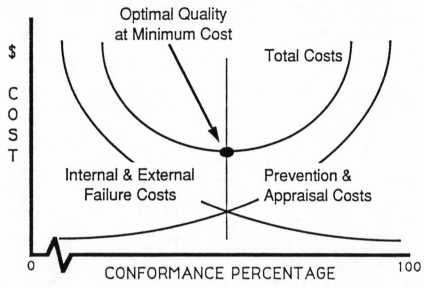

Source: J. H. Atkinson, Jr., G. Hohner, B. Mundt, R. B. Troxel, and W. Winchell, *Current Trends in Cost of Quality: Linking the Cost of Quality and Continuous Improvement* (Montvale, N.J.: National Association of Accountants [now Institute of Management Accountants], 1991), p. 12. Reprinted with permission.

NOTES

1. John S. Oakland, *Total Quality Management* (Oxford: Heineman, 1989), p. 5.
2. William A. Band, *Crediting Value for Customers* (New York: John Wiley, 1991), p. 80.
3. Ibid, pp. 146–148.
4. A. H. Hayes, S. C. Wheelwright, and K. B. Clarke, *Dynamic Manufacturing: Creating the Learning Organization* (New York: Free Press, 1988), p. 164.
5. Ibid.
6. David A. Garvin, *Managing Quality: The Strategic and Competitive Edge* (London: The Free Press, 1988), pp. 40–48.
7. R. M. Pirsig, *Zen and the Art of Motorcycle Maintenance* (New York: Bantam Books, 1974).
8. K. B. Geffler, "Ambiguous Changes in Product Quality," *American Economic Review* (December 1988), pp. 956–967.
9. Garvin, *Managing Quality,* p. 43.

10. B. T. Ratford, "The New Economic Theory of Consumer Behavior: An Interpretive Essay," *Journal of Consumer Research* (September 1975), pp. 65–75.

11. L. J. White, "Quality Variation When Prices Are Regulated," *Bell Journal of Economics and Management Science* (Autumn 1972), pp. 425–436.

12. H. L. Gilmore, "Product Conformance Cost," *Quality Progress* (June 1974), pp. 16–19.

13. Crosby, Philip B., *Quality Is Free* (New York: McGraw-Hill, 1984).

14. Garvin, *Managing Quality*, p. 46.

15. Andrea Gabor, *The Man Who Discovered Quality: How A. W. Edwards Deming Brought the Quality Revolution to America—The Stories of Ford, Xerox and GM* (New York: Times Books, 1990).

16. Laura B. Forker, "Quality: American, Japanese, and Soviet Perspectives," *The Executive* (November 1991), p. 65.

17. J. M. Juran, "Product Quality: A Prescription for the West, Part II: Upper-Management Leadership and Employee Relations," *Management Review* (July 1981), p. 61.

18. J. M. Juran and F. M. Cyrna, eds., *Juran's Quality Control Handbook*, 4th ed. (New York: McGraw-Hill, 1988), p. 6.

19. Genichi Taguchi, "The Evaluation of Quality," *48th Annual Quality Congress Transactions* (New York: American Society for Quality Control, Inc., 1987), p. 8.

20. Forker, "Quality: American, Japanese, and Soviet Perspectives," p. 68.

21. Garvin, *Managing Quality*, pp. 49–50.

22. Ibid., p. 51.

23. Ibid., p. 52.

24. Ibid., p. 53.

25. Ibid., p. 57.

26. Ibid., p. 59.

27. Martin Smith, "Management Communication," in L. Walsh, R. Wurster, and R. J. Kimber, *Quality Management Handbook* (New York: Marcel Dekker, 1986), p. 56.

28. J. M. Groocock, *The Cost of Quality* (London: Pitman, 1979), p. 30.

29. Ibid., p. 33.

30. Oakland, *Total Quality Management*, p. 42.

31. Ibid.

32. Groocock, *Cost of Quality*, p. 33.

33. J. H. Rogerson, *Quality Assurance in Process Plant Manufacture* (London: Elsevier Applied Science Publishers, 1986), p. 4.

34. Ibid., p. 14.

35. "The Quality World of Allis Chalmers," *Quality Assurance* (December 1970), pp. 13–17.

36. Dale H. Besterfield, *Quality Control* (Englewood Cliffs, N.J.: Prentice-Hall, 1979), p. 9.

37. Groocock, *The Cost of Quality*, p. 23.

38. Ibid., p. 24.

39. "Where Did They Go Wrong?" *Business Week* (October 25, 1991), p. 35.

40. "Top Products for Less Than Top Dollar," *Business Week* (October 25, 1991), p. 66.

41. "The Prize and the Passion," *Business Week* (October 25, 1991), p. 58.

42. "Leading the Total Quality Effort," Speech given by John A. Saxton, Vice-President, Noxell (Procter & Gamble Company), April 27, 1990.

43. D. Gavin, "Japanese Quality Management," *Columbia Journal of World Business* 19, no. 3 (1982), p. 4.

44. John Hawley Atkinson, Jr., Gregory Hohner, Barry Mundt, Richard B. Troxel, and William Winchell, *Current Trends in Cost of Quality: Limiting the Cost of Quality and Continuous Improvement* (Montvale, N.J.: National Association of Accountants [now Institute of Management Accountants], 1991), p. 11.

45. Ibid., p. 13.

46. Ibid., p. 13.

47. Jack Campanella and Frank J. Corcoran, *Principles of Quality Costs* (Milwaukee: ASQC Quality Press, 1983), p. 10.

REFERENCES

Atkinson, John Hawley, Jr., Gregory Hohner, Barry Mundt, Richard B. Troxel, and William Winchell. *Current Trends in Cost of Quality: Limiting the Cost of Quality and Continuous Improvement.* Montvale, N.J.: National Association of Accountants [now Institute of Management Accountants], 1991.

Crosby, Phillip B. *Quality Is Free.* New York: McGraw-Hill, 1984.

Deming, W. Edwards. *Quality, Productivity, and Competitive Position.* Boston: MIT Press, 1982.

Forker, Laura B. "Quality: American, Japanese, and Soviet Perspectives," *The Executive* (November 1991), pp. 63–74.

Garvin, David H. *Managing Quality: The Strategic and Competitive Edge.* New York: The Free Press, 1988.

Groocock, J. M. *The Cost of Quality.* London: Pitman, 1979.

Juran, J. M. *Juran on Leadership for Quality: An Executive Handbook.* New York: The Free Press, 1989.

Morse, Wayne J. and Harold P. Roth. "Why Quality Costs Are Important." *Management Accounting* (November 1987), pp. 42–43.

Noori, Hamid. "The Taguchi Methods: Achieving Design and Output Quality." *The Executive* (November 1989), pp. 322–326.

Tyson, Thomas N. "Quality and Profitability: Have Controllers Made the Connection?" *Management Accounting* (November 1987), pp. 38–43.

Walsh, Loren, Ralph Wurster, and Raymond J. Kimber. *Quality Management Handbook.* New York: Marcel Dekker, 1986.

2

ACCOUNTING FOR QUALITY COSTS

INTRODUCTION

The concern with quality is evident by the increasing number of U.S. companies that are establishing new positions called "vice-president for quality" and by pegging executive pay partly to quality. Clearly excellence is now the norm rather than the exception, and that means as few defects as possible. In reality, U.S. corporations still face several quality problems generally identified as scrap and waste, defective work, spoilage, and lost units. This chapter elaborates the methods used to account for these quality costs, and introduces the new manufacturing accounting with the ultimate aim of reducing or eliminating quality costs and insuring a zero defect policy.

ACCOUNTING FOR LACK OF QUALITY

Most manufacturing operations are expected to be subject to possible production losses due to scrap, spoilage, or defective work. To be fully informative, a good cost accounting system must recognize such losses.

Scrap and Waste

Scrap and waste are material residues of manufacturing operations that are believed to have minor resale value to scrap dealers. If the amount of scrap is relatively significant, scrap tickets are prepared to support entries to scrap reports usually expressed in terms of quantities of scrap delivered to the storeroom. At the time of sale, the possible entries are as follows.

| Cash (or Accounts Receivable) | xxx |
| Income from sale of scrap (or Department Factory Overhead Control account) | xxx |

This entry shows that in case the scrap is not identifiable to a particular job or department, the credit entry can be made either to a special income account or to reduce the Department Factory Overhead Control account. The posting made to the subsidiary ledger is recorded in the Sale of Scrap column on the departmental cost sheet.

| Cash (or Accounts Receivable) | xxx |
| Work-in-Process | xxx |

If the scrap is identifiable to a specific job or department, an alternative treatment is to credit the appropriate work-in-process account. This treatment is justifiable when an agreement exists between the manufacturer and the customer that specifies the crediting of jobs with all scrap and spoilage losses. Accordingly, the posting made to the subsidiary ledger is recorded in the specific job-order cost sheet.

From a critical point of view, timely and continuous reporting of scrap losses is advisable for the proper functioning of a responsible accounting system. At the time of occurrence, the recording of not only the scrap quantity but also the scrap value at an "estimated" resale value may even be advisable. The entry would be

| Scrap Inventory | xxx |
| Factory Overhead (or Work-in-Process) | xxx |

This last entry is more justifiable when there is a significant time lag between the incurrence and sale of scrap.

Scrap as an aspect of total manufacturing cost should not be ignored. It needs to be identified, monitored, and the full expense segregated in department, plant, division, and corporate management reports. Operating measures that can be used to monitor scrap include quality-incoming material inspection, material cost as a percentage of total cost, actual scrap, scrap by part/production/operation, and scrap percentage of total cost.[1] Beyond monitoring, the objective should be to eliminate scrap. Witness the following statement:

Ironically, if the new manufacturing environment really means high incoming quality and tight in-process control, then you should expect that scrap would be at a minimum. That is the ultimate goal and, in fact, more world class manufacturers have set zero scrap as their objectives. That means no scrap allowances. Until a manufacturer gets there, however, the measurement of scrap is critical.[2]

Defective Work

Defective goods result from failure to meet the production standard established for a good unit. When defects occur, the supervision can authorize either rework or resale. If the decision is to rework the defective units at added costs of material, labor, and overhead, the accounting treatment will depend on whether the cost of defective units is to be charged to the total production and consequently debited to the Department Factory Overhead Control account, or if it is to be charged to a specific job and consequently to Work-in-Process. In either case, the entries will be as follows:

Department Factory Overhead (or Work-in-Process)	xxx
Materials	xxx
Labor	xxx
Overhead Applied	xxx

Spoilage

Spoilage and lost units result from either (1) production that does not meet the standard established for good units, that cannot be reworked, and, consequently, that is sold for disposal value; or (2) shrinkage or evaporation of the materials used so completed production has a smaller volume than the total of basic inputs. Normal spoilage is an expected, inherent result of the production process that cannot be controlled. It should be internalized logically in the computation of the predetermined overhead rate to be prorated to the total period production. Abnormal spoilage is an unexpected production loss resulting from controllable factors; as such, it should be recognized by a loss account called Loss from Abnormal Spoilage. To illustrate, assume the following example:

Units Completed:		2,200 Units
Goods Units	2,000	
Normal Spoilage	50	
Abnormal Spoilage	150	
Total		2,200 Units
Unit Cost:	$3	

The accounting entries for this example could be as follows:

Work-in-Process	xxx
Material, Factory Payroll, Manufacturing Overhead	6,600

to record the input of material and conversion costs.

Cost of Spoiled Goods	600
Work-in-Process	600

to record the spoilage of 200 units.

Finished Goods	6,000
Work-in-Process	6,000

to record the normal spoilage of 50 units.

Loss from Abnormal Spoilage	450
Cost of Spoiled Goods	450

to record the abnormal spoilage of 150 units.

Note that the second entry recognizes a cost of spoiled goods and is, in a way, a clearing account that allows the recognition of both normal and abnormal spoilage as product costs first, and then as either a loss or an expense. In practice, such an entry can be skipped for expediency.

Lost Units

Accounting for lost units depends on whether the units were lost in the first department or after the first department. If the units are lost in the first department, the number of units decreases; this leads to a higher unit cost, and no adjustments are necessary. If the units are lost in subsequent departments, adjustment for lost units must be made. Such an adjustment can be computed according to two possible methods.

Method 1: The adjustment for lost units is equal to the difference between the new unit cost and the old unit cost, where the unit cost is computed as follows:

$$\text{New unit costs} = \frac{\text{Transferred-in cost}}{\text{Units transferred from preceding department} - \text{Lost units}}$$

Method 2: The adjustment for lost units is computed by allocating the total cost lost over the number of units actually produced:

$$\text{Adjustment for lost units} = \frac{\text{Lost units} \times \text{Old unit cost}}{\text{Units transferred from preceding department} - \text{Lost units}}$$

As an example, assume the following information for departments 1 and 2:

Transferred-in Costs from Department 1	$120,000
Units Transferred from Department 1	30,000
Units Lost in Department 2	6,000

The adjustment for lost units is computed using method 1 as follows:

New unit cost: $120,000/(30,000 − 6,000) = $5

Old unit cost: $120,000/30,000 = $4

Adjustment: $5 − $4 = $1

Using method 2,

$$\text{Adjustment: } \frac{6,000 \times \$4}{30,000 - 6,000} = \$1$$

Besides requiring an adjustment to the unit cost, the possibility of units lost in production or units added in the process requires an adjustment in the flow of units in the production equation. Hence the production equation will be as follows for the weighted average method:

Units in process at the beginning + Units started + Units added

$$= \frac{\text{units}}{\text{completed}} + \frac{\text{Units still in}}{\text{process at the end}} + \text{Units lost}$$

For the FIFO (first in, first out) method, the production equation will be:

$$\frac{\text{Units in process}}{\text{at the beginning}} + \frac{\text{Units}}{\text{started}} + \frac{\text{Units}}{\text{added}} = \frac{\text{Units completed from}}{\text{the beginning inventory}}$$

$$+ \frac{\text{Units started}}{\text{and completed}} + \frac{\text{Units still in}}{\text{process at the end}} + \text{Units lost}$$

Notice that units added increase the left side of the production equation, while units lost increase the right side. Using method 1, the following adjustment for lost units is made for another example:

New unit cost: $300,000/(60,000 − 12,000) = $6.25

Old unit cost: $300,000/60,000   = $5.00

Adjustment for lost units: $6.25 − $5   = $1.25

Using method 2,

$$\text{Adjustment for lost units} = \frac{18,000 \text{ units} \times \$5}{60,000 - 12,000} = \$1.25$$

PROCESS COSTING AND SPOILAGE (SHRINKAGE, EVAPORATION, WASTE, AND LOST UNITS)

Initial and Terminal Spoilage

Process costing for spoilage (shrinkage, evaporation, waste, and lost units) differs depending on where in production the spoilage takes place. If spoilage occurs in the beginning of operations, the condition is called initial spoilage. The costs of spoiled goods from normal spoilage are allocated to good production and units in the Ending Work-in-Process Inventory. If spoilage occurs at the end of operations, the condition is called terminal spoilage, and the costs of spoiled goods from normal spoilage are only allocated to Units Completed and Transferred Out of the Department. The following example illustrates the accounting treatment of spoilage in a process cost system under either the FIFO or the weighted average method and assuming either initial or terminal spoilage.

Assume that the ABEL Manufacturing Company produces a product alpha with costs accumulated on a process cost basis. Material for alpha are added in at the beginning of the process, and the conversion costs are added evenly throughout the process. Normal spoilage represents about one-tenth of the good output. Additional relevant production statistics for December are as follows:

Beginning Inventory (Units)	2,000 ($\frac{1}{4}$ Complete)
Total Costs	$29,250
Material	$17,000
Labor	$8,500
Overhead	$3,750
Processing Costs	
Total Costs	$90,000
Material	$60,000
Labor	$24,000
Overhead	$6,000
Production	
Units Started	5,000
Units Completed	5,000
Ending Inventory (Units)	1,000 ($\frac{1}{2}$ Complete)
Normal Spoilage (Units)	500
Abnormal Spoilage (Units)	500

Exhibits 2.1 and 2.2 show the process cost summary under the weighted average method and the FIFO method, respectively. On the basis of these two process cost summaries, accounting for spoilage (either initial or terminal) can be initiated.

Exhibit 2.1

ABEL Manufacturing Company, Ltd., Process Cost Summary: Weighted Average Method

1. Costs Charged to the Department

	Material	Labor	Overhead	Total
Current Costs	$60,000	$24,000	$6,000	$ 90,000
Beginning Work-in-Process	17,000	8,500	3,750	29,250
Total Costs to Be Accounted for	$77,000	$32,500	$9,750	$119,250

2. Equivalent Unit Processing Costs

	Units	Material	Labor	Overhead
Beginning Work-in-Process (1/4)	2,000			
Units Started	5,000			
To Account for	7,000			
Units Completed	5,000	5,000	5,000	5,000
Ending Work-in-Process (1/2)	1,000	1,000	500	500
Spoilage	1,000	1,000	1,000	1,000
Equivalent Units		7,000	6,500	6,500
Total Costs to Be Accounted for		$77,000	$32,500	$9,750
Equivalent Unit Processing Costs		$11.00	$5.00	$1.50

3. Costs Applicable to the Work of the Department

Goods Completed: 5,000 ($11 + $5.00 + $1.50)			$87,500
Ending Work-in-Process			
Material:	1,000 ($11.00)	$11,000	
Conversion Costs:	500 ($ 6.50)	3,250	14,250
Normal Spoilage:	500 ($17.50)		8,750
Abnormal Spoilage:	500 ($17.50)		8,750
Total Costs Accounted for			$119,250

Exhibit 2.2

ABEL Manufacturing Company, Ltd., Process Cost Summary: FIFO Method

1.   Costs Charged to the Department

	Material	Labor	Overhead	Start-up	Total
Current Costs	$60,000	$24,000	$ 6,000	--	$90,000
Beginning Work-in-Process	--	--	--	$29,250	29,250
Total Costs to Be Accounted for	$60,000	$24,000	$ 6,000	$29,250	$119,250

2.   Equivalent Unit Processing

		Equivalent Units		
	Total Units	Material	Labor	Overhead
Beginning Work-in-Process (1/4)	2,000			
Units Started	5,000			
To Account for	7,000			
Units Completed				
Beginning Inventory	2,000	--	1,500	1,500
Started and Completed	3,000	3,000	3,000	3,000
Ending Work-in-Process (1/2)	1,000	1,000	500	500
Spoilage	1,000	1,000	1,000	1,000
Equivalent Units		5,000	6,000	6,000
Total Costs to Be Accounted for		$60,000	$24,000	$6,000
Equivalent Unit Processing Costs		$12.00	$4.00	$1.00

3.   Cost Applicable to the Work of the Department

Goods Completed	29,250 + 1,500 ($4.00 + $1.00)	$36,750
Beginning Inventory: 3,000	($17.00)	
Started and Completed: 500	($17.00)	
Normal Spoilage:		
Abnormal Spoilage:		
Ending Work-in-Process		
Materials:	1,000 ($12.00)	$12,000
Conversion Costs:	500 ($ 5.00)	2,500 14,500
Total Costs Accounted for		$119,250

If the spoilage in the ABEL Manufacturing Company was an initial spoilage, the costs of spoiled goods from normal spoilage would be allocated to good production and units in the Ending Work-in-Process. The allocation using the weighted average results would be as follows:

1. Ending Work-in-Process before normal spoilage: $14,250
2. Goods Completed before normal spoilage loss: $87,500
3. Normal spoilage per unit ($8,750/6,000 units): $1,458
4. Normal spoilage allocated to Goods Completed ($1,458 × 5,000): $7,292
5. Normal spoilage allocated to Ending Work-in-Process ($1,458 × 1,000): $1,458
6. Goods Completed after normal spoilage (2 + 4): $94,790
7. Ending Work-in-Process after normal spoilage (1 + 5): $15,708

The allocation using the FIFO results would be as follows:

1. Ending Work-in-Process before normal spoilage: $14,500
2. Goods Completed before normal spoilage: $87,750
3. Normal spoilage per unit ($8,500/6,000 units): $1,416
4. Normal spoilage allocated to Goods Completed ($1,416 × 5,000): $7,084
5. Normal spoilage allocated to Ending Work-in-Process ($1,416 × 1,000): $1,416
6. Goods completed after normal spoilage (2 + 4): $96,569.25
7. Ending Work-in-Process after normal spoilage (1 + 5): $15,734.525

The journal entries will be as follows:

	Weighted Average		FIFO	
Work-in-Process	90,000		90,000	
Raw Material Inventory		60,000		60,000
Factory Payroll		24,000		24,000
Factory Overhead		6,000		6,000
to record the input of material and conversion costs.				
Cost of Spoiled Goods	17,500		17,000	
Work-in-Process		17,500		17,000
to record the completion of 1,000 units.				
Finished Goods	87,500		87,500	
Cost of Spoiled Goods		87,500		87,500
to record the completion of 5,000 units.				

	Weighted Average		FIFO	
Finished Goods	7,292		7,084	
Work-in-Process	1,458		1,416	
Cost of Spoiled Goods		8,750		8,500

to allocate normal spoilage to good production and units in the Ending Work-in-Process.

	Weighted Average		FIFO	
Loss from Abnormal Spoilage	8,750		8,500	
Cost of Spoiled Goods		8,750		8,500

to record the abnormal spoilage of 500 units.

If the spoilage in the ABEL Manufacturing Company were a terminal spoilage, the costs of spoiled goods from normal spoilage would be allocated only to the units completed and transferred out of the department. In such a case, the journal entries would be as follows:

	Weighted Average		FIFO	
Work-in-Process	90,000		90,000	
Raw Material Inventory		60,000		60,000
Factory Payroll		24,000		24,000
Factory Overhead		6,000		6,000

to record the input of material and conversion costs.

	Weighted Average		FIFO	
Cost of Spoiled Goods	17,500		17,000	
Work-in-Process		17,500		17,500

to record the spoilage of 1,000 units.

	Weighted Average		FIFO	
Finished Goods	87,500		87,750	
Work-in-Process		87,500		87,750

to record the completion of 5,000 units.

	Weighted Average		FIFO	
Finished Goods	8,750		8,500	
Cost of Spoiled Goods		8,750		8,750

to record the normal spoilage of 500 units.

	Weighted Average		FIFO	
Loss from Abnormal Spoilage	8,750		8,500	
Cost of Spoiled Goods		8,750		8,750

Inspection at a Degree of Completion

The example so far assumes that the spoilage is either initial or terminal. However, the spoilage may be detected at a certain degree of completion. In such a case the cost of spoilage will receive a percentage of the conversion costs equal to the degree of completion. For example, let's assume that the spoilage has been detected with an inspection at 40 percent of the ABEL Manufacturing Company operations. In such a case the equivalent units for spoilage under the weighted average method should be 1,000 units for material and 400 units (1,000 units × 40%) of conversion costs. Similarly, the equivalent units for spoilage under the FIFO method would be 0 units of material and 150 units ([.40 − .25] 1,000) of conversion costs if we assume that the spoiled units originated from the beginning inventory of 1,000 units of material and 400 units of conversion costs if we assume that the spoiled units originated from the units started in the period. The assignment of the cost of normal spoilage when the inspection is done at a certain degree of completion (40 percent in this case) would depend on one of two situations:

1. If the ending inventory was less than the degree of completion as far as the production cycle was concerned, then the cost of normal spoilage will be assigned only to the units that have passed inspection.

2. If the ending inventory was more than the degree of completion as far as the production cycle was concerned, then the cost of normal spoilage will be assigned to both completed units and ending inventory.

Thus, a comparison of the stage in operations at which inspection occurs and the stage of completion of the ending inventory is crucial in deciding whether to allocate some of the costs of normal spoilage to the partially completed units in the ending inventory.

Exhibits 2.3, 2.4, and 2.5 show the process cost remaining under the weighted average method and the FIFO method. Under different conditions:

Condition 1: Exhibit 2.3 shows the process cost summary under the weighted average method. The spoilage is assumed to have been discovered at 40 percent of the operations of the firm. The allocation using the weighted average method results and assuming the ending inventory was more than 40 percent completed are:

1. Ending Work-in-Process before normal spoilage: $14,579.325

2. Goods completed before normal spoilage: $90,793.25

3. Normal spoilage per unit: $6,931.73/6,000 = $1.1552

4. Normal spoilage allocated to goods completed: $1.1552 × 5,000 = $5,776

5. Normal spoilage allocated to ending Work-in-Process: $1.1552 × 1,000 = $1,155.20

Exhibit 2.3

ABEL Manufacturing Company, Ltd., Process Cost Summary: Weighted Average Method

1. Costs Charged to the Department

	Material	Labor	Overhead	Total
Current Costs	$60,000	$24,000	$6,000	$90,000
Beginning Work-in-Process	17,000	8,500	3,750	29,250
Total Costs to Be Accounted For	$77,000	$32,500	$9,750	$119,250

2. Equivalent Unit Processing Costs

		Equivalent Units		
	Total Units	Material	Labor	Overhead
Beginning Work-in-Process (1/4)	2,000			
Units Started	5,000			
To Account For	7,000			
Units Completed	5,000	5,000	5,000	5,000
Ending Work-in-Process (1/2)	1,000	1,000	500	500
Spoilage	1,000	1,000	400	400
Equivalent Units		7,000	5,900	5,900
Total Costs to Be Accounted For		$77,000	$32,500	$9,750
Equivalent Unit Processing Costs		$11.000	$5.5084	$1.65025

3. Costs Applicable to the Work of the Department

Goods Completed: 5,000 ($11 + $5.5084 + $1.65025) = $90,793.25

Ending Work-in-Process

  Material   1,000 ($11) = $11,000

  Conversion Costs: 500 ($5.5084 + $1.65025) = $3,579.325

                    $14,579.325

Normal Spoilage: (500 x 11) + 200($5.5084 + $1.65025)   6,931.73

Abnormal Spoilage: (500 x 11) + 200($5.084 + $1.65025)   6,931.73

6. Goods completed after normal spoilage (2 + 4): $94,790

7. Ending Work-in-Process after normal spoilage (1 + 5): $15,708

Condition 2: Exhibit 2.4 shows the process cost summary under the FIFO method and assuming the spoiled units come from the beginning inventory. The spoilage is assumed to have been discovered at 40 percent of the firm's operations. The allocation using the FIFO method results and assuming the ending inventory was more than 40 percent completed are:

1. Ending Work-in-Process before normal spoilage: $17912.57

2. Goods completed before normal spoilage: $100,463.13

3. Normal spoilage per unit: $436,8855/6,000 = $0.0728

4. Normal spoilage allocated to goods completed = $0.0728 × 5,000 = $364

5. Normal spoilage allocated to Ending Work-in-Process: $0.0728 × 1,000 = $72.80

6. Goods completed after normal spoilage (2 + 4): $100,827.13

7. Ending Work-in-Process after normal spoilage (1 + 5): $17,985.37

Condition 3: Exhibit 2.5 shows the process cost summary under the FIFO method and assuming the spoiled units come from the units started in the period. The spoilage is assumed to have been discovered at 40 percent of the firm's operations. The allocation using the FIFO method results and assuming the ending inventory was more than 40 percent completed are:

1. Ending Work-in-Process before normal spoilage: $14,777.75

2. Goods completed before normal spoilage: $90,249.75

3. Normal spoilage per unit: $7,111.10/6,000 = $1.1851

4. Normal spoilage allocated to goods completed: $1.1851 × 5,000 = $5,925.50

5. Normal spoilage allocated to ending Work-in-Process: $1.1851 × 1,000 = $1,185.10

6. Goods completed after normal spoilage (2 + 4): $96,175.25

7. Ending Work-in-Process after normal spoilage (2 + 5): $15,962.85

NEW MANUFACTURING ACCOUNTING

New manufacturing accounting has emerged as a result of new technologies and intense global competition. Examples of these technologies include computer-integrated manufacturing (CIM), flexible manufacturing systems (FMS), and just-in-time (JIT systems). Their introduction is motivated by the need to increase product quality and reduce product costs. The new manufacturing accounting is considered to have caused the superior performance of some Japanese manufacturing firms. Some of the improvements brought by the new manufacturing accounting are explored next.

Exhibit 2.4

ABEL Manufacturing Company, Ltd., Process Cost Summary: FIFO Method

1. Costs Charged to the Department

	Material	Labor	Overhead	Start up	Total
Current Costs	$60,000	$24,000	$6,000	---	$90,000
Beginning Work-in-Process	---	---	---	$29,250	29,250
Total Costs to Be Accounted For	$60,000	$24,000	$6,000	$29,250	$119,250

2. Equivalent Unit Processing Cost

		Equivalent Units		
	Total Units	Material	Labor	Overhead
Beginning Work-in-Process (1/4)	2,000			
Units Started	5,000			
To Account For	7,000			
Units Completed				
Beginning Inventory	2,000	--	1,500	1,500
Started and Completed	3,000	3,000	3,000	3,000
Ending Work-in-Process (1/2)	1,000	1,000	500	500
Spoilage	1,000	--	150	150
Equivalent Units		4,000	5,150	5,150
Total Costs to Be Accounted For		$60,000	$24,000	$6,000
Equivalent Unit Processing Costs		$ 15	$4.6601	$1.16504

3. Costs Applicable to the Department

Goods Completed:

Beginning Inventory: $29,250 + 1,500 (44.6601 + $1.16504)

= $37,987.71

Started and Completed: 3,000 ($15 + $4.6601 + $1.16504)

= 436.8855

Normal Spoilage: 75($4.660 + $1.16504)

= $436.8855

Abnormal Spoilage: 75($4.660 + 1.16504)

= $436.8855

Ending Work-in-Process

Materials: 1,000 x $15 = $15,000

Conversion Costs: 500 ($4.6601 + $1.16504) = $2,912.57

Exhibit 2.5

ABEL Manufacturing Company, Ltd., Process Cost Summary: FIFO Method

1. <u>Costs Charged to the Department</u>

	Material	Labor	Overhead	Start up	Total
Current Costs	$60,000	$24,000	$6,000	---	$90,000
Beginning Work-in-Process	---	---	---	$29,250	$29,250
Total Costs to be Accounted For	$60,000	$24,000	$6,000	$29,250	$119,250

2. <u>Equivalent Unit Processing Cost</u>

		Equivalent Units		
	Total Units	Material	Labor	Overhead
Beginning Work-in-Process (1/4)	2,000			
Units Started	5,000			
To Account For	7,000			
Units Completed				
Beginning Inventory (1/4)	2,000	--	1,500	1,500
Started and Completed	3,000	3,000	3,000	3,000
Ending Work-in-Process (1/2)	1,000	1,000	500	500
Spoilage	1,000	1,000	400	400
Equivalent Units		5,000	5,400	5,400
Total Costs to Be Accounted For		$60,000	$24,000	$6,000
Equivalent Unit Processing Costs		$ 12	$4.4444	$1.1111

3. <u>Costs Applicable to the Department</u>

Goods Completed $90249.75

  Beginning Inventory: $29,250 + 1,500 ($4.4444 + 1.1111)

    = $37583.25

  Started and Completed: 3,000 ($12 + $4.4444 + $1.1111)

    = $52666.5

Normal Spoilage: 500 ($12) + 200 ($4.4444 + $1.1111)

    = $7111.1

Abnormal Spoilage: 500 ($12) + 200 ($4.4444 + $1.1111)

    = $7111.1

Ending Work-in-Process

     $14777.75

  Materials: 1000 ($12) = $12,000

  Conversion Costs: 500 ($4.4444 + $1.1111) = $2777.75

Inventory and Production Control Systems

Two systems, push and pull, form the extreme points of inventory and production control systems. The *push system* has been defined as follows:

A push system in reality is simply a scheduled-based system. That is, a multi-period schedule of future demands for the company's products (called a master production schedule) is prepared and the computer breaks that schedule down into detailed schedules for making or buying the component parts. It is a push system in that the schedule pushes the production people into making the required parts and then pushing the parts out and onward. The name given to this push system is material requirements planning (MRP).[3]

Under the push system, following a forecast of demand, production begins in the first department (or subassembly) and is pushed to the work-in-process buffer inventory separating the department from the next one. In the present department, production is pushed to another buffer inventory. The sequence started in the first department continues till the end of the assembly line. The work-in-process inventories accumulated between departments or workstations serve as a cushion for inaccurate forecasting, line imbalances, and inefficiencies. The workers are left decoupled from each other and the production goals.

Under *the pull system,* or just-in-time control system, the production is controlled by a forecast of current demand and the level of finished goods inventory. When the finished goods inventory falls below a specified level, production is started. The work-in-process buffer between workstations is kept low or at zero. The last worker dictates his or her part of the subassembly, removing it from the work-in-process buffer inventory; the next-to-last worker indicates the production of his or her part of the subassembly. Production is therefore pulled from the end of the subassembly line. Unlike the push system, the workers under the pull system are tightly coupled and sensitive to the production goal.

In short, under the pull or JIT system, the production system initiates the work in a component of a production line as soon as it is needed by the next step in the production line. The main objective is to have a zero inventory system, which explains other terms given to the JIT system as MAN (Materials as Needed), MIPS (Minimum Inventory Production System), Pull Through Production (PTP), and ZIPS (Zero Inventory Production System). The pull-system-based production control technique is also known as the kanban system. It has the advantage of eliminating and reducing inventory cost. Traditionally the cost of inventory is perceived to be a financial one—the inventory on hand multiplied by the cost of capital. In fact other indirect and qualitative costs are associated with holding inventory: "Examples include: increased space requirements, increased materials handling costs, increased recordkeeping costs, increased insurance and tax obligations, slower throughput, higher scrap and obsolescence, and more costly inventory write-downs."[4] Reducing these costs frees up cash for investment in productive assets and improves profitability.

In fact, just-in-time is more than a technique, it is a philosophy. The four pivotal aspects of a JIT system are as follows:

- The elimination of all activities that do not add value to a product or service. In the context of JIT, "not adding value" is a buzz phrase loosely used to describe any activities or resources that are targets for reduction or elimination.
- A commitment to a high level of quality. Doing things right the first time is crucial if no time is allowed for rework.
- A commitment to continue improvement in the efficiency of an activity.
- "Simplification and increased visibility to identify activities that do not add value."[5]

A good example of the type of new manufacturing environment is provided by Nummi (New United Motors of Manufacturing Inc.), a General Motors–Toyota venture. At their plant a team concept allows workers to be involved in manufacturing planning. The system—known as "management by stress," "team concept," or "synchronous manufacturing"—centers on target specifications and monitoring of how jobs are to be done, tight control of work, and JIT manufacturing. A description of the system follows:

Under management by stress, the aim is to methodically locate and remove protections against glitches. Glitches are in fact welcomed because they identify where methods must be changed, perhaps a way found to perform a particular bottleneck operation more quickly. Just as important, points that never break down are assumed waste resources. They are targeted as well—human or material resources are removed until the station can keep up, but just barely.[6]

A lighted board above the assembly line—called the andon board—is used to show the status of each workstation. If a worker can not keep up, he or she pulls a cord to ring a bell and light up the board, allowing management to redesign the job to make it more efficient. An unlighted board is an indicator of inefficiencies and management has to speed up the line to stress the system and thereby find the inefficiencies. The system is assumed to allow for "kaizen," or continuous improvement.

Management by stress is in fact a reinforcement of Taylorism with a bigger role for the workers themselves. Witness the following statement:

In fact, management by stress is an intensification of Taylorism. Engineers and group and team leaders break the required assembly tasks down into the tiniest of separate "acts" and come up with a detailed written specification of how each worker is to do each job. This chart is posted near the line so the group leader can check to see that the worker does not vary his or her methods. Workers are not allowed to work faster for a short time to create some breathing space—although the jobs are so "loaded" that this is not possible anyway. If they discover a method, on their own, that makes the job easier, they must ask the supervisor's permission to use it. The catch, of course, is that another task will be found to fill the time.[7]

Costing Under a Just-in-Time Production System

Under a just-in-time production system there are no works-in-process and finished good inventory. Basically the amount produced conforms exactly to the customers' order and is shipped immediately to the customers. The costing system, known as JIT Costing, will be definitively simpler than the costing procedures examined in Chapters 4–6 of this book. Basically under JIT Costing, department costs are accumulated for control purposes before being charged directly to cost of goods sold. The procedures may be as follows:

1. For the raw material, a JIT Costing system will combine the new material accounts and work-in-process account into a "resources in process" account. This new account will be debited by the material purchases and credited for the raw materials assigned directly to finished goods. A comparison of the journal entries between JIT Costing and Operations Costing follows. Operations Costing or specification costing is a system that collects both direct labor and factory overhead to operations by using a simple average unit conversion cost for the operation. Accounting for material follows the same procedures as in a job costing system.

a. Operation Costing			b. JIT Costing		
Stores	$10,000		Raw and In-Process		
			Inventory		$9,500
Accounts Payable	$10,000		Accounts Payable		$9,500
to record the purchases.			to record the purchases.		
Work-in-Process	$10,000		Finished Goods		$9,500
Stores	$10,000		Raw and In-Process		
to record the purchases.			Inventory		$9,500
Finished Goods	$9,500				
Work-in-Process	$9,500				

2. Conversion costs are charged to departments upon occurrence, then applied directly to cost of goods sold as follows:

Cost of goods sold	$5,000	
Factory Overhead Applied		$5,000

3. At the end of each period, an adjustment is made for the overhead applicable to raw and in-process inventory and finished goods as follows:

Raw and in-process inventory	$200	
Finished goods	$800	
Cost of Goods Sold		$1,000
to reallocate irrelevant costs		
from costs of goods sold		
to ending inventory.		

In the above illustration, the figures are assumed. The journal entries shown are not necessary, they are the only approach available under JIT Costing.[8] Other approaches will surely be devised in the future.

Quality Control Systems

Process-based and output-based systems form the extreme points of quality control systems. Under the *output-based* quality control system, the product is inspected for quality when it leaves the assembly line. At the time of this inspection, defective products, scrap, and spoilage are identified. Under this system, there is also the suspicion that because of uncooperative relationships between production and quality control, undetected problems by quality control may be deliberately ignored by production, with the result of inefficiencies and heavy losses to companies.[9]

Under the *process-based* quality control known as Jikoda, the responsibility for quality control is given to the production worker who can stop the total production process when he or she detects a production problem. Therefore quality control takes place at each stage of the process because each worker checks every part sent to him or her to detect any errors before proceeding to work on it. This system is assumed to have eliminated all errors in output in Japanese manufacturing firms. The situation in U.S. manufacturing firms is sometimes different, per the following comment:

> In contrast, in many U.S. firms, management tries very hard to avoid downtime and workers who persist in pointing out problems leading to downtime may be chastised. Worker-based process quality control results in relatively high performance efficiency (i.e., the ratio of good output to total output) because errors are detected and converted before completion of the output. In contrast, output-based quality control has relatively lower performance efficiency because errors are not necessarily detected and converted before the output is completed. Thus, in this latter case, a lower percentage of the total output may not be good output.[10]

Total Quality Control

The Japanese have revamped their concepts of quality control into a set of techniques labeled total quality control (TQC). When implemented in concert with a JIT system and various other productivity improvements, they have the potential of improving industrial management. The emphasis in a total quality control system is:

1. A goal of continual quality improvement, project after project (rejection of the Western notion of an "acceptable quality level").

2. Worker (not QC Department) responsibility.

3. Measurers of quality that are visible, visual, simple, and understandable, even to the casual observer.

4. Automatic quality measurement drives (self-development).[11]

There are seven basic principles of quality control:[12]

1. Process control, as stated earlier, focuses on checking the quality of the product while the work-in-process is being done.

2. Easy-to-see quality refers to the display of easy-to-understand, visual obvious indicators of quality, resulting in a principle of "measurable standards of quality" at every process.

3. Insistence on compliance refers to an unconforming position on quality first and output second.

4. Line stop refers to giving each worker the authority to stop the production line to correct quality problems.

5. Correcting one's errors forces the responsible worker who made the bad product to perform the rework.

6. 100 percent check refers to the inspection of every item, rather than just a random sample, and to the rejection of lot acceptance inspection.

7. Project-by-project improvement.

Measuring and Reporting Quality Costs

If a final product fails to meet the appropriate specifications, there is a failure to maintain quality. Four types of costs are associated with quality conformance: prevention costs, appraisal costs, internal failure costs, and external failure costs.[13] They have been defined as follows:

> Prevention costs are the costs associated with designing, implementing, and maintaining the quality system. These costs include engineering quality control systems, quality planning of various departments, and quality training programs. Appraisal costs use the costs incurred to insure that materials and products meet quality standards. These costs include inspection of raw materials, laboratory tests, quality audits and field testing. Internal failure costs are the costs associated with materials and products that fail to meet quality standards and result in manufacturing losses. They include the costs of scrap, repair, and rework of defective products identified before they are shipped to consumers.
>
> External failure costs are the costs incurred because inferior quality products are shipped to consumers. They include the costs of handling complaints, warranty replacement, repairs of returned products and so forth.[14]

These costs need to be measured and reported to highlight the cost quality of conformance. An example of a quality cost report is shown in Exhibit 2.6. It shows the cost of nonconformance as an aggregation of all the implicit costs that are attributable to manufacturing a nonquality product.[15]

Quality Cost Relationship

A model proposed by J. T. Godfrey and W. R. Pasewark views quality costs as being composed of defect control costs, failure costs, and cost of lost sales.[16]

Exhibit 2.6
Quality Cost Report

	Current Month's Loss	% of Loss
Prevention Costs		
Quality Training	$ 3,000	1.5
Reliability Engineering	15,000	7.5
Pilot Studies	6,000	3
System Development	9,000	4.5
Total Prevention Costs	$ 33,000	16.5
Appraisal Costs		
Materials Inspection	$ 8,000	4
Supplies Inspection	4,000	2
Reliability Testing	6,000	3
Laboratory	28,000	14
Total Appraisal Costs	46,000	23
Internal Failure Costs		
Scrap	13,000	6.5
Repair	23,000	11.5
Rework	13,000	6.5
Downtime	7,000	3.5
Total Internal Failure	$ 56,000	28
External Failure Costs		
Warranty Costs	$ 13,000	6.5
Out-of-Warranty Repairs & Replacement	7,000	3.5
Customer Complaints	10,000	5
Product Liability	10,000	5
Transportation Losses	25,000	12.5
Total External Failure Costs	$ 65,000	32.5
Total Costs of Nonconformance	$200,000	100.0

Defect control costs (Q) are defined as equal to prevention costs (K) plus appraisal costs (A), or $Q = K + A$. Failure costs (F) are defined as equal to rework costs, profit lost by selling units as defective, and the costs of processing customer returns. The profit lost by selling units as defective (Z) is:

$$Z = \text{Total defective units } (D) - \text{Number of units reworked } (Y)$$
$$*(\text{Profit for good unit } [p1] - \text{Profit for defective unit } [p2])$$

or

$$Z = (D - Y)*(p1 - p2).$$

The rework costs (R) are equal to the costs of reworking a unit (r) multiplied by the number of units reworked, or $R = r*Y$. The cost of processing customer returns (*W*) is equal to the cost of a single customer return (*w*) multiplied by the number of defective units returned by customers (*D2*), or $W = w*D2$. Therefore, the total failure costs (*F*) are:

$$F = R + Z + W$$

or

$$F = (r*y) + [(D - Y)*(p1 - p2)] + (w*D2).$$

Cost of lost sales (*L*) is defined as the cost of current and future sales that will be lost if defective units are received by customers.

Total quality costs (*T*) can now be expressed as:

$$T = K + A + R + Z + W + L$$

or

$$T = K + A + (Y*r) + [(D - Y)(p1 - p2)] + (D2*w) + L.$$

Appraisal costs, rework costs, profit foregone by selling units as defective, cost of processing customers' returns, and cost of lost sales increase as the percentage of defective units increases. However, prevention costs decrease as the percentage of defective units increases.

Assuming that the number of defective units discovered by customers is a constant percentage of total defective units and that the number of defective units discovered by customers is a constant percentage of total defective units, the quality cost relationship may be illustrated as in Exhibit 2.7. Management, in this case, would opt for case D, where the total quality costs are minimized at $220.00.

Exhibit 2.7
Quality Cost Relationships

Case	Defect Control Costs		Percent Defective	Failure Costs			Cost Lost of Sales	Total Quality Costs
	Prevention Costs (K)	Appraisal Costs (A)		Rework Costs (R)	Cost of not Re-work ing (Z)	Cost of pro- cess ing (W)		
A	$250	$ 50	2.5%	$25.0	$2.5	$1.25	$3.25	$332.00
B	260	45	2.00%	20.0	2.0	1.00	3.00	331.00
C	270	40	1.50%	15.0	1.5	0.75	2.25	329.00
D	275	32	1.00%	10.0	1.0	0.50	1.50	220.00
E	290	30	0.50%	5.0	0.5	0.25	0.30	325.00
F	320	20	0.00%	0.0	0.0	0.00	0.00	340.00

Zero-Defect Policy

In an earlier section on "Accounting for Lack of Quality," we have assumed that scrap and waste, defective work that has to be reworked, spoilage, and lost units are unavoidable phenomena in the production process. That assumption explains the attitude known as "produce-and-rework-if-defective" program that expects a certain level of error compatible with a tolerance level of authority set by managers. This assumption is severely criticized in favor of a zero-defect policy that expects every produced unit to be a good unit. Any spoilage in rework is therefore treated as an abnormal spoilage and written off as a loss.

EMERGING ISSUES IN PERFORMANCE MEASUREMENT

The success of the firm's activities rests on not only achieving a denied level of profitability but also meeting new critical factors of the new manufacturing environment. These factors include a good record on quality, a minimization or elimination of inventories, an increase in manufacturing flexibility, and the provision of excellent service to customers. In response to concerns, a different kind of performance measurement is required to include a greater focus on global rather than departmental performance measures, a greater reliance on nonfinancial measures, a classification of costs as value added or nonvalue added, and production control by observation rather than accounting report.[17] Each of these data issues will be examined.

Use of Global Evaluation Techniques

While the measurement of departmental performance is still part of the control process, the focus in the new manufacturing strategy is to emphasize plant-wide performance. Measures that focus in the flexibility and performance of all departments include cycle time/amount of throughput, set-up time by product, and downtime (other than set-up).[18]

The degree of automation also dictates a shift from an emphasis on an individual performance to one on group performance. Witness the following comment:

> In an automated manufacturing process as well, the whole system is so integrated and controlled by computers that individuals' performance would be confined to following the preprogrammed flow of the process. The system's productivity would be affected very little by the varying degrees of individual employees' ability, once the employees acquire the proficiency needed to operate in that setting.[19]

Greater Reliance on Nonfinancial Measures

Return on investment (ROI) and residual income capture important aspects of performance. But they are not sufficient, because other aspects need to be accounted for if a firm adopts a basic goal of providing the best product at the best price. Exchange of critical factors that need to be measured at every level of activity include cost, quality, delivery, and people.[20] Performance measurement in these critical aspects of the new multifaceted firms have to be derived by management accounting and control systems. For example, the criteria for evaluating management accounting and control systems in an advanced manufacturing environment are:

- Rapid feedback;
- Sensitivity to profit contribution of various activities and products;
- Flexible and migratory measurement systems;
- Holistic product costing and control measures;
- Identification, measurement, and elimination of non-value-added costs;
- Focus on variance reduction in such areas as quality, cycle time, and product complexity (e.g., total parts);
- Reclassification of costs based on assignability and value-added characteristics;
- Enhanced traceability of costs to specific products and processes to decrease allocations and their distortions.[21]

A second example is provided by Harley Davidson's adoption of the following ten measurements to assess manufacturing effectiveness:

1. Schedule Attainment
2. Manning Requirements
3. Conversion Costs
4. Overtime Requirements as a measurement of flexibility
5. Inventory Levels
6. Material Cost Variance
7. Scrap/Rework
8. Manufacturing Cycle Time as a measure of flexibility
9. Quality Level
10. Productivity Improvement

These measures are deemed more appropriate for inclusion in a cost management system within a JIT environment than the traditional measures of direct labor efficiency, direct labor utilization, direct labor productivity, and machine utilization.

Charles Horngren and George Foster provide the following examples of nonfinancial performance measures used by Texas Instruments (TI):

- First-span calibration yield (percentage of products passing quality tests first time)
- Outgoing quality level for each product line (defective parts per million as assessed by TI Quality Control)

- Returned merchandise (percentage of shipments returned from customers because of poor quality)
- Customer report card (sample of customers interviewed to get feedback on quality)
- Competitive rank by TI marketing and field sales personnel (ranking of product relative to a number of competitors in that product line)
- On-time delivery (percentage of shipment made on or before the scheduled delivery date).[22]

Throughput in the New Manufacturing Accounting

The new manufacturing accounting puts a heavy emphasis on throughput, a measure of how many good units are produced during a particular period. It can be calculated by dividing good units produced by the total time, or by multiplying the three components of throughput—namely, productive capacity, productive processing time, and yield. These three components of the throughput have been adequately defined as follows:

1. *Productive capacity* is the maximum a particular manufacturing cell or segment can produce given the technology in place. It is measured by dividing total units processed by the processing time.

2. *Productive processing time* shows how much time is spent on activities that add value to the product. It is computed by dividing processing time by the total time the product spends in a particular segment of the factory.

3. *Yield* shows the percentage of good units. It is determined by dividing the good units produced in a particular time period by the total units started during the period.[23]

Based on these definitions, C. Cheatham offers two formulas:

1. Good units produced per two periods = Productive capacity × productive processing time × yield

2. Good units/total time = (Total units/processing time) × (processing time/total time) × (good units/total units)[24]

Classification of Cost as Value Added or Non-Value Added

A new feature of performance measurement is the separation of value-added costs from non-value-added costs. Non-value-added is any cost resulting from an activity or procedure that does not add a value to the product or to the firm. The desired goal is to minimize the value-added costs subject to the quality level sought by the firm and to eliminate non-value-added costs. For example, let's consider the following general steps that comprise the lead time associated with manufacturing a salable product:

- *Process Time* is the amount of time that a product is actually being worked on.
- *Inspection Time* is the amount of time spent either assuring that the product is of high quality or actually spent reworking the product to an acceptable quality level.

- *Move Time* is the time spent moving the product from one location to another.
- *Queue Time* is the amount of time the product waits before being processed, moved, or inspected, or whatever.
- *Storage Time* is the amount of time a product spent in stock before further processing or shipment.[25]

Within a JIT philosophy, only process time adds value to the product. Given that process time is generally around 10 percent of lead time, 90 percent of the lead time adds costs but no value to the product.[26]

Use of Observation in Operational Control

Without discounting the importance of accounting reports in the area of performance measurement and reporting, they should be supplemented and sometimes replaced by observation. Richard Ortman and David Buehlmann cite the example of the immediate observation of production problems with material and assembly "because they cause bottlenecks, which occur because there is no inventory to 'cushion' errors."[27]

NOTES

1. Robert A. Howell and Stephen R. Soucy, "Operating Controls in the New Manufacturing Environment," *Management Accounting* (October 1987), p. 16.

2. Ibid.

3. Richard J. Schonberger, *Japanese Manufacturing Techniques* (New York: The Free Press, 1982), p. 220.

4. Robert A. Howell and Stephen Soucy, "The New Manufacturing Accounting: Major Trends for Management Accounting," *Management Accounting* (July 1982), p. 20.

5. George Foster and Charles T. Horngren, "Cost Accounting and Cost Management Issues," *Management Accounting* (June 1987), p. 19.

6. Mike Parker and Jane Slaughter, "Behind the Scenes at Nummi Motors," *New York Times* (December 4, 1988), p. 2F.

7. Ibid.

8. R. Hunt, L. Garrett, and C. M. Mertz, "Direct Labor Cost Not Always Relevant at H.P.," *Management Accounting* (February 1985), p. 61.

9. R. H. Hayes, "Why Japanese Factories Work," *Harvard Business Review* (July-August, 1981), pp. 57–66.

10. Mark S. Young, Michael D. Shields, and G. Wolf, "Manufacturing Controls and Performance: An Experiment," *Accounting, Organizations and Society* (October 1988), p. 610.

11. R. J. Schonberger, *Japanese Manufacturing Techniques: Nine Hidden Lessons in Simplicity* (London: The Free Press, 1982), p. 7.

12. Ibid., p. 55.

13. Harold P. Roth and Wayne J. Moore, "Let's Help Measure and Report Quality Costs," *Management Accounting* (August 1983), pp. 50–53.

14. Ibid., p. 50.

15. See also John Clark, "Costing for Quality at Celanese," *Management Accounting* (March 1985), pp. 42–46.

16. James T. Godfrey and William R. Pasewark, "Controlling Quality Costs," *Management Accounting* (March 1988), pp. 48–51.

17. Richard Ortman and David Buehlmann, "Supplementing Cost Accounting Courses in Response to the Changing Business Environment," *Issues in Accounting Education* 4, no. 1 (Spring 1989), p. 172.

18. Ibid., p. 174.

19. John Y. Lee, *Managerial Accounting Changes for the 1990s* (Reading, Mass: Addison Wesley, 1987), p. 70.

20. C. J. McNain and William Mosconi, "Measuring Performance in an Advanced Manufacturing Environment," *Management Accounting* (July 1987), pp. 28–31.

21. Ibid., p. 25.

22. Charles T. Horngren and George Foster, *Cost Accounting: A Managerial Emphasis*, 7th ed. (Englewood Cliffs, N.J.: Prentice-Hall, 1992), p. 256.

23. C. Cheatham, "Measuring and Improving Throughput," *The Journal of Accountancy* (March 1990), pp. 89–91.

24. Ibid., p. 90.

25. Robert D. MacIlhattan, "The JIT Philosophy," *Management Accounting* (September 1987), p. 20.

26. Ibid., p. 21.

27. Ortman and Buehlmann, "Supplementing Cost Accounting Courses," p. 174.

REFERENCES

Chalos, P. "High-Tech Production: The Impact on Cost Reporting Systems." *Journal of Accountancy* (March 1986), pp. 106–112.

Clark, John. "Costing for Quality at Celanese." *Management Accounting* (March 1985), pp. 42–46.

Clark, Ronald L. and James B. McLaughlin. "Controlling the Cost of Product Defects." *Management Accounting* (August 1986), pp. 32–35.

Crosby, P. *Quality Without Tears* (New York: McGraw-Hill, 1984).

Foster, George and Charles T. Horngren. "Cost Accounting and Cost Management Issues." *Management Accounting* (June 1987), pp. 19–25.

Gosset, T. E. and M. F. Usry. "Process Costing and Diagrammatical Outlines." *The Accounting Review* (January 1968).

Hunt, R., L. Garrett, and C. Mertz. "Direct Labor Cost Not Always Relevant at H-P." *Management Accounting* (February 1985).

Johansson, H. "The Effect of Zero Inventories on Cost (Just-In-Time)." In *Cost Accounting for the '90's: The Challenge of Technological Change.* Montvale, N.J.: National Association of Accountants, 1986.

Koch, Alfred P. "A Fallacy in Accounting for Spoiled Goods." *The Accounting Review* (July 1960), pp. 501–502.

Luh, Frank S. "Graphical Approach to Process Costing." *The Accounting Review* (July 1967).

Maskell, B. "Management Accounting and Just-In-Time." *Management Accounting* (England) (September 1986), pp. 32–34.

Morse, W. "Measuring Quality Costs." *Cost and Management* (July–August 1983), pp. 16–20.

Newman, B. and P. Jaouen. "Kamban, Zips and Cost Accounting: A Case Study." *Journal of Accountancy* (August 1986), pp. 132–141.

Rogoff, D. L. "Scrap into Profits: How to Fully Exploit Scrap as Revenue Source." *Journal of Accountancy* (February 1987), pp. 106–113.

Roth, Harold P. and Wayne J. Morse. "Let's Help Measure and Report Quality Costs." *Management Accounting* (August 1983), pp. 50–53.

Schwarzbach, W. P. "The Impact of Automation on Accounting for Indirect Costs." *Management Accounting* (December 1985).

Seglund, R. and S. Ibarreche. "Just-In-Time: The Accounting Implications." *Management Accounting* (August 1984), pp. 34–45.

Stallman, James C. "Framework for Evaluating Cost Control Procedures for a Process." *The Accounting Review* (October 1972), pp. 774–790.

3

CONTROL PRINCIPLES AND QUALITY: CONTROL OF DIRECT COSTS

The realization of adequate quality levels for products and services produced by firms rests on the exercise of control. The process of control is the attempt by a manager or accountant to reach a state of control, where actual results conform to planned results. The process of control traditionally has been visualized as a series of examinations of the deviations between actual and planned performances. However, a manager may decide to bring about control by altering the planned results to conform to actual results—*a feedback control system*. Similarly, a manager may elect to adjust the anticipated results through a compensatory action—*a feedforward control system*. Each of these control systems has distinct conceptual and operational advantages over the traditional control system.

The process of control is to be examined in the next three chapters. This chapter begins with the examination of the control process and its use for the control of direct costs.

NATURE OF THE CONTROL PROCESS

Types of Control

Control is a central factor in the management of any organization. Leonard Sayles illustrates its importance:

> After all controls are the techniques by which the manager decides how to expend his most valuable assets, his time. Be they formal or informal, it is through controls that he knows where things are going badly that require his intervention—and where and when he can relax because things are going well. All managers from presidents to foreman made use of controls, some more effectively than others.[1]

Sayles lists four distinct types of control that serve very different functions for the manager:

1. Reassurances to sponsors, whereby stakeholders are informed of the efficient conduct of operations.
2. Closing the loop, whereby the managers are informed that both technical and legal requirements have been met.
3. Guidance to subordinates from managers, whereby the subordinates are informed of "what is important and what they should concentrate on."
4. Guidance to lower-level management by higher-level management, whereby managers are informed of "where accomplishment is lagging and management action is needed."[2]

A more operational classification is provided by W. H. Newman, who recognizes three different types of control:

Steering controls, whereby management is provided signals indicating what will happen if it continues its present operations. Steering controls enable management to take either a corrective or an adaptive response before the total operation is completed. A corrective response implies the source of the error is inside the organization and can be corrected. An adaptive response implies that the source of the error is outside the organization and cannot be corrected. In the latter case, the solution is to redesign the operations to adapt to the new environmental situations.

Yes/no controls, whereby management is provided rules indicating the conditions that must be met before work may proceed to the next step. Yes/no controls provide management with checkpoints at different levels of the total operation. The technique is a defensive strategy aimed at controlling the size of the errors to be made by lower-level management and subordinates in general. In other words, yes/no controls are comparable to safety devices.

Postaction controls, whereby management is provided with performance reports or scorecards upon completion of the operations, indicating the differences or variances between the actual and planned performance. In general, postaction controls and steering controls make use of the feedback mechanism for the correction of any deviations, except that the response in steering controls concerns the completion of the total operation. Steering controls may be labeled as a feedback control system, while postaction controls are a traditional control system.[3]

Stages of Control

The control process involves the following stages:

1. Setting of goals for the performance of the activity or function. These goals help direct and channel human efforts. Organizational goals are desired ends or states of

affairs for whose achievement system policies are committed and resources allocated.[4]

2. Establishing standards of performance for each specified goal of the activity or function. Standards are basically statements of the results that will exist when the performance is satisfactory.

3. Monitoring or measurement of actual performance. Monitoring can be expressed in monetary and accounting terms such as profits, costs, and revenues; by other accounting indicators such as rate of return on investment or residual income; and in nonmonetary terms such as the quality of the product, the nature of the market response, or any other social indicator. Measurement is accomplished by human or mechanical means such as *sensors*.

4. Reviewing and comparing the actual with the planned performance. This is also known as the *comparator process,* which determines whether differences exist between the activities and the results that are taking place and what should be occurring.

5. Investigating and then correcting the deviations.

6. Administering rewards to motivate and reinforce good performance. This is known as the *evolution/reward process.*

Nature of the Deviations

There are five possible causes that can lead to a difference between the actual and standard performance.

1. An *implementation failure* is a human or mechanical failure to obtain or maintain a specific action or standard. For example, the ordering or the use of a wrong quantity of a given input, material, labor, or overhead will result in an implementation failure. Given that the standard is assumed to be obtainable, the deviation caused by the implementation failure may be immediately corrected once its existence is known. The decision to correct such a variance depends on a comparison between the cost of correction and the resulting savings.

2. A *prediction error* is a failure to correctly predict one of the decision model's parameter values. Again, the decision to correct the variance depends on a comparison between the cost of developing a better prediction model and the resulting cost savings.

3. A *measurement error* in determining the actual cost of operations occurs because of improper classification, recording, or counting. The correction of the variance involves improving the work habits of employees and motivating them to maintain proper records.

4. A *model error* arises from an incorrect function representation in the decision model, resulting in a failure to capture reality. The decision to correct the variance depends on a comparison between the cost of reformulating the model and the resulting cost savings.

5. A *random deviation* results from minor variations in the input or output process. Random variations are inevitable and need no corrective action.

TRADITIONAL CONTROL MODEL

A firm using a traditional control model first establishes performance standards for each operational activity in a budget-setting phase. At the end of the period, it compares these standards with the actual results, using the variance analysis technique to assess the nature of the obtained deviations and the possibility of any corrective action. Therefore, a proper selection of the types of standards and the variance analysis technique is essential to the success of a traditional control system.

Standard Setting

A standard is a norm set for a given activity in the plan. It reflects the expectations of managers as developed from the following sources:

- Internally generated *actual costs* from the most recent period.
- *Actual cost* of the most recent period *adjusted* for expected improvement.
- Internally generated *budgeted cost* (often called *standard cost*) numbers based on an analysis of an efficiently operating manufacturing facility.
- Externally generated *target cost* numbers based on an analysis of the cost structure of the leading competitor in an industry.
- Externally generated *most-efficient* plant costs for a company with multiple plants having the same operations or producing the same product. For example, Yamazaki Masak compares actual costs at its U.S. and U.K. plants against the actual costs of its Japanese plant that produces similar products.[5]

A standard also represents the best and most operational working method for the activity, given the state of the art. Consequently, the standard represents a normative expression of the performance related to a given activity, while the actual results represent a descriptive expression. The difference between standard performance and actual performance lies in the distinction defined by management between what should be and what is acceptable behavior.

To avoid semantic problems, the standard is generally considered a unit concept, while the budget is a total concept. For example, the standard cost of direct labor is $3 per direct-labor hour (DLH), whereas the budgeted cost of direct labor is $24,000 if 8,000 direct-labor hours are needed at a standard cost of $3 per direct-labor hour. In general, the standard cost is used for the control of direct material and direct labor, while the budgeted cost is used for the control of overhead. This is because prime costs are identifiable with individual units of output, whereas overhead is identifiable only with total production.

Different types of standards have been presented in the literature and in practice. Standards are either basic or current. Basic standards are historical performance standards that are not changed unless there are important modifications in the nature or sequence of the manufacturing operations. Current standards might be changed to reflect environmental changes. Basic standards are useful to short-run analysis.

There are three different levels of current and basic standards: expected actual, normal, and theoretical. The expected actual standard is set for an expected capacity for the coming year and reflects predictions about the expected actual results. The normal standard, or currently attainable standard, is set for a normal capacity. This is the level of operations attainable by normal operating procedures, allowing for extraordinary events such as normal spoilage, ordinary machine breakdowns, and lost time. The theoretical, or ideal, standard is set for a theoretical capacity—the level of operations possible under the best operating conditions without any unusual events. It is a perfect, maximum efficiency standard.

There are four broad classes of current and basic standards: imposed, those set through participation, those set with consultation, and those reinforced by financial rewards. Imposed standards are derived without any input from subordinates. They reassert the superior's power in the budgeting process and emphasize the goals of the organization. Standards set through participation are derived with direct input for subordinates. They can increase motivation, and they emphasize both the organizational and individual goals. Standards set with consultation are derived with indirect input from subordinates. They represent a trade-off between the imposed and the participative approaches to standard setting. Standards reinforced by financial rewards are derived with a commitment from subordinates secured by linking rewards to organizational performance. An often-cited example is the Scanlon plan.[6]

Types of Budgets and Types of Analysis of Variance

The standards as expressed in the master budget are static standards in the sense that they refer to a single planned level. That is why the master budget illustrated in Chapter 6 may be referred to as a static budget. As shown in Exhibit 3.1, a comparison of actual performance with the static (master) budget results in a static budget variance. The assumption is that the standard performance is as formulated in the static (master) budget. The variances illustrated in Exhibit 3.1 are just informative enough for a good control of the activities of the firm. What would be required at the end of the period is a flexible or variable budget that would indicate how the budget would be for a range of activity. The flexible budget is illustrated in Exhibit 3.2 for the relevant range of from 1,200 to 1,700 units. Notice that these budgets are based on the mathematical function used to estimate the cost or formula: $10,000 fixed cost per month plus $30 variable cost per unit of product. With a knowledge of the flexible budget, the analysis of variance can proceed to different levels to identify two new variances: (1) Sales volume variance—the difference between the flexible budget performance and the static (master) budget performance with selling prices and unit variable costs held constant. (2) Flexible budget variance—the difference between actual per-

Exhibit 3.1
Variance Analysis Based on a Static Budget

	Budgeted Amount Per unit	Static (Master) Budget (1)	Actual Performance (2)	Variance (2) - (1)
Units		1,000	1,500	500F
Revenue	$50	$50,000	$82,500	$32,000
Variable Cost				
Direct Material	$10	$10,000	$12,000	$2,000U
Direct Labor	5	5,000	9,000	4,000U
Variable Factory Overload	12	12,000	22,500	10,500U
Variable Manufacturing Costs	27	$27,000	$43,500	$16,500U
Variable Selling and Administrative Costs	3	3,000	6,000	3,000U
Total Variable Cost	$30	$30,000	$49,000	$19,500U
Contribution Margin	$20	$20,000	$33,000	$13,000F
Fixed Costs				
Manufacturing		$8,000	$10,000	$2,000U
Selling and Administrative		2,000	4,000	2,000U
Total Fixed Costs		$10,000	$14,000	$4,000U
Total Costs		$40,000	$63,500	$23,500U
Operating Income		$10,000	$19,000	$9,000F

F=Favorable,   U=Unfavorable effect on operating income

formance and the flexible budget performance based on the actual output achieved.

The computation of these two variances is shown in Exhibit 3.3. The sales variances result from changes in sales unit, market share, and market size. They will be fully explained in Chapter 4. The flexible budget variances for direct costs will be explained in this chapter; the flexible budget variance for overhead costs will be explained in Chapter 5.

Expressions of Standards

Standard cost systems are generally expressed in terms of standard units of input allowed for a good output product where the input chosen is a common denominator for the type of activity in question. The standard unit of input allowed for good output is computed as follows:

Units of good output * Input allowed per unit of output = Standard units of input allowed for good output

Exhibit 3.2
Flexible Budget Performance

	Budgeted Amount Per Unit	Various Levels of Volume		
Units		1,200	1,500	1,700
Revenue	$50	$60,000	$75,000	$85,000
Variable Cost				
Direct Material	$10	$12,000	$15,000	$17,000
Direct Labor	5	6,000	7,500	8,500
Variable Factory Overload	12	14,000	18,000	20,400
Variable Manufacturing Costs	27	$32,000	$40,500	45,900
Variable Selling and Administrative Costs	3	3,600	4,500	5,100
Total Variable Cost	30	36,000	45,000	51,000
Contribution Margin	20	24,000	30,000	34,000
Fixed Costs				
Manufacturing		8,000	8,000	8,000
Selling and Administrative		2,000	2,000	2,000
Total Fixed Costs		10,000	10,000	10,000
Total Costs		46,000	55,000	61,000
Operating Income		$14,000	20,000	24,000

For example, if the manufacturing of a product required in the budget 5 units of material and 6 hours of labor and if the actual production was 1,000 good units produced, then:

the standard direct material allowed = 5 * 10,000 = 50,000 units

the standard hours allowed = 6 * 10,000 = 60,000 hours

Therefore, in this example, the standard direct material allowed represents the number of units of material that should have been used if actual production was known. Similarly, the standard hours allowed represent the number of hours that should have been used if actual production was known.

DIRECT-COST VARIANCES

Models of Variance Analysis

Actual performance and standard performance can be compared within three models in variance analysis: the one-way, the two-way, and the three-way.

The *one-way model* appraises the total performance for a given activity by

Exhibit 3.3
Variance Analysis Based on Both Flexible and Static Budgets

	(1) Actual Results	(2)=(1)-(3) Budget Variance	(3) Flexible Budget	(4)=(3)-(5) Sales Volume Variance	(5) Static (Master) Budget
Units	1,500		1,500		1,000
Revenue	$82,500	7,500F	$75,000	25,000F	$50,000
Variable Cost					
Direct Material	12,000	3,000F	15,000	5,000U	10,000
Direct Labor	9,000	1,500U	7,500	2,500U	5,000
Variable Factory Overhead	22,500	4,500U	18,000	6,000U	12,000
Variable Manufacturing Costs	43,500	3,000U	40,500	13,500U	27,000
Variable Selling and Administrative Costs	6,000	1,500U	4,500	1,500U	3,000
Total Variable Cost	49,500	4,500U	45,000	15,000U	30,000
Contribution Margin	33,000	3,000F	30,000	10,000F	20,000
Fixed Cost					
Manufacturing	10,000	2,000U	8,000		8,000
Selling and Administrative	4,000	2,000U	2,000		2,000
Total Fixed Costs	14,000	4,000U	10,000		10,000
Total Costs	63,500	8,500U	55,000	15,000U	40,000
Operating Income	$19,000	1,000U	$20,000	10,000F	$10,000

F=Favorable effect on operating income   U=Unfavorable effect on operating income

combining the effects of both price and quantity decisions. It is expressed by a unique variance figure as follows:

$$V^t = P^a Q^a - P^s Q^s$$

where

V^t = total variance
P^a = actual price
Q^a = actual quantity
P^s = standard price
Q^s = standard quantity

The *two-way model* appraises both the price and quantity performance for a given activity. It is expressed by both a price and a quantity variance as follows:

$$V^p = Q^a(P^a - P^s)$$

and

$$V^q = P^s(Q^a - Q^s)$$

where

V^p = price variance
V^q = quantity variance

The *three-way model* formulates the price variance differently than the two-way model to pinpoint the joint responsibility through a joint price/quantity variance. The model is expressed by a price variance, a quantity variance, and a joint price/quantity variance as follows:

$$V^p = Q^s(P^a - P^s)$$
$$V^q = P^s(Q^a - Q^s)$$
$$V^{pq} = (P^a - P^s)(Q^a - Q^s)$$

where V^{pq} = joint price/quantity variance.

The usual breakdown of variances into only price and quantity variances, as advocated by the two-way model, is not conceptually correct because of the existence of a joint price/quantity variance. The graphic analysis of variance depicted in Exhibit 3.4 highlights these differences. The small area in the upper right corner may create problems, because a price-responsible agent may not accept responsibility for the price variance $Q^a(P^a - P^s)$, as computed in the two-

Exhibit 3.4
Analysis of Variances

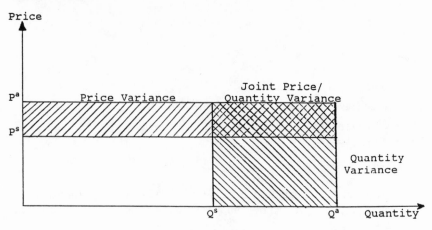

way analysis of variances. However, any of the three analyses of variance models can be used to assess the performance of operational activities pertaining to the acquisition and use of direct manufacturing inputs.

Direct-Material Variances

The master budget must include two standards for material costs: a material price standard and a material quantity standard. A comparison between actual and planned material costs, using a two-way analysis of variance, leads to the computation and evaluation of both a material price variance and a usage variance (material quantity variance). The material price standards set by the purchasing department reflect current market prices. They are intended to be an indicator of both efficient conduct of the purchasing activities and the effects of price changes on the company's profits. The material price standards can be used to evaluate the purchasing department's general performance. The material price variance is computed as follows:

$$\text{in a two-way model: } V^{mp} = Q^a(P^a - P^s),$$
$$\text{in a three-way model: } V^{mp} = Q^s(P^a - P^s),$$

where V^{mp} = material price variance.

The material quantity standard set by the production department reflects basic material specifications for routine production operations. Either the quantity standard at the time of purchase or at the time of usage can be used, and both are indicators of the efficient conduct of production activities. The usage variance is computed in both two- and three-factor models as follows:

$$U = P^s(Q^a - Q^s),$$

where U = usage variance.

Direct-Labor Variances

The master budget specifies two standards for labor: a labor price standard, or rate standard, and a labor quantity standard, or labor efficiency standard. A difference between the actual and planned labor performance will lead—in a two-way analysis of variance—to the computation of both a labor price variance and a labor quantity variance. The rate standard set by the personnel department is the result of collective bargaining agreements, government regulations, and other factors. Consequently, rate variances are rare and occur only in unusual situations. The rate variance is computed as follows:

$$\text{in a two-way model: } R = Q^a(P^a - P^s),$$
$$\text{in a three-way model: } R = Q^s(P^a - P^s),$$

where R = rate variance.

The labor efficiency standard set by the production department reflects production specifications. The production department uses it to evaluate labor management efficiency. The labor efficiency variance can be computed as follows:

$$E = P^s(Q^a - Q^s),$$

where E = labor efficiency variance.

Illustration of Direct-Cost Variances

Input	Actual Quantity	Standard Quantity	Actual Price	Standard Price
Direct Material	5,000 Units	4,000 Units	$15	$20
Direct Labor	2,000 DLH	1,000 DLH	$20	$10

The formal calculation of direct-cost variances is shown in Exhibit 3.5.

STANDARD COST ACCOUNTING SYSTEM

A standard cost accounting system includes at least two phases: the recording of standard costs in the regular accounting system and the isolation of variances; and the disposition of variances.

Exhibit 3.5
Direct-Cost Variances

I. <u>Analysis of Variance</u>

    A.   Total Material Variance

        ($5,000 * $15) - ($4,000 * $20)   = $5,000 (Favorable)

    B.   Total Labor Variance

        ($2,000 * $20) - ($1,000 * $10) = $30,000 (Unfavorable)

    C.   Total Direct-Cost Variance

        $5,000 + ($30,000)   = $25,000 (Unfavorable)

II. <u>Two-Way Analysis of Variance</u>

    A.   Material Variances

        1. Material Price Variance

            5,000 ($15 - $20)   = $25,000 (Favorable)

        2. Usage Variance

            $20 (5,000 - 4,000)   = $20,000 (Favorable)

    B.   Direct-Labor Variances

        1. Rate Variance

            2,000 ($20 - 10)   = $20,000 (Unfavorable)

        2. Labor Efficiency Variance

            $10 (2,000 - 1,000)   = $10,000 (Unfavorable)

III. <u>Three-Way Analysis of Variance</u>

    A.   Material Variances

        1. Material Price Variance

            4,000 ($15 - $20)   = $20,000 (Favorable)

        2. Usage Variance (as above)   = $10,000 (Unfavorable)

        3. Joint Price/Quantity Material Variance

        (5,000 - 4,000) * ($15 - $10) = $5,000 (Favorable)

    B.   Direct-Labor Variances

        1. Rate Variance

          1,000 ($20 - $10)   = $10,000 (Unfavorable)

        2. Labor Efficiency Variance

          $10 (2,000 - 1,000)   = $10,000 (Unfavorable)

        3. Joint Price/Quantity Labor Variance

        (2,000 - 1,000) ($20 - $10) = $10,000 (Unfavorable)

Isolating the Direct-Material Variances

The general ledger entries to record and isolate the material variances arising in a standard cost accounting system generally fit into three categories:

1. Material purchase price variance is recognized at the time of the input purchases, while material usage variance is recognized at the time of the issuance of the input.

2. Material usage price variance and material usage (quantity) variance are both recognized at the time of the input issuance.

3. Material purchase price variance is recognized at the time of the input purchases, while both material usage price variance and material usage (quantity) variance are recognized at the time of the input issuance.

To illustrate the three methods, assume the following data:

Standard Material Cost per Unit	$3.00
Purchases	1,000 Units at $2.50
Issuance for Production	500 Units
Standard Quantity Allowed	450 Units

Method 1. In the first method, the T accounts would appear as follows:

```
          Material Inventory              Work-in-Process Inventory
1. Beginning        | 3. Actual Quantity    3. Standard Quantity |
   Inventory        |    Requisitioned *       Requisitioned *   |
2. Actual Quantity  |    Standard Price        Standard Price    |
   * Standard Price |

                                        Direct-Material Purchase
          Accounts Payable                  Price Variance
            | 2.Actual Quantity     2. Difference in    |
            |   Purchased *            Price * Actual    |
            |   Actual Price           Quantity         |

                   Direct-Material Usage Variance
            3. Difference in Quantity  |
               Issued * Standard Price |
```

The first method recognized the material price variances at the time of incurrence or purchase and the usage variance at the time of issuance. Note that the variances are debited when unfavorable and credited when favorable.

The journal entry at the time of material incurrence would be

Material Inventory	3,000	
Accounts Payable		2,500
Material Purchase Price Variance		500

to record the issuance of 500 units of direct material.

The journal entry at the time of material issuance would be

Work-in-Process	1,350	
Material Usage Variance	150	
Material		1,500

to record the issuance of 500 units of direct material.

Method 2. In the second method, the T accounts would appear as follows:

```
         Material Inventory                Work-in-Process Inventory
1.Beginning          3. Actual Quantity    3. Standard Quantity
Inventory              * Standard Price        Requisitioned *
2.Actual Quantity*                           Standard Price
Standard Price
                                          Direct Material Purchase
        Accounts Payable                        Price Variance
             2. Actual Quantity      2.Difference      4.Difference
                * Actual Price         in Price *        in Price *
                                       Actual Quantity   Quantity
                                       Purchased         Requisitioned

              Direct-Material Usage Variance
        3. Different in Quantity
           Issued * Standard Price

              Direct-Material Usage Price Variance
        4. Difference in Price
            * Quantity Requisi-
            tioned
```

Method 3. The third method recognizes the material purchase price variance at the time of purchase and both the material quantity and price variances at the time of issuance. The journal entry at the time of material incurrence would be

Material Inventory	3,000	
Accounts Payable		2,500
Material Purchase Price Variance		500

to record the purchase of 1,000 units of direct material.

The entry at the time of material issuance would be

Work-in-Process	1,350	
Material Quantity Variance	150	
Materials		1,500

to record the issuance of 500 units of direct material.

The entry to record the material usage price variance would be

Materials Purchase Price Variance	250	
Materials Usage Price Variance		250

Isolating the Direct-Labor Variances

The general ledger entries to record and isolate the direct-labor variances arising in a standard cost accounting system generally fall under two categories: direct labor incurred is recognized on the basis of actual values, and standard direct labor distributed is recognized on the basis of standard values and variances are isolated. To illustrate, assume the following data:

Actual Hours Worked	2,000 Hours
Actual Rate	$5 per Hour
Standard Hours Allowed	1,500 Hours
Standard Rate	$4 per Hour

To isolate the direct-labor variance, the T accounts would appear as follows:

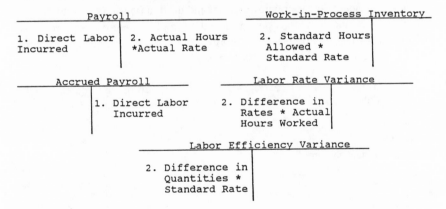

The two journal entries are as follows. The entry at the time of labor incurrence would be

Payroll	10,000	
Accrued Payroll		10,000

to record the incurrence of direct labor.

The entry at the time of labor distribution would be

Work-in-Process	6,000	
Labor Rate Variance	2,000	

Labor Efficiency Variance	2,000
Payroll	10,000

to record the distribution of direct labor.

FEEDBACK CONTROL SYSTEM

In the traditional control system, costs are classified by responsibility, budgeted, and then compared at the end of the period with the actual results, using the techniques of standard analysis. The traditional system does not include any monitoring system to detect and correct errors arising during the accounting period. It is an almost fatalistic approach in which the budget is perceived as a static rather than a continuous and dynamic process. A net separation between the budgeting and control phases dismissed the obvious complementarity of both operations.

One possible method of alleviating these shortcomings is the feedback control system, whereby an error in the system becomes the basis for the correction of the budget estimates. It is used after an error is detected and, therefore, represents a reaction to the error. As Exhibit 3.6 shows, the feedback control system consists of, first, an examination of a sample of operational activities; second, a feedback of observed error or confirmation; and third, a revision of the budget in accordance with the deviations observed in the sample. Therefore, the feedback control system requires both the monitoring of errors and management action.

R. N. Anthony and J. S. Reece observed:

Control reports are feedback devices, but they are only part of the feedback loop.
Unlike the thermostat, which acts automatically in response to information about

Exhibit 3.6
Feedback Control System

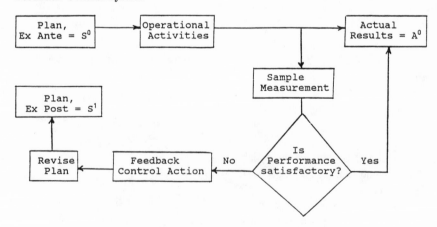

temperature, a control report does not by itself cause a change in performance. A change results only when managers take actions that lead to change. Thus, in a management control, the feedback loop requires both the control report plus management action.[7]

Feedback control systems may be applied to any business operation. For example, in the control of the purchasing manager, the accountant examines the actual prices paid to the supplier (sensor) and compares them to the budgeted prices (controller). If a variance emerges, the purchasing manager is advised to revise the budgeted price (actuator) to correct for the error.

J. S. Demski distinguishes between three types of results: the ex ante budgeted performance (the original budgeted estimates); the ex post budgeted performance (the revised budgeted performance after the feedback); and the observed performance (the actual performance).[8] The total traditional variance between the observed performance and the ex ante performance can be dichotomized as follows: (1) The difference between the ex ante and ex post results is a rough measure of the firm's forecasting ability. This is the difference between what the firm budgeted and what it should have budgeted. (2) The difference between the ex post and the observed results is a measure of the "opportunity cost to the firm" of not using resources to maximum advantage.

Assuming

S^0 = ex ante performance

S^1 = ex post performance

A^0 = observed performance

then

$$(A^0 - S^0) = (A^0 - S^1) + (S^1 - S^0),$$

where

$S^1 - S^0$ = indicator of the efficiency of the planning process

$A^0 - S^1$ = "opportunity cost of nonoptimal capacity utilization."[9]

This feedback control system, also labeled the ex post control system, when based on a linear programming formulation of the planning process, was reported to have been successfully applied in conjunction with a petroleum refinery model in an effort to examine the system's feasibility.

The feedback control system does have some operational limitations. First, it depends heavily on the success of the error detection process. Second, there may be a time lag between error detection, error confirmation, and error revision during which actual results may have changed again. The effectiveness of the feedback control system depends on the rapidity of the error response process.

FEEDFORWARD CONTROL SYSTEM

A feedforward control system must sense a specific error from a specific standard result before initiating a correction, and the process always occurs after the fact. Feedforward control systems do not rely on the examination of errors to recommend a correction. Instead, any correction is based on the anticipation of an error. As Exhibit 3.7 shows, a feedforward control system consists of, first, an examination of a "related" activity based on the anticipation of a possible deviation between the standard and actual performance; second, the feedforward or confirmation of the possibility of such an error; and, third, taking a compensatory action to maintain or adjust the operational activities. In other words, the information from the related activity acts as a surrogate for the operational activity and is fed forward to adjust the actual results through a compensatory action. Thus, the feedforward control system implies the possibility of predicting the effects of future actions and the very existence of a related activity: "Anticipation of deviations from standards depends upon the correlation of two systems such as the change in one enables prediction of change in the other. A controlling

Exhibit 3.7
Feedforward Control System

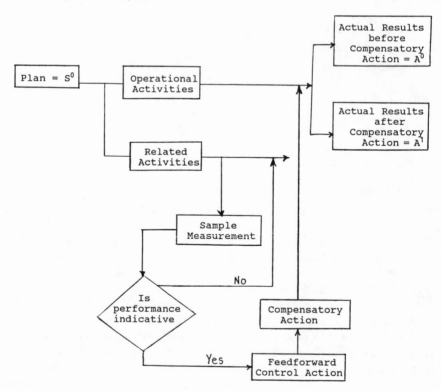

activity, which we shall call the 'related activity,' is ahead of the primary activity and 'feeds forward' information to it."[10]

Norbert Wiener, the father of cybernetics, recognized the limitations of feedback control systems. He pointed out that where there are lags in the system, corrections ("the compensator") must predict or anticipate errors. He referred to this system as an "anticipatory feedback" system. In fact, feedforward control systems have been applied only to specialized engineering processes, mainly chemical process.[11]

In a business setting, a feedforward control system might be used to adjust levels for inventories, production volume, purchase schedules, and employment as sales volume increases or decreases. A change in sales volume could automatically adjust the prescribed levels in the other factors in order to maintain a predetermined relationship of costs and activities to income.[12]

The typical feedforward control system goes through the following stages. At t − 1, an internal or external disturbance is detected by the controller (sensor). Given certain implied business relationships, the impact of such a disturbance on an organizational member's behavior at time t is postulated (controller). Appropriate information is fed forward to the given member for confirmation, and a compensatory action is taken that affects and governs the actual results (actuator).

To put such a system into operation, three figures are needed: the ex ante budgeted performance results (the originally budgeted results), the observed performance results (the actual possible results before the compensatory action), and the ex post actual performance results (the actual results after the compensatory action).

Feedforward control systems apply to management control as long as management can be provided information on forthcoming trouble in time for correction. For example, feedforward control can be used in cash planning, inventory control, and new product development. Mathematical models of these decisions programmed into a computer may be necessary to trace readily the influence of changes of input variables on cash flow, inventory level, and product development.[13]

However, before feedforward can be applied as successfully in management control as it has been in engineering, several guidelines must be followed:

1. Thorough planning and analysis is required.

2. Careful discrimination must be applied in selecting input variables.

3. The feedforward system must be kept dynamic.

4. A model of the control system should be developed.

5. Data on input variables must be regularly collected.

6. Data on input variables must be regularly assessed.

7. Feedforward control requires action.[14]

The feedforward control system has two main limitations: It depends on the reliability of the relationship assumed between the related and operational activities, and it does not discriminate between usual or planned events and unusual events.

In fact, the feedforward and feedback control systems can be linked together, thus reducing the limitations attributed to each system. The general control process of usual events falls under the feedforward control system, while the control process for unusual events will be handled by the feedback control system: "Technical discussions also emphasize that while feedforward systems are useful in dealing with events which may be anticipated, such systems are best linked with feedback mechanisms to handle events which cannot be determined in advance."[15]

NOTES

1. Leonard Sayles, "The Many Dimensions of Control," *Organizational Dynamics* (Summer 1972), p. 21.

2. Ibid.

3. W. H. Newman, *Constructive Control and Use of Control Systems* (Englewood Cliffs, N.J.: Prentice-Hall, 1975), p. 6.

4. Joel S. Demski, *Information Analysis* (Reading, Mass.: Addison-Wesley, 1972), Chap. 6.

5. C. T. Horngren and George Foster, *Cost Accounting: A Managerial Emphasis*, 7th ed. (Englewood Cliffs, N.J.: Prentice-Hall, 1991), pp. 219–220.

6. F. C. Leiseur, ed., *The Scanlon Plan* (Cambridge, Mass.: MIT Press, 1958).

7. R. N. Anthony and J. S. Reece, *Management Accounting: Text and Cases* (Homewood, Ill.: Irwin, 1975), p. 780.

8. J. S. Demski, "An Accounting System Structured on a Linear Programming Model," *Accounting Review* (October 1967), pp. 701–712.

9. Ibid., p. 704.

10. A. C. Filley, F. J. House, and S. Kerr, *Managerial Processes and Organizational Behavior* (Glenview, Ill.: Scott, Foresman, 1976), p. 441.

11. E. C. MacMullen and F. G. Shinskey, "Feedforward Analog Computer Control of a Superfractionator," *Control Engineering* 11 (1964), pp. 69–74; F. G. Shinskey, "Feedforward Control of pH," *Instrumentation Technology* 15 (1968), pp. 65–69; A. E. Nisenfield and R. G. Miyasaki, "Applications Feedforward Control to Distillation Columns," *Proceedings of the IFAC* (June 1972), pp. 1–7.

12. Filley, House, and Kerr, *Managerial Processes*, p. 443.

13. Harold Koontz and Robert W. Bradspies, "Managing through Feedforward Control," *Business Horizons* (June 1972), pp. 25–36.

14. Ibid., pp. 36–37.

15. Filley, House, and Kerr, *Managerial Processes*, p. 463.

REFERENCES

Barnes, John L. "How to Tell If Standard Costs Are Really Standard." *Management Accounting* (June 1983), pp. 50–54.

Beerel, Annabel. "Strategic Financial Control Can Provide Light and Guidance." *Accountancy* (British) (June 1986), pp. 70–74.

Demski, Joel S. "Analyzing the Effectiveness of the Traditional Standard Cost Variance Model." *Management Accounting* (October 1967), pp. 9–19.

Luh, F. S. "Controlled Cost: An Operation Concept and Statistical Approach for Standard Costing." *Accounting Review* (January 1968), pp. 123–132.

Newman, W. H. *Constructive Control and Use of Control Systems.* Englewood Cliffs, N.J.: Prentice-Hall, 1975.

Onsi, Mohamed. "Quantitative Models for Accounting Control." *Accounting Review* (April 1967), pp. 321–330.

Sayles, Leonard. "The Many Dimensions of Control." *Organizational Dynamics* (Summer 1972), pp. 21–31.

4

CONTROL PRINCIPLES AND QUALITY: CONTROL OF OVERHEAD COSTS

The analysis of variance procedure is expanded in this chapter to the control of the quality of factory overhead. The various overheads are presented as well as the required journal entries. The disposition of material, labor, and overhead variances are also illustrated in the cases of no beginning inventory and of beginning inventory. The different treatments covered in accounting textbooks are presented in the Appendix to this chapter.

FACTORY OVERHEAD VARIANCE

As automation increases and overhead adds to a higher part of the total manufacturing costs, the control of overhead becomes crucial in the management and controllable costs of the firm. The control of overhead resides in the determination and investigation of the factory overhead variances, which are equal to the differences between actual factory overhead and the standard factory overhead allowed for good output, which is basically equal to the amount of overhead applied in the product costing process. There are four steps in the process to determine the applied overhead:

Step 1: Determine the volume base that is most highly associated with the variable factory overhead.

Step 2: In the budgetary process, determine the normal activity level and the corresponding factory overhead for the coming year. The estimated overhead is generally a semivariable cost composed of a fixed component and a variable component.

Step 3: Determine the budgeted variable factory overhead rate, the budgeted fixed factory overhead rate, and the budgeted total factory overhead rate.

Step 4: Apply the overhead to jobs and/or production on the basis of the actual activity
level × budgeted total overhead rate.

Exhibit 4.1 illustrates the computation of the predetermined or budgeted overhead rate and the resulting flexible budget. Assuming that 80 percent represents
the normal capacity, the predetermined or budgeted overhead rate can be computed as follows:

$$\text{Budgeted overhead rate} = \frac{\$10,000}{100,000 \text{ hours}}$$

$$= \$.1 \text{ per standard direct labor hour (SDLH)}$$

This determined rate may be divided into a fixed component: $3,000/10,000
hours = $.30 per SDLH; and a variable component: $7,000/10,000 hours =
$.70 per SDLH. Although straightforward, the steps for computing the predeter-
mined overhead rate present some conceptual problems in both the choice of the
activity level and the specification of the denominator level.

The choice of the activity level rests on the choice of an expression of capacity.
Depending on whether a long- or short-range viewpoint is adopted, the activity
level can be expressed as either a normal capacity or an expected annual capacity.

Normal capacity is the level of capacity utilization that will meet average and
trend variations. It covers a period long enough to average consumer demand
over a number of years and includes seasonal, cyclical, and trend variations. Its
time span is sufficiently long to average out sizable changes in activity utilization
and allow a trend for sales.

Exhibit 4.1
Flexible Factory Overhead Budget

	40%	80%	100%
Capacity (Expressed as a Percentage of Normal)	40%	80%	100%
Direct-Labor Hours	5,000	10,000	15,000
Variable Factory Overhead			
Indirect Labor	$2,000	$ 3,000	$ 5,000
Indirect Material	1,000	4,000	5,000
Total Variable Factory Overhead	$3,000	$ 7,000	$10,000
Fixed Factory Overhead			
Machinery Depreciation	$1,000	$ 1,000	$ 1,000
Insurance	500	500	500
Property Taxes	500	500	500
Power and Light	800	800	800
Maintenance	200	200	200
Total Fixed Factory Overhead	$3,000	$ 3,000	$ 3,000
Total Factory Overhead	$6,000	$10,000	$13,000
Overhead Budget Formula	$3,000 + $.7 per Direct-Labor Hour		

Expected annual capacity is the anticipated level of capacity utilization for the coming year. Needless to say, the resulting overhead rate will vary from one period to another with changes in short-term production levels. It may be easily argued that the use of normal capacity avoids capricious changes in unit costs.

The denominator level expressing the activity level must be a useful common denominator for measuring production in all departments. Given the differences in the outputs of several departments, the activity level should be expressed uniformly. There must be a causal relationship between the denominator base and the overhead costs, and the denominator level should be measured in terms of outputs rather than inputs. In general, the denominator level is expressed in terms of standard hours of input allowed for good output produced. That is, if 1 unit of output requires 2 standard direct-labor hours, 800 units of output achieved may be expressed as 1,600 (800 × 2) standard hours of input allowed for good output produced.

OVERHEAD VARIANCE MODELS

One-Way Variance Model

Jobs and products in a standard cost system are charged with overhead on the basis of standard inputs allowed for actual outputs. An example of standard input is the standard hour allowed for one good output. At the end of a period, the applied overhead is compared with the actual overhead incurred. In the one-way variance model, the difference between the actual factory overhead and the applied factory overhead constitutes the total factory overhead variance.

Consider the following example. The Rocchi Company has prepared the following estimates for 19XA:

Budgeted overhead: $3,000 + $.7 per DLH.

Normal capacity in DLH: 10,000 units × 1 DLH per unit: 10,000 DLH.

Standard total overhead rate: $\dfrac{\$3,000 + \$.7(10,000 \text{ DLH})}{10,000 \text{ DLH}}$ = $1 per DLH

= $.3 fixed per DLH +
$.7 variable per DLH

In 19XA the actual data are

Variable Overhead	$4,500
Fixed Overhead	$4,000
Units Produced	8,000 units
Direct-Labor Hours	8,700 DLH

Thus, during 19XA the factory overhead applied to production, based on standard hours allowed for actual production, is equal to 8,000 units × 1 DLH per unit = 8,000 DLH. The total factory overhead variance will be computed as follows:

$$\text{Total factory overhead variance} = \text{Actual factory overhead}$$
$$- \text{Applied factory overhead}$$

The computation of the one-way variance model for the Rocchi Company can be illustrated as follows:

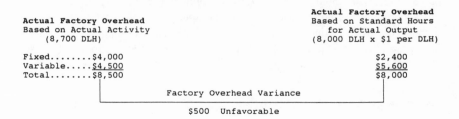

```
                                                          Actual Factory Overhead
Actual Factory Overhead                                   Based on Standard Hours
Based on Actual Activity                                      for Actual Output
      (8,700 DLH)                                         (8,000 DLH x $1 per DLH)

Fixed........$4,000                                                 $2,400
Variable.....$4,500                                                 $5,600
Total........$8,500                                                 $8,000
                   |                                              |
                   |         Factory Overhead Variance           |
                   |_____|
                              $500   Unfavorable
```

This total factory overhead variance needs further analysis to identify the exact causes of its incurrence and help management choose a corrective action. Further analysis may be made by the two-way variance model A or B, the three-way variance model A or B, or the four-way variance model.

Two-Way Variance Model A

The two-way variance model A is analogous to that used for direct costs (material and labor). The total overhead variance is divided into an overhead price variance and an overhead efficiency variance. The computation of the two-way variance model A for the Rocchi Company is as follows:

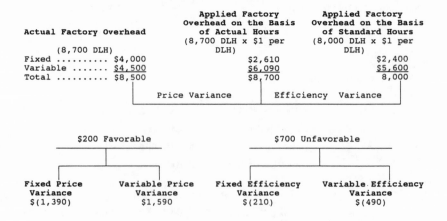

```
                                       Applied Factory          Applied Factory
                                    Overhead on the Basis    Overhead on the Basis
Actual Factory Overhead                of Actual Hours          of Standard Hours
                                    (8,700 DLH x $1 per       (8,000 DLH x $1 per
        (8,700 DLH)                        DLH)                      DLH)
Fixed .......... $4,000                    $2,610                   $2,400
Variable ....... $4,500                    $6,090                   $5,600
Total .......... $8,500                    $8,700                   8,000
                        |                         |                       |
                        |   Price Variance        |  Efficiency  Variance |
                        |_____|_____|


              $200 Favorable                         $700 Unfavorable
         _____                _____
        |                       |              |                        |
Fixed Price        Variable Price       Fixed Efficiency      Variable Efficiency
Variance             Variance             Variance               Variance
$(1,390)             $1,590               $(210)                 $(490)
```

Two-Way Variance Model B

The two-way variance model B distinguishes between a controllable variance and a volume variance (uncontrollable). The computation of the two-way variance model B for the Rocchi company is as follows:

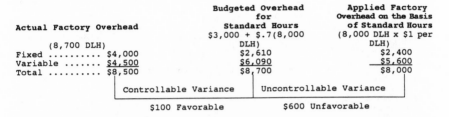

Actual Factory Overhead	Budgeted Overhead for Standard Hours $3,000 + $.7(8,000 DLH)	Applied Factory Overhead on the Basis of Standard Hours (8,000 DLH x $1 per DLH)
(8,700 DLH)		
Fixed $4,000	$2,610	$2,400
Variable $4,500	$6,090	$5,600
Total $8,500	$8,700	$8,000

Controllable Variance	Uncontrollable Variance
$100 Favorable	$600 Unfavorable

The controllable variance and the volume variance can be computed differently. The controllable variance is due to the variable overhead and can be computed as follows:

Variable Overhead at Normal Capacity	$7,000
Standard Hours Allowed (8,000 DLH)	× 80%
Allowable Variable Overhead	$5,600
Actual Variable Overhead ($8,500 − $3,000)	5,500
Controllable Variance	$ 100 (Favorable)

The uncontrollable (or volume) variance is due to the fixed overhead and can be computed as follows:

Normal Capacity	10,000 DLH
Standard Hours	− 8,000 DLH
Capacity Unused	2,000 DLH
Fixed Overhead Rate	×$ .3
	$ 600 (Unfavorable)

The controllable variance is the responsibility of the department manager, given that it is possible to control the causes of variance. The uncontrollable or volume variance arises from the failure to use the total capacity or from the inefficient use of the available capacity.

Three-Way Variance Model A

In the three-way variance model A, the total factory overhead variance is divided into an overhead spending variance, an overhead capacity variance (or idle capacity variance), and an overhead efficiency variance. The three-way variance model A for the Rocchi Company can be computed as follows:

Actual Factory Overhead	Budgeted Overhead for Actual Hours	Applied Overhead on the Basis of Actual Hours	Applied Overhead on the Basis of Standard Hours
	$3,000 +	(8,700 DLH	(8,000 DLH
(8,700 DLH)	$.7(8,700 DLH)	x $1 per DLH)	x 1 per DLH)
Fixed $4,000	$3,000	$2,610	$2,400
Variable . $4,500	$6,090	$6,090	$5,600
Total $8,500	$9,090	$8,700	$8,000

```
         | Spending Variance | Idle Capacity Variance | Efficiency Variance |

           $590 Favorable        $390 Unfavorable        $700 Unfavorable
```

The idle capacity variance can be computed as follows:

Normal Capacity	10,000 DLH
Actual Capacity	− 8,700 DLH
Capacity Unused in Planning	1,300 DLH
Fixed Overhead Rate	×$ .3
	$ 390 (Unfavorable)

The spending variance is again the responsibility of the departmental manager. Performance based on the spending variance appears to be more favorable than that based on the controllable variance ($100 versus $590) because the budgeted overhead is based on the actual rather than the standard hours.

The idle capacity variance is due to the underabsorption or overabsorption of overhead arising from differences between the actual capacity and the normal capacity, on which the overhead rate was based. The efficiency variance results from the differences between the actual hours and the standard hours allowed for actual production. These differences reflect inefficiencies in labor usage if the capacity level is expressed in terms of labor hours, and they reflect inefficiencies in material usage if the capacity level is expressed in terms of machine hours.

Three-Way Variance Model B

The three-way variance model B makes a distinction between overhead spending variance, overhead efficiency variance, and overhead capacity variance. The computation of the three-way variance model B for the Rocchi Company is illustrated as follows:

Actual Factory Overhead	Budgeted Overhead for Actual Hours	Budgeted Overhead for Standard Hours	Applied Overhead on the Basis of Standard Hours
	$3,000 +	$3,000 +	(8,000 DLH
	$.7(8,700 DLH)	$.7(8,700 DLH)	x 1 per DLH)
Fixed $4,000	$3,000	$3,000	$2,400
Variable . $4,500	$6,090	$5,600	$5,600
Total $8,500	$9,090	$8,600	$8,000

```
         | Spending Variance | Efficiency Variance | Idle Capacity Variance |

           $590 Favorable        $490 Unfavorable        $600 Unfavorable
```

Four-Way Variance Model

The four-way variance model is identical to the three-way variance model A, except that the efficiency variance is separated into fixed efficiency variance and variable efficiency variance. The four-way variance model for the Rocchi Company is computed as follows:

Actual Factory Overhead (8,700 DLH)	Budgeted Overhead for Actual Hours $3,000 + $.7(8,700 DLH)	Applied Overhead on the Basis of Actual Hours (8,700 DLH x $1 per DLH)	Applied Overhead on the Basis of Standard Hours (8,000 DLH x 1 per DLH)
Fixed $4,000	$3,000	$2,610	$2,400
Variable . $4,500	$6,090	$6,090	$5,600
Total $8,500	$9,090	$8,700	$8,000

Spending Variance	Idle Capacity Variance	Efficiency Variance
$590 Favorable	$390 Unfavorable	$700 Unfavorable

Fixed Efficiency Variance	Variable Efficiency Variance
.3 x (8,700 – 8,000 DLH) $210 Unfavorable	$.7 x (8,700 – 8,000 DLH) $490 Unfavorable

Note that the sum of the spending variance ($590 favorable) and the variable efficiency variance ($490 unfavorable) equals the controllable variance ($100) of the two-way variance method B. Similarly, the sum of the idle capacity variance ($390 unfavorable) and the fixed efficiency variance ($210 unfavorable) equals the uncontrollable or volume variance ($600) of the two-way variance method B. Exhibit 4.2 summarizes the factory overhead variance analysis methods.

JOURNAL ENTRIES FOR OVERHEAD VARIANCES

The general ledger entries to record and isolate the overhead variances arising in a standard cost accounting system include the following steps:

1. Factory overhead incurred is recognized on the basis of actual values.
2. Factory overhead is applied to the Work-in-Process Inventory (sometimes referred to as Work-in-Process) on the basis of standard or budgeted values.
3. Overhead variances are isolated.

To illustrate, assume the following data (used previously in the "Two-Way Variance Model B" section to illustrate the computation of overhead variances):

Standard overhead = $3,000 + $.7 per SDLH

Normal capacity = 10,000 SDLH

Total predetermined overhead rate (TPOR) = $\dfrac{\$10,000}{10,000}$ = $1 per SDLH

Variable predetermined overhead rate (VPOR) $= \dfrac{\$7,000}{10,000} = \$.7$ per SDLH

Fixed predetermined overhead rate (FPOR) $= \dfrac{\$3,000}{10,000} = \$.3$ per SDLH

Actual overhead = \$4,000 fixed + \$4,500 variable = \$8,500

Actual capacity = 8,700 DLH

Standard hours for actual production = 8,000 SDLH

Exhibit 4.2
Summary of Factory Overhead Variance Analysis Methods

Method	Actual Factory Overhead	Budgeted Overhead for Actual Hours	Budgeted Overhead for Standard Hours	Actual Hours x Standard Rate	Standard Hours x Standard Rate
Two-way Variance Method A	$8,500			$8,700	$8,000
Two-way Variance Method B	$8,500		$8,600		$8,000
Three-way Variance Method A	$8,500	$9,090		$8,700	$8,000
Three-way Variance Method B	$8,500	$9,090	$8,600		$8,000
Four-way Variance Method	$8,500	$9,090	$8,600	$8,700	$8,000

Variances For Each Method	Total Overhead Variance

Variances For Each Method		Total Overhead Variance
Price Variance	= Col. 1 - Col. 4 = $200 Favorable	
Efficiency Variance	= Col. 4 - Col. 5 = $700 Unfavorable	$500 (Unfavorable)
Controllable Variance	= Col. 1 - Col. 3 = $100 Favorable	
Volume Variance	= Col. 3 - Col. 5 = $600 Unfavorable	$500 (Unfavorable)
Spending Variance	= Col. 1 - Col. 2 = $590 Favorable	
Idle Capacity Variance	= Col. 2 - Col. 4 = $390 Favorable	
Efficiency Variance	= Col. 4 - Col. 5 = $700 Unfavorable	$500 (Unfavorable)
Spending Variance	= Col. 1 - Col. 2 = $590 Variance	
Efficiency Variance	= Col. 2 - Col. 3 = $490 Unfavorable	
Idle Capacity Variance	= Col. 3 - Col. 5 = $600 Favorable	$500 (Unfavorable)
Spending Variance	= Col. 1 - Col. 2 = $590 Variance	
Idle Capacity Variance	= Col. 2 - Col. 4 = $390 Favorable	
Variable Efficiency Variance	= Col. 2 - Col. 3 = $490 Unfavorable	
Fixed Efficiency Variance	= $210 Unfavorable	$500 (Unfavorable)

The journal entries obtained by using the four-way variance method are as follows. At the time of factory overhead incurrence, the entry is

Factory Overhead Control		8,500
Cash, Accounts Payable, Accrued Expenses	8,500	

to record the incurrence of actual factory overhead.

At the time of factory overhead application the entry is

Work-in-Process		8,000
Variable Efficiency Variance		490
Fixed Efficiency Variance		210
Factory Overhead Control	8,700	

to record the application of factory overhead.

To record the other variances and close the $200 credit balance of factory overhead, the entry is

Factory Overhead		200
Idle Capacity Variance		390
Spending Variance	590	

Another possible accounting treatment for the second and third entries is as follows:

Work-in-Process		8,000
Factory Overhead Control	8,000	
Variable Efficiency Variance		490
Fixed Efficiency Variance		210
Idle Capacity Variance		390
Spending Variance	590	
Factory Overhead	500	

STANDARD COST ACCOUNTING: PRORATING THE VARIANCES

Methods of Treating Variances

Both the normal and standard costing systems produce accounts valued at standard costs, and a set of variances may be treated as follows: they can be carried as deferred charges or credits on the balance sheet, they can appear as charges or credits on the income statement, and they can be allocated to inventories and cost of goods sold. Each of these methods will be dealt with in turn.

The deferral of variances is supported on the grounds that if the standards in use are based on normal levels of price, efficiency, and output, then positive and negative variances can be expected to offset one another in the long run. Because variance account balances at a given time are due to recurring seasonal and business cycle fluctuations, and because periodic reporting requirements result in arbitrary cutoff dates, variance account balances at a particular cutoff date are not assignable to the operating results of the period then ended. They will cancel out over recurring seasonal and business cycle fluctuations and, therefore, should be carried to the balance sheet. This method is appropriate for interim statements, no matter what method is used for annual statements.

If variances appear as charges or credits on the income statement, they are regarded as appropriate charges or credits in the period in which they arise because they are considered to be the result of favorable or unfavorable departures from normal (standard) conditions. These variances are disclosed separately from cost of goods sold at standard cost and thus provide management with unobscured information permitting immediate corrective action. Inventory valuations and cost of goods sold should not be distorted by variances that represent abnormal efficiencies or inefficiencies. A standard cost represents the amount that is reasonably necessary to produce finished products, and therefore should be considered the best measure of cost of goods manufactured and inventory valuation as long as the underlying operating conditions remain unchanged.

Those who advocate allocation of variances to inventories and cost of goods sold regard standard costs as a useful tool for purposes of managerial control rather than as substitutes for actual historical costs in the financial statements. These people believe that only actual historical costs should be used for financial reporting, even though these costs are greater or less than standard costs and without regard to the reasons for the historical costs' differences from standard costs. Standard cost variances are not gains or losses; they are costs (or reductions thereof) of goods manufactured and, as such, should be allocated to inventories and cost of goods sold. To treat standard cost variances as gains or losses in the period in which they arise distorts both the inventory and gross profit figures. This distortion would be even greater if the standards lacked accuracy or reliability. Further, to substitute standard costs for actual historical costs in the financial statements represents an unwarranted sacrifice of objectivity. In fact, *Accounting Research Bulletin No. 43* requires that standard costs, to be acceptable for financial reporting purposes, be "adjusted at reasonable intervals to reflect current conditions so that at the balance-sheet date standard costs reasonably approximate costs computed under one of the recognized bases."[1] The recognized bases are first in, first out (FIFO); last in, first out (LIFO); and weighted average cost-flow patterns.

Prorating Variances: No Beginning Inventory

As a general rule, each variance on a given factor (labor, material, or overhead) is prorated to each relevant ending inventory and cost of sales proportionally to the standard cost for that factor in each account. The first example to
be used assumes that there are no beginning inventories to simplify the presenta-
tion. The data for a fictional example appear in Exhibit 4.3. The allocation of the
variances, shown in Exhibit 4.4, was accomplished on the basis of the following
steps:

1. The materials price variances were prorated proportionally to the standard costs of
   materials in each affected account: usage variance, materials inventory, work-in-
   process inventory, finished goods inventory, and cost of sales. Note that the allocation to the usage variance was negative because the usage variance was favorable.

Exhibit 4.3
Data for a Fictional Example

Standard Cost of Product

      Materials: 2 pounds at $5 = $10
      Conversion Costs   20
      Total $30

Production and Sales Data

	Units	Standard Cost of Material at $10	Standard Conversion Cost at $20	Total Standard Costs
Units Sold	30,000	$300,000	$600,000	$900,000
Finished Goods, Ending Inventory	20,000	200,000	400,000	600,000
Work-in-Process, Ending Inventory				
Materials, 6,000 Units 100% Complete		60,000		
Conversion Costs, 6,000 Units 80% complete			96,000	
Total Work-in-Process				156,000

Material Data

    The inventory of materials at the end of the period was 20,000 pounds with
a standard cost of $100,000. There were no beginning inventories.

Variance Data

      Material Price Variance: $ 40,000 unfavorable
      Material Usage Variance: 60,000 favorable
      Conversion Cost Variance: 100,000 unfavorable

Exhibit 4.4
Schedule of Proration of Variances, No Beginning Inventory

	Total	Material Usage Variance	Material Inventory	Work-In Process Inventory	Finished Cost Inventory	Cost of Goods Sold
1. Standard Cost of Materials	$600,000	($60,000)	$100,000	$60,000	$200,000	$300,000
2. Percentage of Total			16.66%	10.00%	33.34%	50.00%
3. Proration of Material Price Variance	40,000	(4,000)	$ 6,664	4,000	13,336	20,000
4. Adjusted Usage Variance		($64,000)				
5. Percentage of Total	$560,000	--	--	10.714%	35.714%	53.572%
6. Proration of Material Usage Variance		($64,000)	--	$(6,856.96)	$(22,856.96)	$(34,286.08)
7. Standard Conversion Cost	1,096,000	--		$ 96,000	$400,000	$600,000
8. Percentage of Total				8.760%	36.496%	54.744%
9. Proration of Conversion Cost Variance	100,000			8.760%	36,486	54,744
10. Actual Cost	--	--	$106,664	$161,903.04	$626,975.04	$943,457.92

2. The usage variance is then adjusted before being prorated to the work-in-process inventory and the finished goods inventory and to the cost of goods sold.

3. The conversion cost variances are then prorated in proportion to the standard costs in each of the affected accounts—namely, finished goods inventory, work-in-process inventory, and cost of goods sold.

Prorating Variances: With Beginning Inventory

With beginning inventory present, a cost-flow assumption becomes very important. The example to be used assumes that FIFO is used, meaning that all

Exhibit 4.5
Data for Illustration

Standard Cost per Unit

Materials:	$1.50
Conversion Costs:	3.00
	$4.50

Equivalent Production

	Materials	Conversion Costs
Completed	18,000	18,000
Ending Inventory	15,000	10,000
Beginning Inventory	(3,000)	(1,000)
Equivalent Production	30,000	27,000

Inventories

	Materials	Conversion Costs
Beginning Inventory	20,000	10,000
Added during the period	50,000	18,000
Used or Sold	(30,000)	(20,000)
Ending Inventory	40,000	8,000

Variances

Material price :	$50,000 unfavorable
Usage :	10,000 favorable
Conversion cost:	20,000 unfavorable

beginning material inventory is used in production first, all beginning work-in-process inventory is completed first, and all beginning finished goods inventory is sold first. The data for the fictional example appear in Exhibit 4.5. The allocation of the variances proceeds as follows:

1. The materials price variance is allocated first to the ending inventory of materials as follows:

   • Ending inventory of materials: 40,000 gallons

   • Materials price variance per gallon:
     ($50,000/50,000 gallons): $1

   • Materials price variance allocated to ending inventory:
     $40,000 (40,000 gallons × $1)

   • Materials price variance remaining:
     ($50,000 − $40,000): $10,000

2. The next step is to determine where the current period equivalent production for materials and conversion cost finished. The computation may proceed as follows:

	Disposition of Current Period Production	
	Materials	*Conversion Costs*
Total Equivalent Production for Period	30,000	27,000
Equivalent Units in Ending Inventory of Work-in-Process	15,000	10,000
Ending Inventory of Finished Goods	8,000	8,000
Total Current Period Equivalent Production in Ending Inventory	23,000	18,000
Equivalent Production in Cost of Sales	7,000	9,000

3. The third step is to prorate the materials price variance proportionally to the standard costs of materials in usage variance, the work-in-process inventory, the finished goods inventory, and the cost of goods sold. The results are shown in Exhibit 4.6.

4. The fourth step is to prorate the adjusted usage variance proportionally to the standard costs of materials in the work in process inventory, the finished goods inventory, and the cost of goods sold. The results are shown in Exhibit 4.6.

5. The conversion costs are then prorated in proportion to the standard conversion costs in the work-in-process inventory, the finished goods inventory, and the cost of goods sold. The results are shown in Exhibit 4.7.

6. The variances are prorated to determine the actual costs of materials inventory,

Exhibit 4.6
Schedule of Proration of Variances, with Beginning Inventory

	Total	Usage Variance	Work-In Process Inventory	Finished Cost Inventory	Cost of Goods Sold
1. Standard Cost of Materials	$35,000	($10,000)	$22,500	$12,000	$10,500
2. Percentage of Total	100%	(28.57%)	64.28%	34.28%	30.00%
3. Proration of Material Price Variance	10,000	(2,857)	$ 6,428	3,428	3,000
4. Unadjusted Usage Variance	10,000				
5. Adjusted Usage Variance	$ 2,857				
6. Percentage of Total	100%	--	50.00%	26.66%	23.33%
7. Proration of Usage Variance	$12,857	--	(6,428.5)	(3,497.67)	(2,999.54)
8. Standard Conversion Cost	$81,000	--	$30,000	$24,000	$27,000
9. Percentage of Total	100%	--	37.03%	29.62%	3.33%
10. Proration of Conversion Cost Variance	$20,000		7,406	5,924	6,666

Exhibit 4.7
Proration of Variances

	Materials Inventory	Work-in Process Inventory	Finished Cost Inventory	Cost of Goods Sold
Standard Cost	$45,000	$52,500	$36,000	$90,000
Material Price Variance	40,000	6,429	3,428	3,000
Material Usage Variance		(6,428.5)	(3,427.67)	(2,999.54)
Conversion Cost Variance		7,406	5,924	6,666
Actual Costs	$85,000	$59,906	$41,924	$96,666

work-in-process inventory, finished goods inventory, and cost of goods sold. The results are shown in Exhibit 4.7. Note that the standard figure used for cost of sales is total cost of sales at standard costs rather than just the standard cost of sales related to current period production.

NOTE

1. Committee on Accounting Procedure, *Accounting Research Bulletin No. 43, Restatement and Revision of Accounting Research Bulletins* (New York: American Institute of Certified Public Accountants, 1953), p. 17.

APPENDIX—Teaching Standard Costs: A Look at Textbook Differences in Overhead Variance Analysis

William B. Pollard

APPALACHIAN STATE UNIVERSITY

Abstract: Procedures for calculating the two-way, three-way, and four-way analysis of overhead variances can differ significantly among cost accounting textbooks. This study uses a common problem framework to compare the isolation of overhead variances in 20 cost accounting textbooks that present the current, yet different methods of overhead variance analysis.

INTRODUCTION

Standard costs and the corresponding isolation of variances is an integral part of any cost accounting course. While there is relative consistency among cost accounting textbooks for procedures to isolate materials and labor variances, the procedures for calculating the two-way, three-way, and four-way analysis of overhead variances can differ significantly. This difference in methodologies is acceptable since no absolute procedure must be followed. However, it cannot only prove confusing when switching from one textbook to another, it can also leave students feeling they have mastered the topic of overhead variance analysis when, in fact, they have mastered only their particular textbook author's procedures.

The analysis presented in this study compares the isolation of overhead variances in 20 cost accounting textbooks. In the following sections, the two-way, three-way, and four-way analysis of overhead variances for each of the 20 texts is presented and the different techniques of determining the overhead variances are compared.

TEXTBOOK SELECTION

The textbooks analyzed in this study represent the current, yet different methods of overhead variance analysis. The textbooks include all cost accounting textbooks listed in *Subject Guide To Books In Print, 1983-84* (including supplements) under "Cost Accounting" with a copyright date of 1980 or later. Accordingly, the following 20 textbooks are analyzed: Asch

[1983], Belkaoui [1983], Brock and Palmer [1984], Cashin and Polimeni [1981], Chatfield and Neilson [1983], Deakin and Maher [1984], Dopuch, Birnberg, and Demski [1982], Gray and Ricketts [1982], Hartley [1983], Horngren [1982], Killough and Leininger [1984], Louderback and Hirsch [1982], Matz and Usry [1984], Moriarity and Allen [1984], Morse [1981], Most and Lewis [1982], Rayburn [1983], Schmiedicke and Nagy [1983], Shillinglaw [1982], and Walker [1982].

GENERAL FRAMEWORK

To facilitate the discussion of each textbook's treatment of overhead variance analysis, the following problem framework will be used and partially solved to the point of textbook disagreement.

PROBLEM   The following information is available:
Budgeted Production . . . . 9,000 units
Actual Production . . . . 9,450 units
Standard DIRECT LABOR HOURS (DLHs)
  per unit 3
Actual DLHs (total) 28,000
Standard DLHs (total) . . . (9,450 x 3) 28,350
Actual FIXED OVERHEAD (FOH) $56,700
Actual VARIABLE OVERHEAD (VOH) . . $30,300
Budgeted FOH $54,000
FOH Rate (per DLH) $2
VOH Rate (per DLH) $1

Shown in Table 1 is a partial solution to the problem. The information used in Table 1, while usually well hidden in a problem, is all given above. It should be emphasized that none of the textbooks use this solution procedure. It has been used here to illustrate that, to a point, the analyses are relatively similar. The differences emerge in the treatment of Table 1, items A through E, (see next page).

SIMILARITIES AND DIFFERENCES

A comparison of the two-way, three-way, and four-way analysis of overhead variances for each of the twenty textbooks is shown in Table 2. An examination of Table 2 shows that, while there is some agreement, differing views do exist on (1) which variances exist, (2) how the variances should be calculated, and (3) what the variances should be named.

TABLE 1

Partial Analysis of Overhead Variances

VARIABLE OVERHEAD:

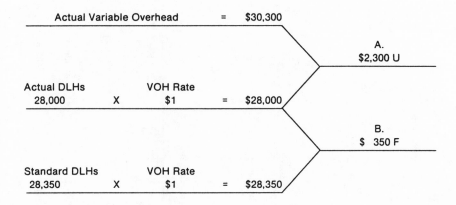

Actual Variable Overhead = $30,300

A.
$2,300 U

Actual DLHs VOH Rate
28,000 X $1 = $28,000

B.
$ 350 F

Standard DLHs VOH Rate
28,350 X $1 = $28,350

FIXED OVERHEAD:

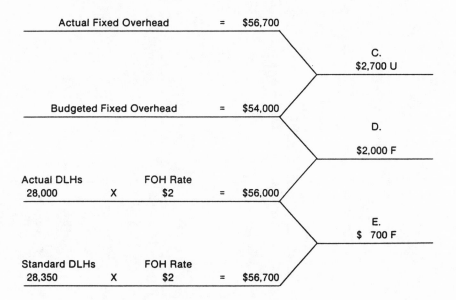

Actual Fixed Overhead = $56,700

C.
$2,700 U

Budgeted Fixed Overhead = $54,000

D.

$2,000 F

Actual DLHs FOH Rate
28,000 X $2 = $56,000

E.
$ 700 F

Standard DLHs FOH Rate
28,350 X $2 = $56,700

TABLE 2

Overhead Variance Analysis—Comparison

	ASCH [1983]	BELKAOUI [1983] Model A	BELKAOUI [1983] Model B	BROCK and PALMER [1984]	CASHIN and POLIMENI [1981]	CHATFIELD and NEILSON [1983]
TWO-WAY						
1.	None	Price A+C+D	Controllable A+B+C	OH Budget A+B+C	Controllable A+B+C	OH Budget A+B+C
2.	None	Efficiency B+E	Uncontrollable D+E	OH Volume D+E	Volume D+E	FOH Volume D+E
THREE-WAY						
1.	None	Spending A+C	Spending A+C	Spending A+C	Spending A+C	Combined OH Spending A+C
2.	None	Efficiency B+E	Efficiency B	Efficiency B	Efficiency B+E	VOH Efficiency B
3.	None	Idle Capacity D	Idle Capacity D+E	OH Volume D+E	Idle Capacity D	FOH Volume D+E
FOUR-WAY						
1.	VOH Expenditure A	Spending A+C		None	Spending A+C	VOH Spending A
2.	VOH Efficiency B	VOH Efficiency B		None	VOH Efficiency B	VOH Efficiency B
3.	FOH Expenditure C	Idle Capacity D		None	Idle Capacity D	FOH Spending C
4.	FOH Volume D+E	FOH Efficiency E		None	FOH Efficiency E	FOH Volume D+E

122

TABLE 2 (Continued)

Overhead Variance Analysis—Comparison

	DEAKIN and MAHER [1984]	DOPUCH, BIRNBERG and DEMSKI [1982]	GRAY and RICKETTS [1983]	HARTLEY [1983]	HORNGREN [1982]
TWO-WAY					
1.	None	None	Budget A+B+C	Controllable A+B+C	Flexible Budget A+B+C
2.	None	None	Volume D+E	Noncontrollable D+E	Production Volume D+E
THREE-WAY					
1.	None	Price A+C	Spending A+C	Spending A+C	Price (Spending) A+C
2.	None	Quantity B	Efficiency B	Efficiency B	Efficiency B
3.	None	Volume D+E	Volume D+E	Noncontrollable D+E	Production Volume D+E
FOUR-WAY					
1.	VOH Price A	None	None	VOH Spending A	Price (Spending) A
2.	Efficiency B	None	None	VOH Efficiency B	Efficiency B
3.	FOH Price C	None	None	FOH Spending C	Budget C
4.	Production Volume D+E	None	None	Noncontrollable D+E	Production Volume D+E

123

TABLE 2 (Continued)
Overhead Variance Analysis—Comparison

	KILLOUGH and LEININGER [1984]	LOUDERBACK and HIRSCH [1982]	MATZ and USRY [1984]	MORIARITY and ALLEN [1984]	MORSE [1981]
TWO-WAY					
1.	Controllable A+B+C	None	Controllable A+B+C	None	OH Budget A+B+C
2.	Volume D+E	None	Volume D+E	None	OH Volume D+E
THREE-WAY					
1.	Spending A+C	Spending A+C	Spending A+C	Combined Price A+C	OH Spending A+C
2.	Efficiency B	Efficiency B	Efficiency B+E	VOH Quantity B	OH Efficiency B
3.	Volume D+E	Application D+E	Idle Capacity D	Volume (Denominator) D+E	OH Volume D+E
FOUR-WAY					
1.	VOH Spending A	VOH Price A	Spending A+C	VOH Price A	VOH Spending A
2.	Efficiency B	VOH Efficiency B	VOH Efficiency B	VOH Quantity B	VOH Efficiency B
3.	FOH Spending C	FOH Budget C	Idle Capacity D	FOH Price C	FOH Budget C
4.	Volume D+E	FOH Application D+E	FOH Efficiency E	Volume (Denominator) D+E	FOH Volume D+E

TABLE 2 (Continued)

Overhead Variance Analysis—Comparison

MOST and LEWIS [1982]	RAYBURN [1983]	SCHMIEDICKE and NAGY [1983]	SHILLINGLAW [1982]	WALKER [1982]
TWO-WAY	**TWO-WAY**	**TWO-WAY**	**TWO-WAY**	**TWO-WAY**
1. Spending A+B+C	Controllable A+B+C	Budget A+B+C	Spending A+B+C	None
2. Volume D+E	Volume D+E	Volume D+E	Volume D+E	None
THREE-WAY	**THREE-WAY**	**THREE-WAY**	**THREE-WAY**	**THREE-WAY**
1. Spending A+C	OH Spending A+C	Budget (Spending) A+C	Spending A+C	None
2. Efficiency B+E	VOH Efficiency B	Efficiency B+E	Labor Efficiency B	None
3. Volume D	Volume D+E	Capacity D	Volume D+E	None
FOUR-WAY	**FOUR-WAY**	**FOUR-WAY**	**FOUR-WAY**	**FOUR-WAY**
1. None	VOH Spending A	None	None	VOH Expenditure A
2. None	VOH Efficiency B	None	None	VOH Efficiency B
3. None	FOH Spending C	None	None	FOH Expenditure C
4. None	Volume D+E	None	None	FOH Volume D+E

The names of the overhead variances in Table 2 are the primary names used by the authors. Even though Horngren [1982], Moriarity and Allen [1984], and Schmiedicke and Nagy [1983] use two primary names for some of the variances, the remaining authors use only one for each variance. Most authors, however, do briefly note additional names for the variances.

Also, some authors do not explicitly call their analysis of overhead variances a "two-way," "three-way," or "four-way" analysis. However, they show a four-variance breakdown followed by combinations of the variances that result in a two-way, three-way, or four-way analysis. The terms "two-way," "three-way," and "four-way" are used in this study and applied to each textbook to facilitate comparisons.

The two-way analyses in Table 2 indicate that all cost accounting textbooks that present a two-way analysis show an A+B+C and D+E combination except Belkaoui's [1983] Model A which combines the differences between actual hours and standard hours for both variable and fixed overhead (B+E) for an overhead "Efficiency"variance. The remaining elements (A+C+D) comprise a "Price" variance.

Even though most authors present their particular analysis without detailing their arguments for selecting one approach over another, the differences in calculating the three-way and four-way analysis of overhead variances center around two major areas of disagreement. First is whether items D+E should be subdivided. Horngren [1982, p. 209] does specify reasons for his choice and disagrees with a subdivision of items D+E. Horngren [1982, p. 210] states that "the breakdown of the Production Volume variance really attempts to separate the cost of *misused* facilities (E) from the cost of *unused* facilities (D)." Even though Horngren [1982, p. 210] does show how to isolate a "Fixed Overhead Efficiency" variance (E), he states that variances are for a short-term analysis and that (in bold type) "short-run fixed-overhead cost is not affected by efficiency." Other authors, however, such as Matz and Usry [1984], do show a breakdown of items D+E into an "Idle Capacity" variance (D) and a "Fixed Overhead Efficiency" variance (E).

The second area of disagreement concerns the possibility of a variance between actual and budgeted fixed overhead (C). For example, Matz and Usry [1984, p. 481] disagree with the separate isolation of an item C variance and state that in their analysis, only budgeted fixed overhead is used. They note that if a difference between actual and budgeted fixed overhead were to occur, it would become a part of the variable overhead variances. Even though Matz and Usry [1984, p. 481] note that any difference between actual and budgeted fixed overhead could be separately isolated as a "Fixed Overhead Spending" variance, their analysis, by including item C (if it exists) as part of the variable overhead variances, causes item C to be continually linked to item A. One advantage to this method is that total actual overhead does not have to be subdivided into its exact fixed and variable overhead components to analyze the overhead variances.

Based on these areas of disagreement, the three-way analyses show that while most authors (including Horngren [1982]) present a breakdown of A+C, B, and D+E, Matz and Usry [1984], Belkaoui's [1983] Model A, Cashin and Polimeni [1981], Most and Lewis [1982], and Schmiedicke and Nagy [1983] show a breakdown of A+C, B+E, and D.

The four-way analyses also reflect the areas of disagreement. All textbooks with a four-way analysis present an A, B, C, and D+E analysis except for Matz and Usry [1984], Belkaoui [1983] and Cashin and Polimeni [1981] who present an A+C, B, D, and E analysis.

In addition, while each textbook has its own unique style, rather distinct differences are found in some texts. For example, Most and Lewis [1982, p. 358] present a "Fixed Budget Approach" which generally treats all overhead as fixed. They state that "firms will use fixed budgets even though output may vary substantially from period to period because the bulk of overheads are fixed for long periods of time . . . . The problems associated with overheads have led some cost accountants to conclude that overheads should be controlled by means of budgets and not by means of standards." Thus, Most and Lewis [1982, p. 375] present a flexible budget analysis of overhead variances. Most and Lewis [1982, p. 365], however, do show a calculation for a "Variable Overhead Spending" variance and generally link variable overhead, if present, to fixed overhead. Accordingly, items A and B are linked to items C and E in this analysis.

Belkaoui [1983] presents a Model A and B approach for the two-way and three-way analyses. Even though Belkaoui's two-way, Model A is not presented by other authors, his two-way, Model B is widely used. Also, Belkaoui's three-way, Model A corresponds to Matz and Usry [1984] who allow a subdivision of items D+E while Belkaoui's three-way, Model B corresponds to Horngren [1982] who does not agree on an item D+E subdivision.

Asch [1983, p. 175] and Walker [1982, p. 250] present five different variances for overhead that generate a "five-way" analysis as follows:

1. VOH Expenditure	A
2. VOH Efficiency	B
3. FOH Expenditure	C
4. FOH Capacity	D
5. FOH Efficiency	E

In addition, Walker [1982, p. 247] presents a "Calendar" variance for use when annual fixed overhead is divided into equal quarters or months for analysis. For example, suppose budgeted fixed overhead was $180,000 ($15,000 per month) and normal work days per year were 240 (20 per month). If February had 17 work days because of the length of the month and/or holidays, there would be a $2,250 unfavorable [$15,000/20) x 3 = $2,250] "Calendar" variance.

The 20 textbooks analyzed in this study show that there is disagreement in current cost accounting textbooks concerning which overhead variances exist, how the variances should be calculated or combined, and what the variances should be named. Many similarities, however, do exist. The largest area of agreement shows that six of the 20 textbooks (Chatfield and Neilsen [1983], Hartley [1983], Horngren [1982], Killough and Leininger [1984], Morse [1981], and Rayburn [1983]) use identical variances for the two-way, three-way, and four-way analysis of overhead variances, even though different names are used. There is not, nor necessarily should be, any final authority on these issues. However, when teaching cost accounting, care should be taken to recognize the differing views. An analysis as done in this study, of some of the similarities and differences among cost accounting textbooks, could prove beneficial in alerting students to alternate overhead variance analysis alternatives.

REFERENCES

Asch, D. C., *Cost Accounting and Budgeting*, (Macdonald and Evans Ltd, 1983).

Belkaoui, A., *Cost Accounting, A Multidimensional Emphasis*, (The Dryden Press, 1983).

Brock, H. R. and C. E. Palmer, *Cost Accounting: Principles & Applications*, Fourth Edition, (McGraw-Hill Book Company, 1984).

Cashin, J., and R. S. Polimeni, *Cost Accounting*, (McGraw-Hill Book Company, 1981).

Chatfield, M., and D. Neilson, *Cost Accounting*, (Harcourt Brace Jovanovich, 1983).

Deakin, E. B., and M. W. Maher, *Cost Accounting*, (Richard D. Irwin, Inc., 1984).

Dopuch, N., J. G. Birnberg, and J. S. Demski, *Cost Accounting, Accounting Data for Management's Decisions*, Third Edition, (Harcourt Brace Jovanovich, 1982).

Gray, J. and D. E. Ricketts, *Cost and Managerial Accounting*, (McGraw-Hill Book Company, 1982).

Hartley, R. V., *Cost and Managerial Accounting*, (Allyn and Bacon, Inc., 1983).

Horngren, C. T., *Cost Accounting: A Managerial Emphasis*, Fifth Edition, (Prentice-Hall, Inc., 1982).

Killough, L. N., and W. E. Leininger, *Cost Accounting, Concepts and Techniques for Management*, (West Publishing Company, 1984).

Louderback, J. G., III, and M. L. Hirsch, Jr., *Cost Accounting, Accumulation, Analysis, and Use*, (Kent Publishing Company, 1982).

Matz, A., and M. F. Usry, *Cost Accounting, Planning and Control*, Eighth Edition, (South-Western Publishing Company, 1984).

Moriarity, S., and C. P. Allen, *Cost Accounting*, (Harper & Row, 1984).

Morse, W. J., *Cost Accounting, Processing, Evaluating, and Using Cost Data*, Second Edition, (Addison-Wesley Publishing Company, 1981).

Most, K. S., and R. J. Lewis, *Cost Accounting*, (Grid Publishing, Inc., 1982).

Rayburn, L. G., *Principles of Cost Accounting: Managerial Applications*, Revised Edition, (Richard D. Irwin, Inc., 1983).

Schmiedicke, R. E., and C. F. Nagy, *Principles of Cost Accounting*, Seventh Edition, (South-Western Publishing Company, 1983).

Shillinglaw, G., *Managerial Cost Accounting*, Fifth Edition, (Richard D. Irwin, Inc., 1982).

Subject Guide To Books In Print 1983-84, Volume 1, (R. R. Bowker Company, 1983).

Walker, C. J., *Principles of Cost Accounting*, (Macdonald and Evans Ltd., 1982).

Source: Reprinted with permission from *Journal of Accounting Education*, 4, no. 1 (Spring 1986), Pergamon Press Ltd., Oxford, England.

5

CONTROL PRINCIPLES AND QUALITY: CONTROL OF MIX AND YIELD FACTORS

The subjects of control and the use of variance analysis are continued in this chapter to cover the following four advance control subjects: (1) control of nonmanufacturing variance through the analysis of contribution mix variance and sales variances (sales volume variance, sales quantity variance, and sales mix variance); (2) the analysis of market size and market share variances; (3) the analysis of production mix variances using the partial linear substitution model; and (4) the analysis of production mix variances using the fixed proportion substitution model. A more elaborate treatment of this topic is presented in the Appendix to this chapter.

CONTROL OF NONMANUFACTURING ACTIVITIES

The analysis of variance can be extended to nonmanufacturing activities in general and to sales and profit analysis in particular. Because organizations generally produce more than one product or service, the analysis will rely on the sales mix that is the relative proportion or combination of the quantities of products that compose total sales.

Total Marketing Variance

The first variance used to control manufacturing activities is the total marketing variance:

$$\sum_{i=1}^{n} [(\text{Actual sales volume} \times \text{Actual contribution margin per unit}) - \text{Standard sales volume} \times \text{Standard contribution margin per unit}]$$

where n = number of products i in the sales mix.

Contribution Margin Variance and Sales Volume Variance

The total marketing variance is equal to the sum of the contribution margin variance and the sales volume variance. Contribution margin variance is computed as follows:

$$\sum_{i=1}^{n} [(\text{Actual number of units sold}) \times (\text{Actual contribution margin per unit} - \text{Standard contribution margin per unit})]$$

where n = number of products i in the sales mix.

The total contribution margin variance is a measure of the variation caused by the difference between the actual and standard contribution margin per unit of each product.

Sales volume variance is computed as follows:

$$\sum_{i=1}^{n} [(\text{Actual sales volume} - \text{Standard sales volume}) \times (\text{Standard contribution margin per unit})]$$

where n = number of products i in the sales mix.

The sales volume variance shows the impact of a change in unit sales measured at the standard contribution margin per unit of each product.

Sales Quantity Variance and Sales Mix Variance

The sales volume variance can be decomposed into a sales quantity variance and a sales mix variance. In other words, a favorable (unfavorable) sales volume variance may be due either to an increase (decrease) in the total number of units sold to be measured by the sales activity variance or to a favorable (unfavorable) mix of products to be measured by the sales mix variance. Sales quantity variance is computed as follows:

$$\sum_{i=1}^{n} [(\text{Actual sales volume} - \text{Static budgeted sales volume}) \times (\text{Standard average contribution margin per unit})]$$

where n = number of products i in the sales mix.

The sales quantity variance will be favorable or positive only if actual sales exceed standard sales. It is a measure of the variation caused uniquely by the sale of more or fewer units of products.

Sales mix variance is computed as follows:

$$\sum_{i=1}^{n} [(\text{Actual sales mix percentage} - \text{Standard sales mix percentage}) \times (\text{Actual total sales volume of all products}) \times (\text{Standard individual contribution margin per unit} - \text{Standard average contribution margin per unit})]$$

where n = number of products i in the sales mix.

Exhibit 5.1
Input Data: Control of Nonmanufacturing Activities

Kinds of cookies	Standard Sales	Actual Sales	Standard Contri- bution Margin	Actual Contri- bution Margin	Total Standard Contri- bution Margin	Total Actual Contri- bution Margin
Chocolate Chip	200	180	$60	$56	$12,000	$10,080
Oatmeal Raisin	120	128	68	72	8,160	9,216
Coconut	60	56	80	68	4,800	3,808
Peanut Butter	20	28	140	136	2,800	3,808
Total	400	392			$27,760	$26,912

The sales mix variance is a measure of the variation in the total contribution margin caused by the differences between the actual and standard sales mix, taking into account how the product's contribution margin differs from the standard average contribution margin per unit. The products that have a contribution margin greater than the average standard contribution margin are known as "high-profit products," and those that have a lower than average margin are known as "low-profit products." Consequently, a move from low-profit products to high-profit products will increase profits and vice versa.

Illustration of the Control of Nonmanufacturing Activities

To illustrate the control of nonmanufacturing activities, let us use the example of a chain of cookie stores with four kinds of cookies: chocolate chip, oatmeal raisin, coconut, and peanut butter. The data for 19 × 5 are shown in Exhibit 5.1. The analysis of variance may proceed as follows:

Total Marketing Variance

$$\$26,912 - \$27,760 = \$(848) \text{ unfavorable.}$$

Contribution Margin Variance

Chocolate chip	($56 − $60)	× 180 =	(720) unfavorable
Oatmeal raisin	($72 − $68)	× 128 =	512 favorable
Coconut	($68 − $80)	× 56 =	(672) unfavorable
Peanut butter	($136 − $140)	× 28 =	(112) unfavorable
Total contribution margin variance			(992) unfavorable

Sales Volume Variance

Chocolate chip	$(180 - 200) \times \$60$	$= \$(1,200)$	unfavorable
Oatmeal raisin	$(128 - 120) \times \$68$	$= \$544$	favorable
Coconut	$(56 - 60) \times \$80$	$= \$(320)$	unfavorable
Peanut butter	$(28 - 20) \times \$140$	$= \underline{\$1,120}$	favorable
Total sales volume variance		$\$144$	favorable

Notice that the total marketing variance of $(848) (unfavorable) is equal to the sum of the total contribution margin of (992) and the sales volume variance of $144.

Sales Quantity Variance

The standard average contribution margin per unit is equal to

$$\frac{\$27,760}{400} = \$69.4$$

Therefore, the sales quantity variances are computed as follows:

Chocolate chip	$(180 - 200) \times \$69.4 = \$(1,388)$	unfavorable
Oatmeal raisin	$(128 - 120) \times \$69.4 = \$\ \ 555.2$	favorable
Coconut	$(56 - 60)\ \ \times \$65.4 = \$\ \ (277.6)$	unfavorable
Peanut butter	$(28 - 20)\ \ \times \$69.4 = \underline{\$\ \ 555.2}$	favorable
Total sales quantity variance	$\$\ \ (555.2)$	unfavorable

Sales Mix Variance (formula 1)

Chocolate chip $\quad \dfrac{180}{392} - \dfrac{120}{400} \times 392 \ (\$60 - \$69.4) = \$150.4 \qquad$ favorable

Oatmeal raisin $\quad \dfrac{128}{392} - \dfrac{120}{400} \times 392 \ (\$68 - \$69.4) = \$(14.56) \qquad$ unfavorable

Coconut $\quad \dfrac{56}{392} - \dfrac{60}{400} \times 392 \ (\$80 - \$69.4) = \$(29.68) \qquad$ unfavorable

Peanut butter $\quad \dfrac{28}{392} - \dfrac{20}{400} \times 392 \ (\$140 - \$69.4) = \dfrac{\$593.04 \text{ favorable}}{\$699.20 \text{ favorable}}$

MARKET SIZE AND MARKET SHARE VARIANCES

The overall market demand for the products of an industry as well as the company's ability to maintain its market share are important to a company. Hence the sales quantity variance of a company can be subdivided into a market size variance and a market share variance.[1] They may be computed as follows:

Market size variance = (Standard market share percentage) × (Actual industry sales volume in units − Standard industry sales in units) × (Standard average contribution margin per unit).

Market share variance = (Actual market share percentage − Standard market share percentage) × (Actual industry sales volume in units) × (Standard average contribution margin per unit).

To illustrate these variances, let us return to the example used before for the computation of nonmanufacturing variances. Let us also assume that the standard sales of 400 units represents 1 percent of the expected industry sales of 40,000 units and that the actual sales of 392 units represents 1.25 percent of the actual industry sales of 31,360 units. What follows are the computations of the market size and market share variances:

$$\text{Market size variance} = (0.01) \, (31,360 - 40,000) \times \$69.4$$
$$= \$5996.16 \text{ unfavorable}$$

$$\text{Market share variance} = (0.0125 - 0.01) \, (31,360) \times \$69.4$$
$$= \underline{5440.96 \text{ favorable}}$$
$$\$552.2 \quad \text{unfavorable}$$

Note that the total of market share variance and market size variance is equal to the sales quantity variance of $552.2 unfavorable obtained earlier.

PRODUCTION MIX AND YIELD VARIANCES: THE PARTIAL LINEAR SUBSTITUTION MODEL

Various manufacturing operations require a combination of different direct materials or a material mix and a number of different direct labor types or a labor mix. What is expected from the use of these mixes is a yield that refers to the quantity of output most probable by the use of material and labor mixes. The variances may result in this situation. The first variance is the mix variance, which refers to the difference between the input quantities expected to be used and the input quantities actually used. The second variance is the yield variance, which refers to the difference between the output expected to be obtained and the output actually obtained. More specifically, the mix variance results from using an actual mix in quantities of input (materials or labor) different from the standard mix. The yield variance results from obtaining a yield (a measure of output) different from the one expected based on the standard input.

The computation of the mix variance and yield variance depends on the assumptions made about the production function, which is the technical relationship among inputs and between input quantities and output quantities. In general, the production function may be such that it allows partial linear substitution among input materials or labor (linear production function); it requires usage of input materials or labor in a fixed proportion only (fixed proportion function); or it allows substitution among inputs at varying rates (nonlinear production function).

Quantity Variance and Mix Variances

If partial linear substitution is assumed, the following variances may be used:

Quantity variance = (Standard quantity of input − Actual quantity) × Standard price.

The quantity variance is equal to the sum of the mix variance and yield variance. The mix variances are computed as follows:

Material mix variance = [(Actual material mix percentage − Standard material mix percentage) × (Actual total units of material inputs used) × (Standard individual price per unit of labor input − Standard average price per unit of material input)]

Labor mix variance = [(Actual labor mix percentage − Standard labor mix percentage) × (Actual total units of labor inputs used) × (Standard individual price per unit of labor input − Standard average price per unit of labor input)]

The material variance for materials (or labor) is a measure of the cost variation caused by using a different mix of materials (or labor). The materials (or labor) that have a standard price higher than the average standard price of materials (or labor) are known as "high-cost inputs," and those that have a standard price lower than the average standard price are known as "low-cost inputs." A move from high-cost to low-cost inputs will render the mix variance more favorable.

Yield Variance

The yield variances in the case of materials can be computed by using the following formulas:

Material Yield Variance (first formula):

$$\sum_{i=1}^{n} \text{[(Standard units of material input allowed for actual outputs − Actual units of material input used)} \times \text{(Standard average price per unit of material input)]}$$

Material Yield Variance (second formula):

(Actual quantity of all material input × Average standard cost of all material input) − (Actual quantity of output produced × Standard material cost of output units)

Material Yield Variance (third formula):

(Expected output − Actual output) × Unit output material cost

Yield variances in the case of labor can be computed by using the following formulas:

Labor Yield Variance (first formula):

$$\sum_{i=1}^{n} \begin{array}{l} \text{[(Standard units of labor input allowed for actual outputs} \\ - \text{ Actual units of labor inputs used)} \times \text{(Standard average} \\ \text{price per unit of labor input)]} \end{array}$$

Labor Yield Variance (second formula):

(Actual quantity of all labor inputs × Average standard cost of all labor inputs) −
(Actual quantity of output produced × Standard labor cost of output units)

Labor Yield Variance (third formula):

(Expected output − Actual output) × Unit output labor cost

Illustration for Production Mix and Yield Variances for Material

Let us use the example of a chemical company that requires the use of two types of materials. The standard quantities and prices per unit of output are:

Materials	Standard Quantity	Standard Price	Total Standard Cost
A	.20	$ 6	$1.20
B	.12	10	1.20
Total	.32		$2.40

The information was based on a standard production of 2,000 good units of output. The actual quantities and prices for the production of 2,200 units of output are as follows:

Materials	Actual Quantity	Actual Price	Actual Material Cost for a Total Production of 2,200
A	240	$7.00	$1,680
B	124	11.00	1,364
Total	364		$3,044

The analysis of variance may proceed as follows:

1. Material usage variance: (Actual quantity − Standard quantity) × Standard price.

A: (240 − 440) × $6 = $1,200 favorable
B: (124 − 264) × $10 = $1,400 favorable
Total $2,600 favorable

Note that the standard quantity used is the standard quantity allowed—that is, the standard quantity to be used for actual production. For example, for material A, it is equal to 2,200 units of output $\times$ 0.20 = 440 standard quantity allowed.

2. Material mix variance: First, the average standard price of all material input is computed as follows:

$$P* = \frac{\$2.40}{.32} = \$7.5.$$

Second, the material mix variances are computed as follows:

Material A: $\frac{240}{364} - \frac{.20}{.32} \times 364$ [$6 - $7.5 = $18.75 favorable]

Material B: $\frac{124}{364} - \frac{.12}{.32} \times 364$ [$10 - $7.5 = $31.25 favorable]

3. Material yield variance: three formulas may be used to determine the material yield variance. The first formula is as follows:

Material A: (240 − 440) × $7.5 = $1,500 favorable
Material B: (124 − 264) × $7.5 = $1,050 favorable
Total $2,550 favorable

The second formula is as follows:

Material yield variance = (Actual quantity of all inputs $\times$ Average standard cost of all inputs) $-$ (Actual activity of output produced $\times$ Standard material cost of output units)
   = (364 $\times$ $7.5) $-$ (2,200 $\times$ $2.40) = ($2,730 $-$ $5,280) = $2,550

The third formula is as follows:

Material yield variance = (Expected output $-$ Actual output)
                                $\times$ (Unit output material cost)

To find the expected output, consider the following relationship:

$$\frac{\text{Standard quantity of material input}}{\text{Standard output}} = \frac{\text{Actual quantity of material input}}{\text{Expected output}}$$

therefore

$$\text{Expected output} = \frac{\text{Standard output} \times \text{Actual quantity of material input}}{\text{Standard quantity of material input}}$$

in other words,

$$\text{Expected output} = \frac{2,000 \times 364}{(.32 \times 2,000)} \text{ or Expected output} = 1,137.5 \text{ units.}$$

Given that the unit output material cost is \$2.40 per unit of output, the material yield variance will be

Material yield variance = $(1,137.5 - 2,200) \times \$2.40 = \$2,550$ favorable.

Illustration for Production Mix and Yield Variances for Labor

Let us use the example of a manufacturing company that requires the use of two types of labor: semiskilled and skilled. The standard quantities and prices are as follows:

Labor	Standard Hours per Unit of Output	Standard Labor Rate	Standard
Semiskilled	2.50	\$5 per hour	\$12.5
Skilled	2.50	30 per hour	75
Total	5.00		\$87.5

The average standard price of labor is then \$17.50 (87.50/5.00). The above information was based on a standard production of 1,000 units of output.

The quantities and prices for the actual production of 1,100 units of output follows:

Labor	Actual Labor in Hours	Actual Labor Rate	Actual Labor for the Total Production of 1,100 Units
Semiskilled	2,480	\$10.50	\$26,040
Skilled	2,640	33.00	87,120
Total	5,120		113,160

The analysis of variance may proceed as follows:

1. Labor quantity variance (labor efficiency variance). Labor efficiency variance = (Actual hours − Standard hours) × Standard rate

Semiskilled: $(2,480 - 2,750) \times \$\ 5 = \$1,350$ favorable
Skilled: $(2,640 - 2,750) \times \$30 = \$3,300$ favorable
Total   \$4,650 favorable

Note that the standard quantity used is the standard quantity allowed—that is, the standard quantity to be used for actual production. For example, for semiskilled labor, it is equal to 1,100 units of output × 2.50 = 2,750 standard hours allowed. For skilled labor, it is also equal to 2,750 (1,100 × 2.50).

2. Labor mix variance.

$$\text{Semiskilled} = \frac{2,480}{5,120} - \frac{2.50}{5.00} \times 5,120 \quad \$5 - \$17.50 = \$1,000 \text{ unfavorable}$$

$$\text{Skilled} = \frac{2,640}{5,120} - \frac{2.50}{5.00} \times 5,120 \quad \$30 - \$17.50 = \$1,000 \text{ unfavorable}$$

3. Labor yield variance: Three formulas may be used to determine the labor yield variance. The first formula is as follows:

Semiskilled: (2,480 − 2,750) × $17.50 =	$4,725 favorable
Skilled: (2,640 − 2,750) × $17.50 =	$1,925 favorable
Total	$6,650 favorable

The second formula is as follows:

Labor yield variance = (Actual quantity of all inputs × Average standard cost of all inputs) − (Actual quantity of output produced × Standard labor cost of output units)
= (5,120 × $17.50) − (1,000 × $87.50) = $6,650.

The third formula is as follows:

Labor yield variance = (Expected output − Actual output) × (Unit output labor cost).

To find the expected output, consider the following relationship:

$$\frac{\text{Standard quantity of labor input}}{\text{Standard output}} = \frac{\text{Actual quantity of labor input}}{\text{Expected output}}$$

$$\text{therefore, Expected output} = \frac{\text{Standard output} \times \text{Actual quantity of labor input}}{\text{Standard quantity of labor input}}$$

$$\text{in other words, Expected output} = \frac{1,000 \times 5,120}{(5 \times 1,000)}$$

$$\text{or, Expected output} = 1,102.4 \text{ units.}$$

Therefore, the labor yield is equal to (1,024 − 1,100) × $87.5 = $6,650 favorable.

PRODUCTION MIX AND YIELD VARIANCES: THE FIXED PROPORTION SUBSTITUTION MODEL

Under a fixed proportion substitution model, the following formula may be used:
1. The mix variance is computed as follows:

Mix variance = (Expected quantity of one input − Actual quantity of one input) × Standard price of one input

2. The yield variance is computed as follows:

Yield variance = (Expected output − Actual output) × Unit output cost

To illustrate the application of the formula to material, let us return to the example used in the "Illustration for Production Mix and Yield Variances for Material" section. The variances, assuming a fixed proportion substitution model, are as follows:

1. Mix variance. To compute the mix variance, the expected quantity of one input has to be computed. The following relationship may be used.

$$\frac{\text{Standard quantity of one input}}{\text{Standard quantity of another input}} = \frac{\text{Expected quantity of one input}}{\text{Actual quantity of another input}}$$

therefore, the Expected quantity of one input = (Standard quantity of one input × Actual quantity of another input)/(Standard quantity of another input). It follows that

$$\text{Expected quantity of material A} = \frac{(.20 \times 2{,}200) \times 124}{(.12 \times 2{,}200)} = 206.66$$

Therefore, the mix variance of material A = (206.66 − 240) × \$6 = \$200.00 unfavorable.

2. Yield variance. To compute the yield variance, the expected output is needed. The following relationship may be used.

$$\frac{\text{Total standard quantity of input}}{\text{Actual output}} = \frac{(\text{Expected quantity of one input} + \text{Actual quantity of another input})}{\text{Expected output}}$$

$$\frac{(.32 \times 2{,}200)}{2{,}200} = \frac{206.66 + 124}{\text{Expected output}}$$

Expected output = 1,033.3125 units

therefore, the yield variance is computed as follows:

$$(1033.3125 - 2{,}200) \times \$2.40 = 2{,}800.04 \text{ favorable}$$

Note that the sum of the mix variance of \$200.04 (unfavorable) and the yield variance of \$2,800.04 (favorable) is equal, as expected, to the material usage variance of \$2,600 favorable.

To illustrate the application of the formula to labor, let us return to the example used in the "Illustration for . . . Labor" section. The variances, assuming a fixed proportion substitution model, are as follows:

1. Mix variance. To compute the mix variance, the expected quantity of one input has to be computed. The following relationship may be used.

$$\frac{\text{Standard quantity of one input}}{\text{Standard quantity of another input}} = \frac{\text{Expected quantity of one input}}{\text{Actual quantity of another input}}$$

Therefore, the Expected quantity of one input = (Standard quantity of one input × actual quantity of another input)/(Standard quantity of another input). It follows that:

$$\text{Expected quantity of skilled labor} = \frac{(2.50 \times 1,100) \times 2,480}{(2.50 \times 1,100)} = 2,480.$$

Therefore, the labor mix variance of skilled labor = $(2,480 - 2,640) \times \$30 = \$4,800$ unfavorable.

2. Yield variance. To compute the yield variance, the expected output is needed. The following relationship may be used:

$$\frac{\text{Total standard quantity of input}}{\text{Actual output}} = \frac{\text{(Expected quantity of one input + Actual quantity of another input)}}{\text{Expected output}}$$

$$\frac{(5.00 \times 1,100)}{1,100} = \frac{2,480 + 2,480}{\text{Expected output}}$$

Expected output = 992 units.

therefore, the yield variance is computed as follows: $(992 - 1,100) \times \$87.5 = \$9,450$ favorable.

Note that the sum of the mix variance of \$4,800 unfavorable and the yield variance of \$9,450 favorable is equal, as expected, to the material usage variance of \$4,650 favorable.

NOTE

1. J. Shank and N. Churchill, "Variance Analysis: A Management-Oriented Approach," *Accounting Review* (October 1977), p. 955.

APPENDIX—Direct Material Variances: Review of the Mix and Yield Variances

Edward A. Becker and K. J. Kim

ABSTRACT

Various articles and textbooks have developed different models for the calculation of the direct material variances. This has led to considerable confusion. This paper examines the area of direct material variance, provides definitions, and establishes evaluation criteria. Correct calculation of direct material variances (i.e., price variance, direct material mix variance [MV], and direct material yield variance [YV]) are a function of the production function assumed and the calculation model's ability to comply with the established variance analysis criteria. The three production functions are: (1) partial linear substitution, (2) the fixed proportion production function, and (3) the nonlinear production function. The three criteria are: (1) the computational models of MV and YV must be constructed in conformity with their definitions, (2) the computational models of MV and YV must be consistent with the characteristics of the underlying production function; and (3) the total of MV and YV must be equal to the total direct material quantity variance. This paper reviews the existing direct material variance calculation models. It suggests that Hasseldine's fixed-proportion production function model is the only one that meets the criteria and recommends its use. For partial linear substitution, this paper recommends the model proposed by Killough and Leininger, and for the nonlinear production function, none of the existing models fit all of the established criteria, so this paper develops a new model and recommends its use.

INTRODUCTION

THE two principal objectives of a standard cost system are cost control and performance evaluation. Therefore, variance analysis is one of the most important features of any cost accounting system. Management's effi-ciency and effectiveness are frequently evaluated on the results of their variance analyses. Favorable variances

Edward A. Becker is a Professor at Nova University and K. J. Kim is an Associate Professor at California State University at Fullerton.

often lead to bonuses, promotions, and/or raises. Accordingly, how the variance calculations are made is important.

This paper examines material variances. For variance analysis purposes, the total material variance is generally divided into two parts: price variance and quantity variance. The problem is that, depending on the model one assumes, several different methods are available to calculate both price and quantity variances. The choice of techniques leads to confusion for accounting educators, students, and practitioners. While rigid conformity is not expected, educators, students, and practitioners would benefit from consistency. This paper examines the extant theories and methods of direct material variance and makes recommendations that would improve consistency.

If the variances are planned to be specific problem indicators, how the variances are defined, partitioned, and measured are critical to understanding the corrective action that should be taken. For a standard cost system to be a beneficial cost control and performance evaluation device, it is essential that variances be precisely defined, and that measurement techniques be properly designed and comprehended.

Background

In a standard cost system the total direct material variance is generally divided into price variance and quantity variance. The quantity variance is further divided into a mix variance (MV) and a yield variance (YV). Such successive divisions of total variance into its components are intended to

identify the causes of the variances and to suggest corrective actions that might be taken. In addition, by establishing different weights on MV and YV, management can more accurately evaluate a specific manager's performance because an individual manager may have only limited control over certain variances. A prerequisite to a standard cost system is to clearly define variances and computational methods consistent with established definitions.

The measurement and analysis of direct material mix and yield variances are areas that need clarification and improvement. Several different direct material mix and yield variance models have appeared in articles and textbooks over the past fifteen years.[1] However, the mix and yield variances computed by those models are not the same for a variety of reasons. Frequently, differences occur because of the methods of partitioning the direct material variance into mix and yield elements; differences also occur from dissimilar measurement techniques; or differences come about because the substitutability among input materials is not specifically considered. As a result, mix and yield variance computations are problematic. More seriously, such problematic measurement may fail to convey the necessary information to management for effective and efficient cost control and performance evaluation.

Accountants find themselves faced with numerous models designed for analysis of direct material mix and yield variances. It is impossible, without

---

[1] See Table 2 and Table 3 for various models.

considerable study, to understand the idiosyncrasies of each, or to determine if they even produce useful measurements.

This paper reviews the partitioning of the total direct material variance into price, mix, and yield variances (using three different models with varying degrees of substitutability among input materials) and suggests improvements where needed. Accordingly: (1) the direct material variance is decomposed and defined, with emphasis on the mix and yield variances; (2) existing mix and yield variance models are reviewed; and (3) improvements are suggested, along with numerical illustrations.

STANDARD COST, PRICE, MIX, AND YIELD VARIANCES DEFINED

Assume that a firm manufactures a single product line, AB, by using two kinds of materials, A and B. Under the normal standard cost system, the standard direct material costs can be expressed as equation (1) and the actual direct material costs as equation (2) below:

$$SP_i \times TSQ_i \qquad (1)$$

$$AP_i \times TAQ_i \qquad (2)$$

where

SP_i = standard price per unit of each input material,

AP_i = actual price per unit of each input material,

TSQ_i = total quantity of each input material allowed for output attained, and

TAQ_i = total quantity of each input material used for output attained.

Given the two equations above, the price variance (PV) can be calculated as: the difference between SP_i and AP_i, multiplied by TAQ_i. The quantity variance (QV) can be calculated as: the difference between TSQ_i and TAQ_i, multiplied by SP_i. Existing models regarding these two variances all agree and, therefore, require no further comment.

Existing models, however, do not agree when decomposing QV into the mix variance (MV) and the yield variance (YV). Expanding equations (1) and (2) above yield the following:

$$TSQ_i = SQ_i \times AY \qquad (3)$$

$$TAQ_i = AQ_i \times AY \qquad (4)$$

where

SQ_i = each input material allowed per unit of output,

AQ_i = each input material used per unit of output, and

AY = actual number of output produced.

Unlike PV and QV, MV and YV cannot be derived directly from equations (3) and (4) above. Instead, two additional concepts are needed. The first concept is the input quantities that are expected to be used for a specific quantity of output actually attained, denoted here as EQ_i. EQ_i is differentiated from SQ_i because EQ_i may or may not be equal to SQ_i, depending on the substitutability assumed among input materials. Normally, EQ_i will equal SQ_i when input quantities are required to be used in a fixed-proportion, or, when input quantities can be substituted for each other in a linear proportion. However, EQ_i may not be equal to SQ_i when input quantities can be substituted for each other at varying rates. Bringing together in parallel the input quantities that are expected to be used (EQ_i) and the input quantities that are actually used (AQ_i), MV computation now is possible. Generally, "mix" refers to the relative proportion of each ingredient (or expected to be used to the total ingredients). The direct material mix variance (MV) is defined as: the difference between EQ_i (input quantities expected to be used) and AQ_i (input quantities actually used) for a given amount of output (AY), multiplied by SP_i. Therefore, MV is an input based concept, the difference between two input quantities.

The second concept is output quantity (yield) that is expected to be produced, for the actual input quantities used, denoted here as EY. The output quantity expected to be produced (EY) from the actual input quantities used is differentiated from the standard output quantity (SY) initially planned to produce because EY may or may not be equal to SY, depending on the specific production process under consideration in the analysis. When the production process is such that its technical relationship between the input materials and output quantity is linear, EY will be equal to SY. EY, however, will not be equal to SY when the relationship is curvilinear. Once again bringing together in parallel both the output quantity that is expected to be produced (EY) and the output quantity that is actually produced (AY), the YV computation now is possible.

Generally, "yield" refers to the output quantity attained (or expected to be attained) from a given quantity of inputs. Accordingly, the direct material yield variance (YV) is defined as the difference between EY (output expected to be attained) and AY (output actually attained) from given quantities of input materials, multiplied by the unit output cost (AOC). Therefore, YV is an output-based concept, the difference between two output quantities.

When applying the definitions of MV and YV for their computations, care should be exercised. As explained earlier, the production function[2] may be such that it allows partial linear substitution among input materials (linear production function); requires usage of input materials in a fixed proportion only (fixed-proportion production function); or allows substitution among input materials at varying rates (nonlinear production function). Furthermore, the technical relationship between input and output quantities may be linear or curvilinear. Consequently, computations of MV and YV should reflect the proper function.

MV AND YV COMPUTATIONS UNDER PARTIAL LINEAR SUBSTITUTION FUNCTION AND FIXED-PROPORTION FUNCTION

Consider a firm that produces a single line of product AB by use of two

---

[2] The production function refers to the technical relationship among input materials and between input quantities and output quantity. See Ferguson [1972] for more details about the production function.

kinds of materials, A and B. Assume that one unit of output requires usages of .10 pounds of material A and .06 pounds of material B. Material A is forecasted at $3 per pound and material B at $5 per pound. The standard bill of materials for producing 1,000 good units of output will be 100 pounds (.10 × 1,000) of A and 60 (.06 × 1,000) pounds of B at the total budgeted costs of $600 (100 × $3 + 60 × $5). Further assume that the firm actually produced 1,000 good units of output at the total costs of $761, using 120 pounds of A and 62 pounds of B at $3.50 and $5.50, respectively.

Many of the textbook models do not specify the substitutability between the input materials, but, they appear to have implicitly assumed the partial linear substitution function. Therefore, their models are in the category of partial linear substitution. (Where a complete linear substitution is possible, management will obviously use only the one material with the lowest cost. Therefore, a partial linear substitution assumption is required.)

Table 1 shows PV, MV, and YV models frequently encountered in the available literature using the partial linear substitution function. All models agree as to PV (i.e., the difference between SP_i and AP_i, multiplied by AQ_i). As to MV, the models suggested by Killough and Leininger [1984], Deakin and Maher [1984], Moriarity and Allen [1984], and Hasseldine [1967] conform to the definition of MV (i.e., the difference between EQ_i and AQ_i, multiplied by SP_i). The other authors' models, including Hasseldine [1967] appear to be at odds with the definition of MV. In the Horngren [1982] and Matz

and Usry [1984] models, the difference in input quantities are multiplied by the difference between SP_i and AIC (average input cost). With some algebraic notations and manipulation, it is possible to prove that their models are equivalent to the Killough and Leininger model. But the Killough and Leininger model is simple, straightforward, and consistent with the MV definition.

The lower portion of Table 1 shows Hasseldine models for PV, MV, and YV when input materials are required to be used only in a fixed-proportion. Note that input quantities expected to be used (EQ_i), are computed by holding either one of the actual input quantities constant, and computing what the other input quantity should have been. This method is consistent with the assumption that usage of input materials is required only in a fixed-proportion. However, MV computed in this way may be a misnomer. Instead, it might be called "input overusage variance."

In conclusion, the Killough and Leininger model (or Deakin and Maher, Moriarity and Allen models) is recommended for use for MV computation when partial linear substitution of input materials is possible and the Hasseldine model is suggested for use when input materials should have been used only in a fixed-proportion. The above models meet the definitions of direct material mix variance.

When a partial linear substitution function is assumed, only the Matz and Usry [1984] model computes YV consistent with the yield variance definition (i.e., the difference between EY and AY, multiplied by AOC, average output cost). The Hasseldine model computes a fixed-proportion function in a

TABLE 1

PV, MV, and YV Under Partial Linear Substitution and Under Fixed-Proportion

Author	Price Variance	Mix Variance	Yield Variance	Total Variance	Comment
PARTIAL LINEAR SUBSTITUTION MODEL					
Killough & Leininger	$\Sigma I(SP, - AP,) \times AQ,]$ $=[(\$3.00 - \$3.50) \times 120]$ $+[(\$5.00 - \$5.50) \times 62]$ $=\$60.00\ U + \$31.00\ U$ $=\$91.00\ U$	$\Sigma I(EQ, - AQ,) \times (SP,)]**$ $=[(113.75 - 120) \times \$3.00]$ $+[(68.25 - 62) \times \$5.00]$ $=\$18.75\ F + \$31.25\ F$ $=\$12.50\ F$	$(\Sigma SQ, - \Sigma AQ,) \times AIC$ $=(160 - 182) \times \$3.75$ $=\$82.50\ U$	$161.00\ U$	$EQ, = \Sigma AQ, \times M, = \begin{bmatrix} 182 \times .625 \\ 182 \times .375 \end{bmatrix} = \begin{bmatrix} 113.75 \\ 68.25 \end{bmatrix}$ $M, = SQ,/\Sigma SQ, = \begin{bmatrix} 100/160 \\ 60/160 \end{bmatrix} = \begin{bmatrix} .625 \\ .375 \end{bmatrix}$ $AIC = \Sigma I(SQ, \times SP,)/\Sigma SQ,$ $=(100 \times \$3.00 + 60 \times \$5.00)/(100 + 60)$ $=\$3.75$ per unit of input
Horngren	Same as the above	$\Sigma I(EQ, - AQ,) \times (SP, - AIC)]$ $=[(100 - 120) \times (\$3.00 - \$3.75)]$ $+[(60 - 62) \times (\$5.00 - \$3.75)]$ $=\$15.00\ F + \$2.50\ U$ $=\$12.50\ F$	$\Sigma I(EQ, - AQ,) \times AIC]$ $=[(100 - 120) \times \$3.75]$ $+[(60 - 62) \times \$3.75]$ $=\$82.50\ U$	$161.00\ U$	$\Sigma SQ, :SY = \Sigma EQ,:AY$ $160 :1,000 = \Sigma EQ,:1,000$ $\Sigma EQ, = (160 \times 1,000)/1,000 = 160$ $EQ, = \Sigma EQ, \times M, = \begin{bmatrix} 160 \times .625 \\ 160 \times .375 \end{bmatrix} = \begin{bmatrix} 100 \\ 60 \end{bmatrix}$ $M, =$ Same as Killough & Leininger $AIC =$ Same as Killough & Leininger
Deakin & Maher, and Moriarity & Allen	Same as the above	$\Sigma I(EQ, - AQ,) \times SP,]$ $=$ Same as Killough & Leininger $=\$12.50\ F$	$\Sigma I(SQ, - EQ,) \times SP,]$ $=[(100 - 113.75) \times \$3.00]$ $+[(60 - 68.25) \times \$5.00]$ $=\$41.25\ U + \$41.25\ U$ $=\$82.5\ U$	$161.00\ U$	$EQ, = \Sigma AQ, \times M, = \begin{bmatrix} 182 \times .625 \\ 182 \times .375 \end{bmatrix} = \begin{bmatrix} 113.75 \\ 68.25 \end{bmatrix}$ $M, =$ Same as Killough & Leininger
Matz & Usry	Same as the above	$\Sigma I(AQ, \times (SP, - AIC)]$ $=[180 \times (\$3.00 - \$3.75)]$ $+[62 \times (\$5.00 - \$3.75)]$ $=\$90.00\ F + \$77.50\ U$ $=\$12.50\ F$	$(EY - AY) \times AOC**$ $=(1,137.50 - 1,000) \times \$.60$ $=\$82.50\ U$	$161.00\ U$	$\Sigma SQ, :SY = \Sigma AQ,:EY$ $160 :1,000 = 182:EY$ $EY = (182 \times 1,000)/160$ $=1,137.50$ units of output $AOC = \Sigma I(SQ, \times SP,)/SY$ $=(100 \times \$3.00 + 60 \times \$5.00)/1,000$ $=\$.60$ per output
Hasseldine	Same as the above	(1) $\Sigma I(EQ, - AQ,) \times SP,]$ $=$ Same as Killough & Leininger $=\$12.50\ F$ (2) $\Sigma I(EQ, - AQ,) \times (SP, - AIC)]$ $=$ Same as Horngren $=\$12.50\ F$	(1) $\Sigma I(SQ, - EQ,) \times SP,]$ $=$ Same as Deakin & Maher $=\$82.50\ U$ (2) $\Sigma I(SQ, - EQ,)] \times AIC$ $=[(100 - 120) + (60 - 62)] \times \$3.75$ $=\$75.00\ U + \$7.50\ U = \$82.50\ U$	$161.00\ U$	$EQ, =$ Same as Deakin & Maher $AIC =$ Same as Horngren

146

TABLE 1—Continued

Author	Price Variance	Mix Variance	Yield Variance	Total Variance	Comment
FIXED-PROPORTION SUBSTITUTION MODEL					
Hasseldine	Same as the above	$(EQ_A - AQ_A) \times SP_A^{**}$ $= (103.33 - 120) \times \$3.00$ $= \$50.00$ U	$(EY - AY) \times AOC^{**}$ $= (1,033.333 - 1,000) \times \$.60$ $= \$20.00$ U	$\$161.00$ U	$SQ_A : SQ_A = EQ_A : AQ_A$ $100 : 60 = EQ_A : 62$ $EQ_A = (100 \times 62)/60 = 103.333$ units of A $\Sigma SQ_i : 1,000 = (EQ_A + AQ_B) : EY$ $160 : 1,000 = (103.333 + 62) : EY$ $EY = [1,000 \times (103.33 + 62)]/160$ $= 1,033.33$ units of output

** Recommended for use.
F:Favorable variance.
U:Unfavorable variance.

147

way consistent with the YV definition. All of the other authors compute YV as the difference between two *input* quantities even though yield variance was defined as an *output* concept. For example, the Horngren model computes YV as the difference between EQ_i and AQ_i multiplied by AIC (average input cost). Algebraically, it is possible to prove that all the other authors' models are equivalent to the Matz and Usry model. However, the Matz and Usry model is simple, straightforward, and directly conforms in format and in substance with the definition of YV. Therefore, the Matz and Usry model is suggested for use for the YV computation when a partial linear substitution model is used, and the Hasseldine model is suggested for use when the fixed-proportion model is required.

MV AND YV COMPUTATIONS UNDER NONLINEAR SUBSTITUTION

Continuing with the example of a firm that produces a single product line, AB, by use of two input materials, A and B, assume that the firm's production process is such that input materials can be substituted at varying rates for producing an equal number of output. Further, assume that the following two equations represent this firm's total direct material costs under a production process that allows nonlinear substitution of input materials at varying rates.

Total costs

$$= (SQ_A SP_A) + (SQ_B SP_B) \qquad (9)$$

Production process

$$= SY = f(SQ_A)^a (SQ_B)^b \qquad (10)$$

Given these two conditions, it is generally logical to assume that management's primary concern is to find input quantities ($SQ_i = [SQ_A, SQ_B]$), that will minimize the total direct material costs. Given the same forecasted prices of A and B as before ($3.00 per pound for A and $5.00 per pound for B) and assume $f = 12$, $a = .5$, and $b = .5$, SQ_i is found by simultaneously solving the two equations above. (See Appendix A.)

Minimize

$$(SQ_A \times \$3.00) + (SQ_B \times \$5.00)$$

Subject to

$$SY = 1000 = 12(SQ_A)^{.5} \times (SQ_B)^{.5}$$

$$SQ_i = {}^{>0}$$

By taking partial derivatives with respect to SQ_i and setting them equal to zero, the following results are obtained: $SQ_i = [107.583, 64.549]$.[3] Assume that the firm actually produced 1,000 units of output, using 120 pounds of A at $3.50 per pound and 62 pounds of B at $5.50 per pound. Obviously, total actual direct material costs will be higher than the total standard direct material costs. In retrospect, the firm could have been optimizing the total material costs by resetting the standard input quantities for a new planned output quantity. This is possible because of the characteristics of the production process that allow substitution of input materials at varying rates for an equal number of output. Such new standard input quantities (SQ_i') that could have been used are determined by simul-

---

[3] For the proof, see Ferguson [1972], p. 156.

taneously solving the following two equations (see Appendix B):

Minimize

$$(SQ'_A \times \$3.50) + (SQ'_B \times \$5.50)$$

Subject to

$$SY = 1000 = 12(SQ'_A)^{.5} \times (SQ'_B)^{.5}$$

$$SQ'_i = ^{>}0$$

As in the first example, by taking partial derivatives with respect to SQ'_i and setting them equal to zero, we obtain $SQ'_i = [104.464, 66.477]$. Notice that SQ'_i can be viewed as an *ex post* standard[4] and that SP'_i is equal to AP_i in the above equations. EY is obtained by inserting the input quantities actually used (AQ_i) into the production function:

$$EY = 12(120)^{.5} \times (62)^{.5}$$
$$= 1035.0652 \text{ units of output.}$$

It is important to note that SY appearing in the standard bill of materials may not equal EY under the nonlinear substitution, due to the nature of the nonlinear production function. Also, EQ_i (input quantities expected to be used for EY) does not equal SQ'_i in the standard bill of materials for the same reason. EQ_i is obtained by inserting both EY and AP_i into the equations and solving them simultaneously (see Appendix C):

Minimize

$$(EQ_A \times \$3.50) + (EQ_B \times \$5.50)$$

Subject to

$$EY = 1035.0652 = 12(EQ_A)^{.5} \times (EQ_B)^{.5}$$

$$EQ_i = ^{>}0$$

Taking partial derivatives with respect

to EQ_i and setting them equal to zero, $EQ_i = [108.127, 68.808]$.

Table 2 illustrates two sets of models assuming a nonlinear substitution function. In the Mensah [1982] model, PV is computed as the difference between SP_i multiplied by SQ_i and SP' multiplied by SQ'. (Recall that $SP'_i = AP_i$). His PV is consistent with the PV definition. He computes MV as the difference between SQ'_i and EQ_i, multiplied by SP'_i. Notice that he uses SQ'_i when AQ_i should have been used. Moreover, the way that he computes EQ_i is at odds with the substitutability assumed. EQ_i is computed by linearly adjusting AQ_i by the technical inefficiency, e. (See the comment column of Table 2 for e and EQ_i computations.) Such adjustment of input quantities is linear and is at odds with the assumed nonlinear substitution that allows substitution at varying rates. He computes YV as the difference between two different input quantities (EQ_i and AQ_i). Instead, the difference should have been computed for two different output quantities (EY and AY) to be consistent with the YV definition.

In the Marchinko and Petri [1984] model, MV is not computed. PV is computed in the same method as in the Mensah model and is titled as "input choice variance." They compute YV as the difference between AQ_B and EQ_B, multiplied by SP_B. Notice how they obtain EQ_B from the comment column of Table 2. They obtain EQ_B by holding input material A at the level actually

---

[4] For more details about an *ex post* standard, see Demski [1967].

TABLE 2
PV, MV, and YV Under Nonlinear Substitution

Authors	Price Variance	Mix Variance	Yield Variance	Total Variance	Comment
Mensah	Standard Error Adjustment Variance: $\Sigma[SQ_sSP_s - SQ_sSP_s^s]$ $=[(107.583 \times \$3.00 - 104.464$ $\times \$3.50) + (64.549 \times \$5.00$ $- 66.477 \times \$5.50)]$ $= \$42.879\ U + \$42.875\ U$ $= \$85.754\ U$	Input Choice Variance: $\Sigma[(SQ_s - EQ_s) \times SP_s^s]$ $=[(104.464 - 115.7922) \times \$3.50$ $+ (66.477 - 59.8260) \times \$5.50]$ $= \$39.6487\ U + \$36.5805\ F$ $= \$3.0682\ U$	Technical Efficiency Variance: $\Sigma[(EQ_s - AQ_s) \times SP_s^s]$ $=[(115.7922 - 120) \times \$3.50$ $+ (59.8260 - 62) \times \$5.50]$ $= \$14.7273\ U + \$11.9570\ U$ $= \$26.6843\ U$	$\$115.51\ U$	$SQ_s = \begin{bmatrix} SQ_A \\ SQ_B \end{bmatrix} = \begin{bmatrix} 107.583 \\ 64.549 \end{bmatrix}$ $SQ_s^s = \begin{bmatrix} SQ_A^s \\ SQ_B^s \end{bmatrix} = \begin{bmatrix} 104.464 \\ 66.477 \end{bmatrix}$ $EQ_s = \begin{bmatrix} EQ_A \\ EQ_B \end{bmatrix} = (1 - e^s)(AQ_s)$ $= (1 - .0351) \times \begin{bmatrix} 120 \\ 62 \end{bmatrix} = \begin{bmatrix} 115.7922 \\ 59.8260 \end{bmatrix}$ $e^s = (EY - AY)/AY$ $= [(AQ_s)^s(AQ_s)^s - AY]/AY$ $= [12(120)^s(62)^s - 1,000]/1,000$ $= .0351$
Marchinko & Petri	Input Choice Variance: $\Sigma[SQ_sSP_s - SQ_sSP_s^s]$ = Same as Mensah $= \$85.754\ U$	Not Applicable	Waste Variance: $(AQ_s - EQ_s) \times SP_s$ $= (62 - 72) \times \$5.00$ $= \$50.00\ F$	$\$35.754\ U$	SQ_s = Same as Mensah SQ_s^s = Same as Mensah $SQ_s : SQ_s = AQ_s : EQ_s$ $107.583 : 64.549 = 120 : EQ_s$ $EQ_s = 64.549 \times 120/107.583$ $= 72$ units of B

F:Favorable variance.
U:Unfavorable variance.

used and finding what quantity of input material B should have been, had the input quantities been maintained at standard mix. This method is similar to the method used by Hasseldine under the fixed-proportion assumption.

Table 3 illustrates MV and YV models earlier suggested under fixed-proportion and models suggested for MV and YV under nonlinear substitution. For nonlinear substitution, the suggested model computes MV as the difference between EQ_i and AQ_i, multiplied by SP_i'. As stated earlier in this section, EQ_i is obtained by inserting SP_i' and EY into the production function and the total cost function and solving them simultaneously. YV is computed as the difference between EY and AY, multiplied by average output cost (AOC). EY is obtained by inserting AQ_i in the production function and solving for EY. The suggested models of MV and YV are consistent with their definitions and with the underlying assumptions about input substitutability.

SUMMARY

Variance analysis is one of the most important facets of a good standard cost accounting system. For direct material variance, the analyses of price and quantity variances depends on the production model that is assumed. However, whichever production model is assumed, many textbooks present different theories and calculations.

We posit that material variance analysis should satisfy three criteria: (1) the computational models of MV and YV must be constructed in conformity with standard definitions; (2) the computational models of MV and YV must be consistent with the characteristics of the underlying production function; and (3) the total of MV and YV must be equal to the total direct material quantity variance.

This treatise examined the definitions of MV and YV, the characteristics of the two production functions, and the existing theories of how to calculate the direct material variances. It found that most of the existing models did not satisfy each of the three criteria that had been established. This paper did, however, recommend calculation models, for fixed-proportion and the partial linear substitution, nonlinear substitution production functions, that meet the desired criteria and should satisfy the needs of accountants.

TABLE 3
PV, MV, and YV Models Suggested Under Various Substitutability

Substitutability	Price Variance	Mix Variance	Yield Variance	Total Variance	Comment
Partial Linear Substitution	$\Sigma[(SP_i - AP_i) \times 120]$ $= [(\$3.00 - \$3.50) \times 120]$ $+ [(\$5.00 - \$5.50) \times 62]$ $= \$60.00\ U + \$31.00\ U$ $= \$91.00\ U$	$\Sigma[(EQ_i - AQ_i) \times SP_i]$ $= [(113.75 - 120) \times \$3.00]$ $+ [(68.25 - 62) \times \$5.00]$ $= \$18.75\ U + \$31.25\ F$ $= \$12.50\ F$	$(EY - AY) \times AOC$ $= (1,137.50 - 1,000) \times \$.60$ $= \$82.50\ U$	\$161.00 U	$EQ_i = AQ_i \times M_i = \begin{bmatrix} 182 \times 100/160 \\ 182 \times 60/160 \end{bmatrix} = \begin{bmatrix} 113.75 \\ 68.25 \end{bmatrix}$ $EY = (182 \times 1,000)/160 = 1,137.50$ units $\Sigma SQ_i : SY = \Sigma AQ_i : EY$ $160 : 1,000 = 182 : EY$ $AOC = \Sigma(SQ_i SP_i)/SY = \$.60$ per output
Fixed-Proportion	Same as the above	$(EQ_a - AQ_a) \times SP_a$ $= (103.333 - 120) \times \$3.00$ $= \$50.00\ U$	$(EY - AY) \times AOC$ $= (1,033.333 - 1,000) \times \$.60$ $= \$20.00\ U$	\$161.00 U	$EY = 1,000 \times (103.333 \times 62)/160$ $\Sigma EQ_i : 1,000 = (EQ_a + AQ_b) : EY$ $EQ_a = (100 \times 62)/60 = 103.33$ of A $SQ_a : SQ_b = EQ_a : AQ_b$ $100 : 60 = EQ_i : 62$
Nonlinear Substitution	$\Sigma[(SQ_i SP_i) - (SQ_i'SP_i')]$ $= [(107.583 \times \$3.00)$ $- [(104.464 \times \$3.50)$ $+ [(64.549 \times \$5.00)$ $- (66.477 \times \$5.50)$ $= \$42.875\ U + \$42.879\ U$ $= \$85.754\ U$	$\Sigma[(EQ_i - AQ_i) \times SP_i']$ $= [(108.127 - 120) \times \$3.50]$ $+ [(68.808 - 62) \times \$5.50]$ $= \$41.5555\ U + \$37.4440\ F$ $= \$4.1115\ U$	$(EY - AY) \times AOC$ $= (1,035.06522 - 1,000$ $\times \$.731248$ $= \$25.6414\ U$	\$115.51 U	$EY = f(AQ_a)^{.H}(AQ_b)^{.H} = 12(120)^{.H}(62)^{.H}$ [a] $EQ_i = \begin{bmatrix} 108.127 \\ 68.808 \end{bmatrix}$ from Min $\$3.50(EQ_a) + \$5.50(EQ_b)$ S.T. $EY = 1,035.0652 = 12(EQ_a)^{.H}(EQ_b)^{.H}$ [a] $AOC = \Sigma EQ_i SP_i'/EY$ $= [(108.127 \times \$3.50 + 68.808 \times \$5.50)/1,035.06522$ $= \$.731248$

F:Favorable variance.
U:Unfavorable variance.

APPENDIX A

SQ_i Computation

Minimize

$$3SQ_A + 5SQ_B$$

Subject to

$$1000 = 12(SQ_A)^{.5}(SQ_B)^{.5}$$

Converting the above equation into Lagrangian multiplier form, we obtain

$$F(SQ_A, SQ_B, \lambda) = 3SQ_A + 5SQ_B - \lambda(12SQ_A^{.5}SQ_B^{.5} - 1000)$$

Taking the first partial derivatives with respect to each variable and setting them equal to zeroes, we obtain

$$\partial F/\partial SQ_A = 3 - 6\lambda SQ_A^{-.5}SQ_B^{.5} = 0 \tag{1}$$

$$\partial F/\partial SQ_B = 5 - 6\lambda SQ_A^{.5}SQ_B^{-.5} = 0 \tag{2}$$

$$\partial F/\partial \lambda = 12(SQ_A^{.5}SQ_B^{.5}) - 1000 = 0 \tag{3}$$

From (1)

$$\lambda = 3(6SQ_A^{-.5}SQ_B^{.5})^{-1} = .5SQ_A^{.5}SQ_B^{-.5}$$

Substitute λ into (2)

$$5 - 6(.5SQ_A^{.5}SQ_B^{-.5})SQ_A^{.5}SQ_B^{-.5} = 0$$

$$5 - 3(SQ_A^{1}SQ_B^{-1}) = 0$$

$$SQ_A = 5/3SQ_B$$

Substitute SQ_A into (3)

$$12(5/3SQ_B)^{.5}SQ_B^{.5} - 1000 = 0$$

$$SQ_B = 1000/12(5/3)^{.5}$$

Therefore

$$SQ_A = 107.583$$

$$SQ_B = 64.549$$

APPENDIX B

SQ_i' Computation

Minimize

$$3.5SQ_A' + 5.5SQ_B'$$

Subject to

$$1000 = 12(SQ_A')^{.5}(SQ_B')^{.5}$$

Converting the above equation into Lagrangian multiplier form, we obtain

$$F(SQ_A', SQ_B', \lambda) = 3.5SQ_A' + 5.5SQ_B' - \lambda(12SQ_A'^{.5}SQ_B'^{.5} - 1000)$$

Taking the first partial derivatives with respect to each variable and setting them equal to zeroes, we obtain

$$\partial F/\partial SQ_A = 3.5 - 6\lambda SQ_A'^{-.5}SQ_B'^{.5} = 0 \tag{1}$$

$$\partial F/\partial SQ_B = 5.5 - 6\lambda SQ_A'^{.5}SQ_B'^{-.5} = 0 \tag{2}$$

$$\partial F/\partial \lambda = 12(SQ_A'^{.5}SQ_B'^{.5}) - 1000 = 0 \tag{3}$$

From (1)

$$\lambda = 3.5(6SQ_A'^{-.5}SQ_B'^{.5})^{-1} = 3.5/6SQ_A'^{.5}SQ_B'^{-.5}$$

Substitute λ into (2)

$$5.5 - 6(3.5/6SQ_A'^{.5}SQ_B'^{-.5})SQ_A'^{.5}SQ_B'^{-.5} = 0$$

$$5.5 - 3.5((SQ_A')^1(SQ_B')^{-1}) = 0$$

$$SQ_A' = 5.5/3.5SQ_B'$$

Substitute SQ_A' into (3)

$$12((5.5/3.5SQ_B')^{.5}(SQ_B')^{.5}) - 1000 = 0$$

$$SQ_B' = 1000/12(5.5/3.5)^{.5}$$

Therefore

$$SQ_A' = 104.464$$

$$SQ_B' = 66.477$$

APPENDIX C

EQ_i Computation

Minimize

$$3.5EQ_A + 5.5EQ_B$$

Subject to

$$1035.0652 = 12(EQ_A)^{.5}(EQ_B)^{.5}$$

Converting the above equation into Lagrangian multiplier form, we obtain

$$F(EQ_A, EQ_B, \lambda) = 3.5EQ_A + 5.5EQ_B - \lambda(12EQ_A^{.5}EQ_B^{.5} - 1035.0652)$$

Taking the first partial derivatives with respect to each variable and setting them equal to zeroes, we obtain

$$\partial F / \partial EQ_A = 3.5 - 6\lambda EQ_A^{-.5}EQ_B^{.5} = 0 \tag{1}$$

$$\partial F / \partial EQ_B = 5.5 - 6\lambda EQ_A^{.5}EQ_B^{-.5} = 0 \tag{2}$$

$$\partial F / \partial \lambda = 12(EQ_A^{.5}EQ_B^{.5}) - 1035.0652 = 0 \tag{3}$$

From (1)

$$\lambda = 3.5/6EQ_A^{.5}EQ_B^{-.5}$$

Substitute λ into (2)

$$EQ_A = 5.5/3.5EQ_B$$

Substitute EQ_A into (3)

$$EQ_B = 1035.0652/12(5.5/3.5)^{.5}$$

Therefore

$$EQ_A = 108.127$$

$$EQ_B = 68.808$$

REFERENCES

Deakin, E. B., and M. W. Maher, *Cost Accounting* (Homewood: Richard D. Irwin, Inc., 1984).

Demski, J. S., "An Accounting System Structured on a Linear Programming Model," *The Accounting Review* (October 1967), pp. 701–712.

Ferguson, C. E., *Microeconomic Theory* (Homewood: Richard D. Irwin, Inc., 1972).

Hasseldine, C. R., "Mix and Yield Variances," *The Accounting Review* (July 1967), pp. 497–515.

Horngren, C. T., *Cost Accounting* (Englewood Cliffs: Prentice-Hall, Inc., 1982).

Killough, L. N., and W. E. Leininger, *Cost Accounting* (St. Paul: West Publishing Company, 1984).

Marchinko, D., and E. Petri, "Use of the Production Function in Calculation of Standard Cost Variances—An Extension," *The Accounting Review* (July 1984), pp. 488–495.

Matz, A., and M. F. Usry, *Cost Accounting* (Cincinnati: South-Western Publishing Company, 1984).

Mensah, Y. M., "A Dynamic Approach to the Evaluation of Input Variable Cost Center Performance," *The Accounting Review* (October 1982), pp. 681–700.

Moriarity, S., and C. P. Allen, *Cost Accounting* (New York: Harper & Row Publisher, 1984).

Source: Reprinted with permission from *Issues in Accounting Education*, 3, no. 1 (Spring 1988), American Accounting Association.

6

QUANTITATIVE APPROACHES TO CONTROL AND QUALITY

There are numerous variances that can be computed and used to assign responsibility for favorable or unfavorable variances. The major question of interest to a manager is whether to investigate all of these variances or none of them. The most logical answer is to determine an optimal number of variances worthy of investigation and correcting. Models, from rules of thumb to complex techniques, are needed as a decision support system to help the manager decide which variances to investigate that will provide the most benefit to the corporation. Accordingly, the main objective of this chapter is to elaborate on the various cost-variance-investigation models proposed in the literature and in practice. A more exhaustive study of this subject may be found in the Appendix to this chapter.

A DECOMPOSITION APPROACH TO VARIANCE ANALYSIS

All of the variance models and formulas, although seemingly unrelated, constitute different levels of cost analysis. They can be integrated or disaggregated to pinpoint specific levels of control in need of definite attention. Therefore, all of these variances can be organized and integrated to constitute an overall framework of control that in turn can be systematically disaggregated in greater levels of detail and complexity. This framework will be illustrated here using the following simple hypothetical example.[1]

The Karabatsos Computing Company makes four types of monitors. Exhibit 6.1 shows the budgeted and actual performance for 1986. As can be seen, the actual income of the company has declined and it is important to determine the causes. The analysis will proceed according to the following levels.

Exhibit 6.1
Budgeted and Actual Performance: Karabatsos Computing Company

	Monitor 1		Monitor 2		Monitor 3		Monitor 4
Revenues, units	1,000		2,000		3,000		6,000
Revenues, dollars	$ 2,000	$ 6,000		$12,000		$20,000	
Variable expenses	1,000	4,000		6,000		11,000	
Contribution margins	$ 1,000	$ 2,000		$ 6,000		$ 9,000	
Fixed traceable expenses		500		500		4,000		5,000
Traceable margins	$ 500	$ 1,500		$ 2,000		$ 4,000	
Selling and administrative expenses					1,000		
Net income							$ 3,000

Actual (Actual Industry Sales = 29,500 units)

	Monitor 1		Monitor 2		Monitor 3		Monitor 4
Revenues, units	700		2,000		3,200		5,900
Revenues, dollars	$ 1,750	$ 6,000		$16,000		$23,750	
Variable expenses	1,050	5,000		12,800		18,850	
Contribution margins	$ 700	$ 1,000		$ 3,200		$ 4,900	
Fixed traceable expenses		300		100		1,400		1,800
Traceable margins	$ 400	$ 900		$ 2,800		$ 3,100	
Selling and administrative expenses					1,100		
Net income							$ 2,000

Level 0. Profit-variance analysis, in its crudest form, will proceed as follows:

Actual profits	$2,000
Standard profits	3,000
Profit variance	1,000 U

It shows that the actual profits are $1,000 less than expected. This first type of analysis could be refined and expanded in Levels 1–4.

Level 1. At this level, the analysis compares, on as detailed a basis as possible, actual and expected performance for all line items in the income statement. It may proceed as follows:

	Actual	**Expected**	**Variance**
Revenues	$23,750	$20,000	3,750 F
Variable expenses	18,850	11,000	7,850 U
Contribution margin	$ 4,900	$ 9,000	4,100 U
Fixed Expenses	2,900	6,000	3,100 F
Net income	$ 2,000	$ 3,000	1,000 U

Here, it appears that the unfavorable (U) profit variance of $1,000 is a result of differences between the unfavorable variances due to increasing variable expenses and the favorable (F) variances due to increasing revenues and decreasing fixed expenses.

Level 2. At this level the objective is to separate the effects of changes in the level of business activity from those in costs, prices, and operating efficiencies. To do this, we must compute the flexible budget, which is the expected profit assuming an accurate prediction of the actual level of activity in terms of sales volume and sales risk. The flexible budget is computed as follows:

	Actual Sales	Standard Contribution Margin per Unit	Contribution Margin
Monitor 1	700	$1.00	$ 700
Monitor 2	2,000	1.00	2,000
Monitor 3	3,200	2.00	6,400
Contribution margin			9,000
Period expenses			6,000
Net income			$3,100

The Level 2 type of analysis will yield two variances:

Sale-Activity Variance		Cost-Price-Efficiency Variance	
Flexible budget	$3,100	Actual profit	$2,000
Standard profit	3,000	Flexible budget	3,100
	$ 100 F		$1,100 U

The unanticipated change in the actual units and sales mix from the standard levels resulted in a favorable sales-activity variance of $100. At the same time, given the actual level of sales, the changes in unit selling prices and expenses resulted in an unfavorable cost-price-efficiency variance of $1,100.

Level 3. Both the sales-activity variance and the cost-price-efficiency variance can be decomposed further. On the one hand, the sales-activity variance can be decomposed into a sales-volume variance caused by volume changes, and a sales-mix variance caused by a changed composition or mix of items sold. On the other hand, the cost-price-efficiency variance can be decomposed into a sales-price variance due to changes in the sales price, and various cost variances due to changes in the level of costs.

For our example, we start with the decomposition of the sales-activity variance. Given that the weighted contribution margin is equal to:

$$cm^* = \frac{\$1,000 + \$2,000 + \$6,000}{6,000} = \$1.50$$

the sales volume variance is computed as follows:

$$\text{Sales-volume variance} = \sum_i (\Delta x_i) cm^*$$

$$= [(700 - 1{,}000) + (2{,}000 - 2{,}000) \\ + (3{,}200 - 3{,}000)] \times 1.5$$

$$= \$150 \text{ F}$$

Similarly, the sales-mix variance is computed as follows:

$$\text{Sales-mix variance} = \sum_i (\Delta x_i)(Cm - Cm^*)$$

$$= [(700 - 1{,}000)(1.00 - 1.5) \\ + (2{,}000 - 2{,}000)(1.00 - 1.5) \\ + (3{,}200 - 3{,}000)(2.00 - 1.5)]$$

$$= \$250 \text{ F}$$

At the same time, the cost-price-efficiency variance is decomposed into a sales-price variance and a set of cost variances. The sales-price variance is computed as follows:

$$\text{Sales-price variance} = \text{Actual revenues} - \text{Standard revenues at} \\ \text{actual level of sales}$$

$$= \$23{,}750 - [(700 \times 2.00) + (2{,}000 \times 3) \\ + (3{,}200 \times 4)]$$

$$= \$3{,}550 \text{ F}$$

Similarly the cost variances, variable and fixed, are computed as follows:

$$\text{Variable-cost variance} = \text{Actual variable costs} - \text{Budgeted} \\ \text{variable costs at actual level}$$

$$= \$18{,}850 - [(700 \times 1.00) + (2{,}000 \times \\ 2) + (3{,}200 \times 2)]$$

$$= \$7{,}750$$

$$\text{Fixed-cost variance} = \text{Actual fixed costs} - \text{Standard fixed} \\ \text{costs}$$

$$= \$2{,}900 - \$6{,}000$$

$$= \$3{,}100 \text{ F}$$

Level 4. At this level the sales-volume variance is decomposed into a market-size variance caused by changes in overall industry sales, and a market-share variance caused by changes in the company's market share of overall industry sales. Similarly, the sales-mix variance, the sales-price variance, and the cost variances are decomposed by individual products. Note that the cost variances can also be decomposed along the traditional dimensions of labor, material, and overhead.

We start, then, with the decomposition of the sales-volume variance. First, the market-size variance is computed as follows:

$$
\begin{aligned}
\text{Market-size variance} &= \text{(Actual total market} - \text{Expected total} \\
&\quad \text{market) (Expected market share)} \times \\
&\quad \text{(Expected contribution margin per unit} \\
&\quad \text{at standard mix)} \\
&= (29{,}500 - 60{,}000)\ (.10)\ (\$1.50) \\
&= \$4{,}575\ \text{U}
\end{aligned}
$$

Second, the market-share variance is computed as follows:

$$
\begin{aligned}
\text{Market-share variance} &= \text{(Actual market share} - \text{Expected market share)} \\
&\quad \times \text{(Actual market volume)} \\
&\quad \times \text{(Expected contribution margin per unit at standard mix)} \\
&= (\frac{5{,}900}{2{,}500} - 0.10)\ (29{,}500)\ (\$1.50) \\
&= \$4{,}425\ \text{F}
\end{aligned}
$$

The decomposition of the sales-mix variance by individual products proceeds as follows:

Sales-mix variance, Monitor 1: ($\ 700 - 1{,}000$) ($1.00 - 1.5$) = 150 F

Sales-mix variance, Monitor 2: ($2{,}000 - 2{,}000$) ($1.00 - 1.5$) =   0

Sales-mix variance, Monitor 3: ($3{,}200 - 3{,}000$) ($2.00 - 1.5$) = 100 F

The decomposition of the sales-price variance by individual products proceeds as follows:

Sales-price variance, Monitor 1: [\$ 1,750 − ($\ 700 \times 2$)] =   350 F

Sales-price variance, Monitor 2: [\$ 6,000 − ($2{,}000 \times 3$)] =   0

Sales-price variance, Monitor 3: [\$16,000 − ($3{,}200 \times 4$)] = 3,200 F

The decomposition of the variable-cost variances by individual products proceeds as follows:

Variable-cost variance, Monitor 1: [\$ 1,050 − ($\ 700 \times 1.00$)] =   350 U

Variable-cost variance, Monitor 2: [\$ 5,000 − ($2{,}000 \times 3.00$)] =   0

Variable-cost variance, Monitor 3: [\$12,800 − ($3{,}200 \times 2.00$)] = 6,400 U

Finally, the period-cost variance can be decomposed into a traceable fixed variance and a selling and administrative variance as follows:

Traceable fixed component: ($1,800 − $5,000) = $3,200 F

Traceable selling and administrative component: ($1,100 − $1,000) = $100 U

The total multilevel analysis is summarized in Exhibit 6.2. Although it stops at Level 4, it could be expanded to provide more and richer details on the control of the organization. J. K. Shank and N. C. Churchill suggested the following variable improvements: The overall market change could be decomposed into economy-wide factors and industry-specific factors. The market share change could be broken down by products. The sales mix variance could be decomposed by demographic region or customer class. Sales price changes could be decomposed into "list price" changes and discount changes (either early payment discounts or quantity discounts). Cost variances could be broken into controllable and noncontrollable segments by responsibility center. The analysis should stop any time the next level does not produce useful enough management information to warrant the additional complications.[2]

Exhibit 6.2
Multilevel Analysis of Profit Variance

Level 0

Actual Profits	$ 2,000
Standard Profit	3,000
Profit Variance	$ 1,000 U

Level 1

	Actual	Expected	Variance
Revenues	$23,750	$20,000	$ 3,750 F
Variable Expenses	18,850	11,000	7,850 U
Contribution Margin	$ 4,900	$ 3,000	$ 4,100 U
Fixed Expenses	2,900	6,000	3,100 F
Net Income	$ 2,000	$ 3,000	$ 1,000 U

Level 2

Flexible Budget	$ 3,100	Actual profit	$ 2,000
Standard Profit	3,000	Flexible Budget	3,100
Sales Activity Variance	$ 100 F	Cost/Price/Efficiency Variance	$ 1,100 U

Level 3

Sales-Volume Variance = $ 150 U	Variable Cost Variance = $ 7,750 U
Sales Mix Variance = $ 250 F	Final Cost Variance = $ 3,100 F
Sales Price Variance = $5,550 F	

Level 4

Market Size Variance = $14,575 U   Market Share Variance = $14,425 F

	Sales Mix Variance	Sales price Variance	Variable Cost Variance
Monitor 1	150 F	350 F	350 U
Monitor 2	0	0	1,000 U
Monitor 3	100 F	3,200 F	6,400 U

Fixed Cost Variance:	Traceable = 3,200 F
	Selling = 100 U

TRADITIONAL SOLUTIONS FOR VARIANCE
INVESTIGATION: MATERIALITY SIGNIFICANCE

The traditional solutions for variance investigation focus on criteria of materiality significance whereby variances are investigated if they are materially significant in terms of the overall operations of the segment being evaluated. Various traditional solutions for variance investigation have been proposed as follows:

1. Investigate all variances that are unfavorable. This option may be costly and may provide redundant information or information overload.

2. Investigate only the controllable variances. The variances that should be ignored because they are uncontrollable are those that result from prediction error, modeling error, implementation error, and measurement error. The first two signal a need to adjust the standards, whereas the second two signal a need to adjust performance. Again, this option, although superior to the preceding one, may be costly and provide redundant information.

3. Investigate only the controllable variances that exceed the standard by a fixed percentage determined by the manager as being an acceptable measure of materiality significance. Although clearly superior to the two preceding methods, simpler, and less costly to adopt, it may suffer from the following limitations:

- It will not signal when an important account that historically has been controlled very closely, say within 3 percent, suddenly departs from its historical pattern but is still within the preset percentage.

- It will frequently flag accounts where sizeable fluctuation is normal from period to period. An account whose standard deviation is comparable to or larger than the preset percentage will trigger an investigation signal too often.

- The rule may flag many small accounts that are not controlled too closely and that therefore may have larger period-to-period fluctuations.

- There is no attempt to account for investigation of costs and benefits from an investigation that may vary across accounts and that makes some accounts more or less worthwhile to investigate.

- The past history (variances from previous periods) of each account is not incorporated into the fixed-percentage rule when flagging a given account. The manager would have to line up the reports from two or more months to determine whether large deviations have been typical for a given account. The past history of variances for each account is important if we believe that inefficiencies tend to persist once they have crept into the process. Such a persistent inefficiency would be signalled by a sequence of two or more large deviations. In this case, we would be more confident of our investigation's detecting a connectible practice rather than finding that a temporary situation had generated a single large cost variance.[3]

Exhibit 6.3
Areas in One Tail of the Normal Curve

z	0.00	0.01	0.02	0.03	0.04	0.05	0.06	0.07	0.08	0.09
0.0	0.5000	0.4960	0.4920	0.4880	0.4840	0.4801	0.4761	0.4721	0.4681	0.4641
0.1	0.4602	0.4562	0.4522	0.4483	0.4443	0.4404	0.4364	0.4325	0.4286	0.4247
0.2	0.4207	0.4168	0.4129	0.4090	0.4052	0.4013	0.3974	0.3936	0.3897	0.3859
0.3	0.3821	0.3783	0.3745	0.3707	0.3669	0.3632	0.3594	0.3557	0.3520	0.3843
0.4	0.3446	0.3409	0.3372	0.3336	0.3300	0.3264	0.3228	0.3192	0.3156	0.3121
0.5	0.3085	0.3050	0.3015	0.2981	0.2946	0.2912	0.2877	0.2843	0.2810	0.2776
0.6	0.2743	0.2709	0.2676	0.2643	0.2611	0.2578	0.2546	0.2514	0.2483	0.2451
0.7	0.2420	0.2389	0.2358	0.2327	0.2296	0.2266	0.2236	0.2206	0.2177	0.2148
0.8	0.2119	0.2090	0.2061	0.2033	0.2005	0.1977	0.1949	0.1921	0.1894	0.1867
0.9	0.1841	0.1814	0.1788	0.1762	0.1736	0.1711	0.1685	0.1660	0.1635	0.1611
1.0	0.1587	0.1562	0.1539	0.1515	0.1492	0.1469	0.1446	0.1423	0.1401	0.1379
1.1	0.1357	0.1335	0.1314	0.1292	0.1271	0.1251	0.1230	0.1210	0.1190	0.1170
1.2	0.1151	0.1131	0.1112	0.1093	0.1075	0.1056	0.1038	0.1020	0.1003	0.0985
1.3	0.0968	0.0951	0.0934	0.0918	0.0901	0.0885	0.0869	0.0853	0.0838	0.0823
1.4	0.0808	0.0793	0.0778	0.0764	0.0749	0.0735	0.0721	0.0708	0.0694	0.0681
1.5	0.0668	0.0655	0.0643	0.0630	0.0618	0.0606	0.0594	0.0582	0.0570	0.0559
1.6	0.0548	0.0537	0.0526	0.0515	0.0505	0.0495	0.0485	0.0475	0.0465	0.0455
1.7	0.0446	0.0436	0.0427	0.0418	0.0409	0.0401	0.0392	0.0384	0.0375	0.0367
1.8	0.0359	0.0351	0.0344	0.0336	0.0329	0.0322	0.0314	0.0307	0.0300	0.0294
1.9	0.0287	0.0281	0.0274	0.0268	0.0262	0.0256	0.0250	0.0244	0.0238	0.0233
2.0	0.0227	0.0222	0.0217	0.0212	0.0207	0.0202	0.0197	0.0192	0.0188	0.0183

STATISTICAL SOLUTIONS FOR VARIANCE INVESTIGATION: STATISTICAL SIGNIFICANCE

Assuming Normality

The normal distribution has a probability density function that is a smooth, symmetrical, continuous, bell-shaped curve, the area under which sums to 1. It can be completely determined if its mean and its standard deviation are known. If the variances are normally distributed, different probability statements may be made about the expected level of variance. One important feature of any normal distribution is that approximately 50 percent of the area lies within ±0.67 standard deviation of the mean and 0.68 percent of the area lies within ±1.96 standard deviations of the mean. For example, if the cost accountant believes there is roughly a two-thirds (that is, 0.667) chance that the actual costs will be within $500 of the mean, the standard deviation can be set equal to $500, given that two-thirds of the area under a normal curve lies within 1 standard deviation.

Exhibit 6.3 (Continued)

z	0.00	0.01	0.02	0.03	0.04	0.05	0.06	0.07	0.08	0.09
2.1	0.0179	0.0174	0.0170	0.0166	0.0162	0.0158	0.0154	0.0150	0.0146	0.0143
2.2	0.0139	0.0135	0.0132	0.0129	0.0125	0.0122	0.0119	0.0116	0.0113	0.0110
2.3	0.0107	0.0104	0.0102	0.0099	0.0096	0.0094	0.0091	0.0089	0.0087	0.0084
2.4	0.0082	0.0080	0.0078	0.0075	0.0073	0.0071	0.0069	0.0068	0.0066	0.0064
2.5	0.0062	0.0060	0.0059	0.0057	0.0055	0.0054	0.0052	0.0051	0.0049	0.0048
2.6	0.0047	0.0045	0.0044	0.0043	0.0041	0.0040	0.0039	0.0038	0.0037	0.0036
2.7	0.0035	0.0034	0.0033	0.0032	0.0031	0.0030	0.0029	0.0028	0.0027	0.0026
2.8	0.0025	0.0025	0.0024	0.0023	0.0022	0.0022	0.0021	0.0020	0.0020	0.0019
2.9	0.0019	0.0018	0.0017	0.0017	0.0016	0.0016	0.0015	0.0015	0.0015	0.0014
3.0	0.0013	0.0013	0.0013	0.0012	0.0012	0.0011	0.0011	0.0011	0.0010	0.0010
3.1	0.0010	0.0009	0.0009	0.0009	0.0008	0.0008	0.0008	0.0008	0.0007	0.0007
3.2	0.0007	0.0007	0.0007	0.0006	0.0006	0.0006	0.0006	0.0005	0.0005	0.0005
3.3	0.0005	0.0005	0.0005	0.0004	0.0004	0.0004	0.0004	0.0004	0.0004	0.0003
3.4	0.0003	0.0003	0.0003	0.0003	0.0003	0.0003	0.0003	0.0003	0.0002	0.0002
3.5	0.0002	0.0002	0.0002	0.0002	0.0002	0.0002	0.0002	0.0002	0.0002	0.0002
3.6	0.0002	0.0001	0.0001	0.0001	0.0001	0.0001	0.0001	0.0001	0.0001	0.0001
3.7	0.0001	0.0001	0.0001	0.0001	0.0001	0.0001	0.0001	0.0001	0.0001	0.0001
3.8	0.0001	0.0001	0.0001	0.0001	0.0001	0.0001	0.0001	0.0000	0.0000	0.0000
3.9	0.0000	0.0000	0.0000	0.0000	0.0000	0.0000	0.0000	0.0000	0.0000	0.0000
4.0	0.0000	0.0000	0.0000	0.0000	0.0000	0.0000	0.0000	0.0000	0.0000	0.0000

Another important feature of a normal distribution is that it may be standardized, leading to a practical use of the table of normal probabilities. The following formula may be used to standardize a normal distribution:

$$Z = \frac{\text{Actual cost} - \text{Mean cost}}{\text{Standard deviation of cost}}$$

where Z is the number of standard deviations from the mean. Once Z is determined, a table of normal probabilities such as that in Exhibit 6.1 may be used to determine the probability of a cost greater than Z standard deviations from the mean. Thus Exhibit 6.3 shows the right tail of the distribution—that is, the probability of the variable being greater than the standard deviation from the mean.

As an example, suppose that for a given production process we have a standard cost of $500 and an estimated standard deviation of $625. The December result amounts to a cost of $2,375. Z is computed as follows:

$$Z = \frac{\$2,375 - \$500}{\$625} = 3$$

Using Exhibit 6.3 we can state that the probability of cost exceeding $2,375 is equal to 0.0013.

Suppose instead that the cost accountant wants to know the probability that the costs will be equal to $2,375. Exhibit 6.4 gives the relative heights at distances from the mean measured by Z values. Thus:

$$Z = 3 \text{ and } P(Z) = 0.0044$$

Assuming Nonnormality: Using Chebyschev's Inequality

The normal distribution assumed in the preceding section is very practical because it possesses many valuable properties that lend themselves to extensive statistical manipulations. In a control situation, knowledge of the normality of

Exhibit 6.4
Ordinates of the Normal Curve

z	0.00	0.01	0.02	0.03	0.04	0.05	0.06	0.07	0.08	0.09
0.0	0.3989	0.3989	0.3985	0.3988	0.3986	0.3984	0.3982	0.3980	0.3977	0.3973
0.1	0.3970	0.3965	0.3961	0.3956	0.3951	0.3945	0.3939	0.3932	0.3925	0.3918
0.2	0.3910	0.3902	0.3894	0.3885	0.3876	0.3867	0.3857	0.3847	0.3836	0.3825
0.3	0.3814	0.3802	0.3790	0.3778	0.3765	0.3752	0.3739	0.3726	0.3712	0.3697
0.4	0.3863	0.3668	0.3653	0.3637	0.3621	0.3605	0.3589	0.3572	0.3555	0.3538
0.5	0.3521	0.3503	0.3485	0.3467	0.3448	0.3430	0.3411	0.3391	0.3372	0.3352
0.6	0.3332	0.3312	0.3292	0.3271	0.3251	0.3230	0.3209	0.3187	0.3166	0.3144
0.7	0.3123	0.3101	0.3079	0.3056	0.3034	0.3011	0.2989	0.2966	0.2943	0.2920
0.8	0.2897	0.2874	0.2850	0.2827	0.2803	0.2780	0.2756	0.2732	0.2709	0.2685
0.9	0.2661	0.2637	0.2613	0.2589	0.2565	0.2541	0.2516	0.2492	0.2468	0.2444
1.0	0.2420	0.2396	0.2371	0.2347	0.2323	0.2299	0.2275	0.2251	0.2227	0.2203
1.1	0.2179	0.2155	0.2131	0.2107	0.2083	0.2509	0.2036	0.2012	0.1989	0.1965
1.2	0.1942	0.1919	0.1895	0.1872	0.1849	0.1827	0.1804	0.1781	0.1759	0.1736
1.3	0.1714	0.1691	0.1669	0.1647	0.1626	0.1604	0.1582	0.1561	0.1540	0.1518
1.4	0.1497	0.1476	0.1456	0.1435	0.1415	0.1394	0.1374	0.1354	0.1334	0.1315
1.5	0.1295	0.1276	0.1257	0.1238	0.1219	0.1200	0.1182	0.1163	0.1145	0.1127
1.6	0.1109	0.1092	0.1074	0.1057	0.1040	0.1023	0.1006	0.0989	0.0973	0.0957
1.7	0.0941	0.0925	0.0909	0.0893	0.0878	0.0863	0.0848	0.0833	0.0818	0.0804
1.8	0.0790	0.0775	0.0761	0.0748	0.0734	0.0721	0.0707	0.0694	0.0681	0.0669
1.9	0.0656	0.0644	0.0632	0.0620	0.0608	0.0596	0.0584	0.0573	0.0562	0.0551
2.0	0.0540	0.0529	0.0519	0.0508	0.0498	0.0488	0.0478	0.0468	0.0459	0.0449

the distribution is important, because one can make statements concerning the probabilistic relationship between any particular observation and the mean of the universe and thus infer whether there is a need for remedial action.

In fact, lack of normality or of knowledge of distribution is not necessarily a problem as long as the accountant can identify the expected value and the standard deviation of the distribution of interest. That could be enough for making probability statements about the possible outcomes, because in a distribution having finite expectation and variance, there is a close connection between the size of the deviation from the expected value and probability.[4] Chebyschev's inequality uses that connection to make probability statements about a random variable when there is only limited information about the nature of the variable's underlying probability distribution. Chebyschev's inequality allows one to determine the lower bound of the probability that an observation will fall within a certain distance from the mean or the upper bound that it will fall outside, irrespective of the probability law. In mathematical terms, if Pr stands for the probability and X represents the observation, μ the mean of the

Exhibit 6.4 (Continued)

z	0.00	0.01	0.02	0.03	0.04	0.05	0.06	0.07	0.08	0.09
2.1	0.0440	0.0431	0.0422	0.0413	0.0404	0.0396	0.0387	0.0379	0.0371	0.0363
2.2	0.0355	0.0347	0.0339	0.0332	0.0325	0.0317	0.0310	0.0303	0.0297	0.0290
2.3	0.0283	0.0277	0.0270	0.0264	0.0258	0.0252	0.0246	0.0241	0.0235	0.0229
2.4	0.0224	0.0219	0.0213	0.0208	0.0203	0.0198	0.0194	0.0189	0.0184	0.0180
2.5	0.0175	0.0171	0.0167	0.0163	0.0158	0.0154	0.0151	0.0147	0.0143	0.0139
2.6	0.0136	0.0132	0.0129	0.0126	0.0122	0.0119	0.0116	0.0113	0.0110	0.0107
2.7	0.0104	0.0101	0.0099	0.0096	0.0093	0.0091	0.0088	0.0086	0.0084	0.0081
2.8	0.0079	0.0077	0.0075	0.0073	0.0071	0.0069	0.0067	0.0065	0.0063	0.0061
2.9	0.0060	0.0058	0.0056	0.0055	0.0053	0.0051	0.0050	0.0048	0.0047	0.0045
3.0	0.0044	0.0043	0.0042	0.0040	0.0039	0.0038	0.0037	0.0036	0.0035	0.0034
3.1	0.0033	0.0032	0.0031	0.0030	0.0029	0.0028	0.0027	0.0026	0.0025	0.0025
3.2	0.0024	0.0023	0.0022	0.0022	0.0021	0.0020	0.0020	0.0019	0.0018	0.0018
3.3	0.0017	0.0017	0.0016	0.0016	0.0015	0.0015	0.0014	0.0014	0.0013	0.0013
3.4	0.0012	0.0012	0.0012	0.0011	0.0011	0.0010	0.0010	0.0010	0.0010	0.0009
3.5	0.0009	0.0008	0.0008	0.0008	0.0008	0.0007	0.0007	0.0007	0.0007	0.0006
3.6	0.0006	0.0006	0.0006	0.0005	0.0005	0.0005	0.0005	0.0005	0.0005	0.0004
3.7	0.0004	0.0004	0.0004	0.0004	0.0004	0.0004	0.0003	0.0003	0.0003	0.0003
3.8	0.0003	0.0003	0.0003	0.0003	0.0003	0.0002	0.0002	0.0002	0.0002	0.0002
3.9	0.0002	0.0002	0.0002	0.0002	0.0002	0.0002	0.0002	0.0002	0.0001	0.0001
4.0	0.0001	0.0001	0.0001	0.0001	0.0001	0.0001	0.0001	0.0001	0.0001	0.0001

universe, σ^2 the variance, and d a positive measure of the distance, then Chebyschev's inequality states that:

$$Pr(|X - \mu| \le d) \ge 1 - \frac{\sigma^2}{d^2}$$

and the complement of the above is:

$$Pr(|X - \mu| \ge d) \le 1 - \frac{\sigma^2}{d^2}$$

For the example from the preceding section, $\mu = 500$ and $\sigma = 625$. The new observation is 2,375. Using Chebyschev's inequality we can compute the probability of deviation as large as $(2,375 - 500 = 1,875)$ as follows:

$$Pr(|X - 500| \ge 1,875) \le \left(\frac{625}{1,875}\right)^2 = 0.111$$

This result of 0.111 is much higher than the 0.0013 obtained when normality was assumed. This shows a major weakness of Chebyschev's inequality. Chebyschev's inequality can also be expressed differently if the distance is measured in terms of standard deviations. If we let $d = c\sigma$, then:

$$Pr(|X - \mu| \le c\sigma) \ge 1 - \frac{\sigma^2}{c^2}$$

or

$$Pr(|X - \mu| \ge c\sigma) \le 1 - \frac{\sigma^2}{c^2}$$

Returning to the above example, $d = 1,875 = 3(625)$; then:

$$Pr(|X - 500| \ge 3) \le \frac{1}{3^2} = 0.111$$

So in effect 89 percent of the observations will fall within three standard deviations from the mean.

CONTROL-CHART METHOD

Statistical quality control is used to monitor ongoing, repetitive operations in industrial processes and to pinpoint random variations. These variations may be within-piece variations, piece-to-piece variations, or time-to-time variations.

The sources of variation may be one of four factors: the process, the material, the operator, or miscellaneous.

The control-chart method is the basic tool used in statistical quality control. It is a means of visualizing the variations that occur in the central tendency and dispersion of a set of observations. Basically, a standard (or average) is set within an acceptable range, bounded by upper and lower control limits (UCL and LCL). Periodic samples from the output of the production process are plotted, and only observations falling beyond the control limits are considered nonrandom and worth investigating. In short, the control chart is a tool that signals when a variance is due to an assignable cause, and it separates random from nonrandom variances. A control chart can be based on either a categorical measurement such as a good-defective decision for each item (termed *inspection by attributes*) or a qualitative related variable, such as length, weight, or hardness (termed *inspection by variables*). Two types of control charts are used for process control by variables: $\bar{X}$ and $\bar{R}$. Two types of control charts are used for process control by attributes: P and C.

Process Control by Variables: $\bar{X}$ and $\bar{R}$ Charts

Both the $\bar{X}$ and $\bar{R}$ charts are used for variable inspection, which is when a characteristic is measured on a continuous scale. The $\bar{X}$ chart shows variations in the arithmetic mean of the variable being measured, and the $\bar{R}$ chart shows variations in the range of the samples. Thus, whereas the $\bar{X}$ chart focuses on a control of the mean of the process, the $\bar{R}$ chart focuses on a control of the variability of the process.

The general procedures for establishing a control chart are first to draw 20 or more samples and second to compute the upper and lower control limits. The control values for the $\bar{X}$ and $\bar{R}$ charts are obtained using the formulas:

$$\bar{X} = \frac{\sum_{j=1}^{m} \bar{X}_i}{m} \quad \text{and} \quad \bar{R} = \frac{\sum_{j=1}^{m} \bar{R}_j}{m}$$

where

$\bar{X}$ = Mean or average of the subgroup

$\bar{X}_j$ = Mean of the jth subgroup

m = Number of subgroups

$\bar{R}$ = Mean or average of the subgroup ranges

R_j = Range of the jth subgroup

The upper and lower control limits of the control charts are determined as follows:

For $\bar{X}$:

Center line		$\bar{X}$
Upper control limit		$UCL_x = \bar{X} + A_2\bar{R}$
Lower control limit		$LCL_x = \bar{X} - A_2\bar{R}$

A_2 given in Column 2 of Exhibit 6.5.

For $\bar{R}$ when σ is known:

Center line		$d_2\sigma$
Upper control limit		$UCL_R = D_2\sigma$
Lower control limit		$UCL_R = D_1\sigma$

D_1 and D_2 are given in columns 3 and 4 of Exhibit 6.5.

For $\bar{R}$ when σ is known:

Center line		$\bar{R}$
Upper control limit		$UCL_{\bar{R}} = D_4\bar{R}$
Lower control limit		$UCL_{\bar{R}} = D_3\bar{R}$

D_3 and D_4 are given in columns 5 and 6 of Exhibit 6.5.

For the $\bar{X}$ chart the upper and lower control limits are symmetrical about the central value. Theoretically, the control limits for $\bar{R}$ should also be symmetrical about the central value. However, with subgroup sizes of six or less, the lower control limits would need to have a negative value for the control limits for an $\bar{R}$ to be symmetrical. Given that a negative value is impossible, the lower control limit is located at zero by assigning to D_3 the value of zero for subgroup sizes or less.

As an example of process control by variables, assume that the individual weights of cereals for five boxes in each of the ten samples are as shown in Exhibit 6.6. To determine the $\bar{X}$ and $\bar{R}$ charts, the control limits are determined as follows:

For $\bar{X}$:

Center line		$\bar{X} = 7.35$
Upper control limit		$\bar{X} + A_2\bar{R} = 7.35 + 0.58\,(0.85) = 7.843$
Lower control limit		$\bar{X} - A_2\bar{R} = 7.35 + 0.58\,(0.85) = 6.857$

For $\bar{R}$:

Center line		$\bar{R} = 0.855$
Upper control limit		$D_4\bar{R} = 0.855\,(2.11) = 1.804$
Lower control limit		$D_3\bar{R} = 0.855\,(0) = 0$

Exhibit 6.5
Factors Determining Control Limits for X̄ and R̄ Charts

Number of Observations in Subgroup (n)	Factor for X Chart (A₂)	Factors for R̄ Chart (σ known) LCL D₁	Factors for R̄ Chart (σ known) UCL D₂	Factors for R̄ Chart (σ Estimated) LCL D₃	Factors for R̄ Chart (σ Estimated) UCL D₄
2	1.88	0	3.69	0	3.27
3	1.02	0	4.36	0	2.57
4	0.73	0	4.70	0	2.28
5	0.58	0	4.92	0	2.11
6	0.48	0	5.08	0	2.00
7	0.42	0.20	5.20	0.08	1.92
8	0.37	0.39	5.31	0.14	1.86
9	0.34	0.55	5.39	0.18	1.82
10	0.31	0.69	5.47	0.22	1.78
11	0.29	0.81	5.53	0.26	1.74
12	0.27	0.92	5.59	0.28	1.72
13	0.25	1.03	5.65	0.31	1.69
14	0.24	1.12	5.69	0.33	1.67
15	0.22	1.21	5.74	0.35	1.65
16	0.21	1.28	5.78	0.36	1.64
17	0.20	1.36	5.82	0.38	1.62
18	0.19	1.43	5.85	0.39	1.61
19	0.19	1.49	5.89	0.40	1.60
20	0.18	1.55	5.92	0.41	1.59

Source: Adapted from Eugene L. Grant, *Statistical Quality Control*, 3rd ed. Copyright 1964 by McGraw-Hill Book Company. Used with the permission of the publisher.

Exhibits 6.7 and 6.8 show the R̄ and X̄ charts. The X̄ chart shows that the system is out of control for samples 5 and 9. This means that an assignable cause of variation is present. Another approach to explaining the out-of-control points is to think of the subgroup value as coming from a different universe than the one from which the control limits were obtained. In other words, the process that produced samples 5 and 9 is a different process than the stable process from which the control limits were developed. The assignable cause of variation causing this result must be found and corrected before a normal, stable process can continue.

The variation in an out-of-control condition follows generally one of the five

Exhibit 6.6
Weight of Cereals in Boxes (in ounces)

Sample Number	Box Number 1	2	3	4	5	Sum	Average	Range
1	6.50	7.30	7.10	7.00	7.10	35.00	7.00	0.80
2	7.05	7.25	7.25	7.59	7.59	37.09	7.41	0.90
3	6.85	7.31	7.61	7.81	7.38	36.96	7.39	0.96
4	7.15	8.01	7.49	7.39	7.21	37.25	7.45	0.86
5	6.90	6.15	6.35	6.70	6.40	32.50	6.50	0.75
6	7.95	7.06	7.11	7.31	7.55	36.98	7.39	0.89
7	7.10	6.45	7.35	7.10	7.00	35.00	7.00	0.90
8	7.55	7.50	7.06	7.59	8.00	37.70	7.54	0.94
9	7.90	X.90	8.75	7.85	7.95	40.25	8.05	0.90
10	7.27	7.92	7.87	7.87	7.92	38.85	7.77	0.65
						Totals	73.50	8.55

$$\bar{X} = \frac{\Sigma\bar{X}}{n} = \frac{73.50}{10} = 7.35$$

Center line = 7.35

UCL = 7.35 + 0.58 (0.85) = 7.843

LCL = 7.35 - 0.58 (0.85) = 6.857

$$\bar{R} = \frac{\Sigma\bar{R}}{n} = \frac{8.55}{10} = 0.855$$

types of out-of-control $\bar{X}$ and $\bar{R}$ patterns: change or jump in level, trend or steady change in level, recurring cycles, two universes, and mistakes.

1. If the out-of-control pattern of variation is a change or jump in level, the assignable cause for a $\bar{X}$ chart may be an intentional or unintentional change in the process setting, a new or inexperienced operator, a different raw material, or a minor failure of a machine part. For an $\bar{R}$ chart, the assignable cause may be an inexperienced operator, a sudden increase in gear play, or a greater variation in incoming material.[5]

2. If the out-of-control pattern of variation is a trend or steady change in level, the assignable cause for an $\bar{X}$ chart may be tool or die wear, gradual deterioration of equipment, gradual change in temperature or humidity, viscosity in a chemical process, or buildup of chips in a work-holding device. For an $\bar{R}$ chart, the assignable cause may be an improvement in worker skill (downward trend); a decrease in worker skill due to fatigue, boredom, inattention, and so on; or a gradual improvement of the homogeneity of incoming material.[6]

3. If the out-of-control pattern is a recurring cycle, the assignable cause for an $\bar{X}$ chart may be the seasonal effects of incoming material; the recurring effects of temperature and humidity (cold morning start up); any daily or weekly chemical,

Exhibit 6.7
Control Chart for R̄

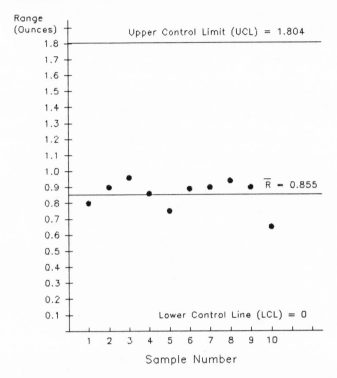

mechanical, or psychological events; or (d) the periodic rotation of operators. For an $\bar{R}$ chart, the assignable cause may be operator fatigue and rejuvenation resulting from morning, noon, and afternoon breaks; or lubrication cycles.[7]

4. If the out-of-control pattern is the presence of two universes, the assignable cause for an $\bar{X}$ chart may be large differences in material quality, two or more machines on the same chart, or large differences in test method or equipment. For an $\bar{R}$ chart the assignable cause may be different workers using the same chart, or materials from different supplies.[8]

5. If the out-of-control pattern results from mistakes, the causes may be measuring equipment out of calibration, errors in calculation, errors in using test equipment, or taking samples from different universes.[9]

Process Control Attributes: *P* and *C* Charts

An attribute refers to those quality characteristics that are either good or bad. A good product is one that conforms to specification. A defective product does not conform to specification because it contains many objects. As such it is not usable and should be rejected.

Exhibit 6.8
Control Chart for X̄

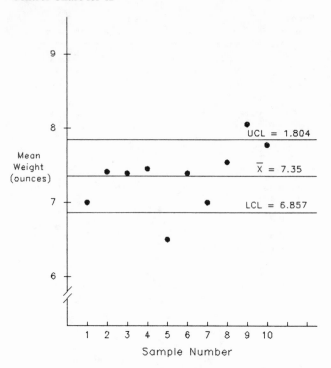

Both *P* and *C* charts are used for attribute inspection. An attribute is a characteristic being measured that can be expressed as a continuous variable—that is, it
is either present in the product, which is considered acceptable, or absent from
the product, in which case the product is not acceptable.

When individual units are judged as either acceptable or defective, a *P* chart is
used. If the attribute is expressed in terms of the number of defects per unit of
output, a *C* chart is used.

P Chart. P is the fraction defective in the sample—that is, the ratio of the
number defective in a sample or subgroup to the total number in the sample or
subgroup. The formula is:

$$P = \frac{np}{n}$$

where

P   = Fraction defective of the subgroup or sample

n   = Number in the sample or subgroup

np = Number defective

Exhibit 6.9
Reconciliation Samples

Date Sampled	Sample Number	Number Sampled	Number Rejected	% Rejected
Jan. 3	1	30	5	0.166
Jan. 4	2	30	6	0.200
Jan. 5	3	30	6	0.200
Jan. 6	4	30	3	0.100
Jan. 7	5	30	2	0.066
Jan. 8	6	30	2	0.066
Jan. 9	7	30	2	0.066
Jan. 10	8	30	6	0.200
Jan. 11	9	30	6	0.200
Jan. 12	10	30	1	0.033
		300	39	

$$\bar{P} = \frac{\text{Total defective}}{\text{Total inspected}} = \frac{39}{300} = 0.13$$

$$\text{UCL} = 0.13 + \sqrt{0.13(1 - 0.13/10)} = 0.419$$

$$\text{LCL} = 0.13 - \sqrt{0.13(1 - 0.13/10)} = -0.219$$

The P chart shows whether the process fraction defective is being maintained. If P is known and the sample size is n, the P chart has the following dimensions:

Center line $\quad \bar{P} = \dfrac{\text{Total defective units}}{\text{Total inspected units}}$

Upper control limit $\quad \bar{P} + 3\sqrt{\dfrac{\bar{p}(1 - \bar{p})}{n}}$

Lower control limit $\quad \bar{P} - 3\sqrt{\dfrac{\bar{p}(1 - \bar{p})}{n}}$

For example, assume that a P chart is used for controlling the quality of operations in a soldering department. The fraction defective is the ratio of improperly soldered connections to total connections examined in 10 samples containing 30 connections each. The control limits derived from data in Exhibit 6.9 would be computed as follows:

Center line $\quad = \quad 39/300 \quad\quad\quad\quad\quad\quad\quad = \quad 0.13$

Upper control limit $= \quad 0.13 + \sqrt{0.13 (1 - 0.13/10)} = \quad 0.419$

Lower control limit $= \quad 0.13 - \sqrt{0.13 (1 - 0.13/10)} = \quad -0.219$

The P control chart is shown in Exhibit 6.10. Sample sizes are typically larger

Exhibit 6.10
Control Chart for P

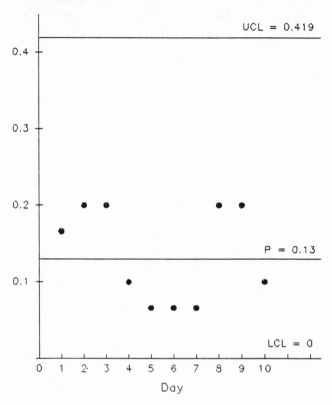

for *P* charts than the one used in this example. In fact, the required sample size can be computed from the following formula:[10]

$$n = \left[\frac{1.645\sqrt{P_1(1 - P_1)} + 3\sqrt{P_0(1 - P_0)}}{P_1 - P_0} \right]$$

where

P_0 = Normal process fraction defective

P_1 = Specified fraction defective that is unacceptable.

C Chart. The other type of attribute chart is a number-of-defects chart, which is referred to as a *C* Chart. Whereas the *P* chart controls the fraction defective, the *C* chart controls the number of defects. The defects could be critical in that they will affect usability, major in that they may affect usability, or minor in that they will not affect usability.

The C chart, where C is the number of defects per unit of output, is established as follows:

Center Line $\qquad \bar{C} = \dfrac{\text{Total defects}}{\text{Number of samples}}$

Upper control limit $\quad \bar{C} + 3\sqrt{C}$

Lower control limit $\quad \bar{C} - 3\sqrt{C}$

For example, assume a C chart is used for controlling the quality of the fabric woven for use as an armchair covering. The number of objects per square yard is represented by C. The control limits derived from the data in Exhibit 6.11 would be computed as follows:

Center line $\qquad\qquad$ 230/10 $\quad = 23$

Upper control limit $\quad 23 + 3\sqrt{23} = 37.38$

Lower control limit $\quad 23 - 3\sqrt{23} = 8.61$

The C chart is shown in Exhibit 6.12.

Exhibit 6.11
Covering Samples

Sample Number	Number of Defects per Square Yard
1	21
2	22
3	23
4	25
5	26
6	23
7	20
8	26
9	22
10	22
	—
	230

Exhibit 6.12
Control Chart for C

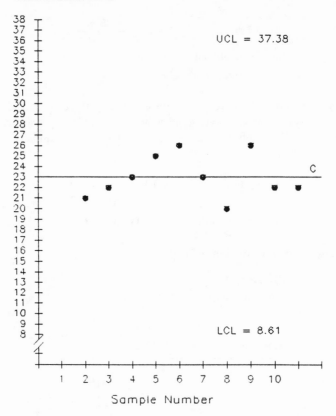

DECISION-THEORY METHOD

The control model based on decision theory tries to minimize some of the limitations generally associated with the classical approach. As such it relies on Bayesian statistics to provide a solution to these problems. Mohammed Onsi stated that a control model based on the Bayesian approach will

1. De-emphasize the confidence-interval estimate. The decision is based on both sample evidence and the consideration of economic loss and prior belief, especially if losses due to one type of error are larger or more serious than those due to the other type of error.

2. Incorporate into the analysis subjective a priori probability as a useful and logically consistent formalization of the prior state of information about the parameter.

3. Not require the determination of α and β as in the classical model. However, the economic importance of each type of error and prior information as to the likelihood of the different parameter values are put in the analysis.

4. Provide a systematic analysis to determine sample size. An optimum sample size can be obtained by balancing the sampling cost against the gains in terms of reduction in risk of error.

5. Provide a procedure to select the best action minimizing expected loss to take in a many-action situation, given the entire subjective probability distribution of the parameter. The model makes explicit and systematic use of the opportunity cost concept to evaluate the worth of each action relative to the best possible action for the given state of nature.[11]

In what follows, three forms of decision-theory method of control are examined: the breakdown probability, which considers only prior probability; the Bayesian approach, which includes both a priori and a posteriori analyses; and formal models for multiple observations.

Break-Even Probability Computation

Both the traditional and the classical approaches of evaluating the significance of variances are of limited value because they fail to consider the costs and losses implicit in the control decision. The basis of any control decision, although not explicitly stated, is that the benefits to be desired from investigation will exceed the costs of investigation. The decision rule will be to choose that act (investigate versus do not investigate) that will minimize the expected cost. Therefore, the decision to investigate a variance can be represented by a two-state action problem as follows:

	States of Nature	
	In-Control	*Out-of-Control*
Actions	*Random Variation*	*Nonrandom Variation*
1. Investigate and correct (a_1)	Cost = C Type I error	Cost = $C + M$ Correct decision
2. Do not investigate (a_2)	Cost = 0 Correct decision	Cost = $C + M$ Type II error
3. Probabilities (a priori)	$_0\Theta_1$	$_0\Theta_2$

where

C = Cost of investigating a variance.

M = Cost of correcting a variance.

L = Opportunity cost, which can be thought of as the future cost savings that might have been realized had the variance being investigated been found to be nonrandom and eliminated. This can be labeled as *out-of-control loss*.

$_0\Theta_1$ = Prior probability that the process is in control and that the variance is due to random and noncontrollable causes.

$_0\Theta_2$ = Prior probability that the process is out of control or that the variance is due to nonrandom and controllable causes.

The expected cost of each act is calculated by multiplying each conditional cost by its respective probability and summing. The results are as follows:

$$\text{Expected cost of } a_1 = E(a_1) = C(_0\Theta_1) + (C + M)_0\Theta_2$$
$$\text{Expected cost of } a_2 = E(a_1) = O(_0\Theta_2) + L_0\Theta_2$$

Therefore, a firm would be indifferent toward investigation if the expected cost of each action were equal to the expected benefit; that is, when:

$$C_0\Theta_1 + (C + M)_0\Theta_2 = O(_0\Theta_2) + L_0\Theta_2$$

or

$$C_0(1 - _0\Theta_2) + (C + M)_0\Theta_2 = L_0\Theta_2$$

Solving for $_0\Theta_2$ yields the break-even or critical probability, which is the probability at which the expected value of a decision to investigate a variance is equal to the expected value of the loss through failure to investigate. The break-even probability $\Theta_2{}^*$ is:

$$\Theta_2{}^* = \frac{C}{L - M}$$

or alternatively, using $\Theta_1{}^*$:

$$\Theta_2{}^* = 1 - \frac{C}{L - M}$$

Therefore, if:

$$\Theta_2 > \Theta_2{}^*$$

or

$$\Theta_1 < \Theta_1{}^*$$

the decision is to investigate, and if

$$\Theta_2 < \Theta_2{}^*$$

or

$$\Theta_1 > \Theta_1{}^*$$

the decision is not to investigate.

For example, assume the following

C = \$ 3,600 = Cost of investigation

L = \$16,000 = Present value of incremental costs that would have been incurred if corrective action were not taken

M = \$10,000 = Cost of corrective action

$_0\Theta_1 = 0.8$ = Prior probability of the process being in control

$_0\Theta_2 = 0.2$ = Prior probability of the process being out of control

Hence, the break-even probability is $\Theta_1{}^* = 1 - 3,000/6,000 = 0.4$

Decision-Control Graph

The decision is to investigate only when the probability of the system being in control drops below 0.4. Since $_0\Theta_1 = 0.8$ and is therefore superior to $\Theta_1{}^*$, the decision is not to investigate.

The critical or break-even probability could be used to develop a cost control chart for unfavorable variances. This could be easily conceived given that L is difficult to determine and can take different values depending on the amount of unfavorable variances. For example, suppose that C (the cost of investigation) is fixed and equal to \$200, M (the cost of correcting a variance), and L (the opportunity cost) is a linear function of the variance. In this case L is equal to twice the variance. Therefore, for different variances it is possible to determine the curve separating the "investigate" and "do not investigate" areas as follows:

Variance	$L = 2(\text{Variance})$	C	M	$\Theta_2{}^* = 1 - \dfrac{C}{L - M}$
\$150	\$ 300	\$200	\$100	0.000
250	500	200	100	0.500
450	900	200	100	0.750
650	1,300	200	100	0.834
850	1,700	200	100	0.875
950	1,900	200	100	0.889

Given these critical probabilities, the decision-control graph in Exhibit 6.13 is prepared. For each observation, the critical probability is depicted and connected with a line, dividing the graph into the "investigate" and "do not investigate" areas.

Bayesian Analysis: First Approach

The prior probabilities ($_0\Theta_1$ and $_0\Theta_2$) used in the break-even probability analysis are based on past information. The manager observing an actual observation from current sample information must determine the revised or a posteriori

Exhibit 6.13
Cost-Control Decision Chart: Unfavorable Variances

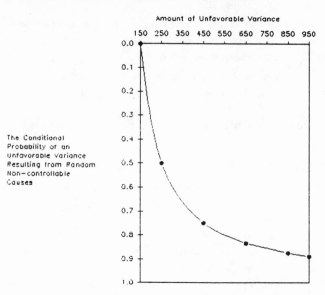

probabilities of the states of nature ($_1\Theta_1$ and $_1\Theta_2$) using the prior information and the actual cost. Bayes's theorem can be used to estimate the revised probabilities for the states. The Bayesian analysis would proceed as follows:

1. First, compute P (cost/in control), the probability of the actual cost observation if the process is in control.

2. Second, compute P (cost/out of control), the probability of the actual cost observation if the process is out of control.

3. Third, use Bayes's theorem to compute $_1\Theta_1$, the revised probability of the process being in control, as follows:

$$_1\Theta_1 = \frac{_0\Theta_2 \times P(\text{cost/in control})}{_0\Theta_2 \times P(\text{cost/in control}) + _0\Theta_2 \times P(\text{cost/out of control})}$$

The procedure is explained using the following example. Suppose that a cost of $10,000 has been incurred. The other information is as follows:

C = $3,600
L = $16,000
M = $10,000
$_0\Theta_1$ = 0.8
$_0\Theta_2$ = 0.2

Assume also that the expected cost when the system is in control is $1,000, with a standard deviation of $1,500, and the expected cost when the system is out of control is $8,000, with a standard deviation of $2,000. The analysis as follows:

First, to compute P (cost/in control) or P ($10,000/in control), compute the standardized value (Z) as follows:

$$Z = \frac{\$10,000 - \$7,000}{1,500} = 2$$

Exhibit 6.4 showed a probability of 0.054 that an observation of $10,000 will occur in a distribution with a mean of $6,000, yielding a Z value of 2. (The ordinate table in Exhibit 6.4 showed the height of an ordinate of the normal curve at nZ_i, or n standard deviations from the mean.)

Second, to compute P (cost/out of control) or P ($10,000/out of control), compute the standardized value (Z) as follows:

$$Z = \frac{\$10,000 - \$8,000}{2,000} = 1$$

Exhibit 6.3 showed a probability of 0.242 that an observation of $10,000 will occur in a distribution with a mean of 8,000 yielding a Z value of 1.

Third, to compute the revised probability of being in control, use Bayes's theorem as follows:

$$_0\Theta_1 = \frac{0.8 \,(0.054)}{0.8 \,(0.054) + 0.2 \,(0.242)}$$

Since $_0\Theta_1 = 0.47$ is greater than the break-even probability

$$\Theta* = 1 - \frac{C}{L - M} = 1 - \frac{3,600}{16,000 - 10,000} = 0.4$$

the decision is not to investigate.

Bayesian Analysis: Second Approach

Setting the Problem. The first approach to Bayesian analysis considers only two possible states of nature: either the system is in control because the unfavorable variances resulted from random, noncontrollable causes; or the system is out of control because the unfavorable variances resulted from nonrandom, controllable causes. The second approach to Bayesian analysis considers various possible states of nature expressed in terms of various percentages of defective items or deviations.

The second Bayesian analysis approach to a control problem includes two steps. The first is an a priori analysis, which consists of choosing the action with the lowest expected cost (or the highest expected benefit) based on the unconditional probabilities of the states of nature (the a priori probabilities). The second step is an a posteriori analysis, which consists of choosing the action with the lowest expected cost (or the highest expected benefit) based on revised or a posteriori probabilities. Bayes's theorem is the basic technique used in reevaluating the a priori probabilities to obtain a posteriori probabilities.

The Bayesian approach to control requires the determination of several factors:

1. The desired objective, such as the maximization of the expected value of benefit or the minimization of the expected value of cost
2. The possible action that can be taken
3. The actuality of possible states of nature
4. The numerical payoff associated with each possible state of nature and decision

To illustrate the second approach to Bayesian analysis of control, let us assume that the XYZ company has to decide which of the following two acts to accept:

1. "Accept" a manufacturing process as being under control; the proportion of deviation of defective units is within normal expectations (say 0.01).
2. "Reject" the process as being out of control; the proportion of deviation of defective units is more than normally expected.

Four states of nature are considered possible, and the firm's objective is to choose the action that minimizes the expected value of cost: $a_1 = 0.01$ defective, $a_2 = 0.05$ defective, $a_3 = 0.10$ defective, $a_4 = 0.15$ defective.

A Priori Analysis. To proceed with a priori analysis, a payoff table such as that in Exhibit 6.14 is required. Such a table shows the possible states of nature, the possible actions, the possible gain (or cost) from the choice of a particular action

Exhibit 6.14
Payoff Table

Decisions	States of Nature			
	$s_1 = .01$ defective	$s_2 = .05$ defective	$s_3 = .10$ defective	$s_4 = .15$ defective
a_1 = Accept the process as being under control	$ 4	$ 20	$ 40	$ 60
a_2 = Reject the process as being out of control	$16	$ 16	$ 16	$ 16
A Priori Probabilities	.5	.2	.2	.1

Exhibit 6.15
Deciding under Uncertainty

Decisions	States of Nature				Expected Cost of Action	Computation
	$_1 = .01$	$s_2 = .05$	$s_3 = .10$	$s_4 = .15$		
a_1	$ 4	$ 20	$ 40	$ 60	$ 20	(4x.5)+(20x.2)+ (40x.2)+(60x.1)
a_2	$ 16	$ 16	$ 16	$ 16	$ 16	(16x.5)+(16x.2)+ (16x.2)+(16x.1)
A Priori Probabilities	.5	.2	.2	.1		

given the state of nature, and the a priori probabilities of the states of nature. This example assumes the following:

1. The production in each period is 400 units.
2. The proportion of normal defective units is 0.01, or 4 defectives.
3. The defective units will cost $1 to rework and the cost of investigation is $12.
4. If the process is rejected, the expected cost of reworking is the same for each value of the states of nature (the proportion of deviation) since we assume that by investigation the deviation will be only within normal expectations—that is, 4 deviations.

The a priori analysis will then proceed as follows:

1. *Deciding under uncertainty.* The expected cost from each action is equal to the sum of the product of each conditional cost multiplied by the corresponding a priori probability of the state of nature. Exhibit 6.15 shows the results of these computations. The assumption that the measure of performance is to minimize the expected cost dictates that the XYZ firm chooses to investigate the process as being out of control.

2. *Opportunity cost under uncertainty.* The same a priori analysis may be performed using an opportunity-cost table as in Exhibit 6.16. The opportunity

Exhibit 6.16
Opportunity-Cost Table

Decisions	States of Nature				Expected Opportunity Costs	Computation
	$s_1 = .01$	$s_2 = .05$	$s_3 = .10$	$s_4 = .15$		
a_1	$ 0	$ 4	$ 24	$ 44	$ 10	(4x.2)+(24x.2)+ (44x.1)
a_2	$ 12	$ 0	$ 0	$ 0	$ 6	(16x.5)+(16x.2)+ (16x.2)+(16x.1)
A Priori Probabilities	.5	.2	.2	.1		

cost for a given action under a given state of nature is equal to the cost of that action minus the cost of the action that would be the best possible for that state of nature. For example, for $s_1 = 0.01$ defective, the opportunity loss is 0 ($4 − $4) for a_1 and 12 ($16 − $4) for a_2.

The expected opportunity loss based on the a priori probabilities are also computed in Exhibit 6.16. Again, the results show that the XYZ firm should investigate the process as being out of control.

A Posteriori Analysis. The a priori analysis was based on past information. New evidence on the proportion of deviations dictates that a posteriori analysis be performed. Assuming that the cost of new information is less than the expected value of perfect information, the a posteriori analysis proceeds as follows:

1. Assume that a new sample is taken from the process showing that the deviation $r = 0$. The conditional probabilities are the following:

$\bar{P}(r/s_1) = 0.818$

$\bar{P}(r/s_2) = 0.358$

$\bar{P}(r/s_3) = 0.122$

$\bar{P}(r/s_4) = 0.039$

2. Based on the new information provided by the conditional probabilities, compute the a posteriori probabilities of the states of nature on the basis of Bayes's theorem.

$$P(s_1/r) = \frac{P(s_1) \times P(r/s_1)}{\sum\limits_{j=1}^{n} P(s_j \times P(r/s_j)}$$

where $P(s_1/r)$ is the probability of the state of nature s_1, given the new evidence r, and s_j is the state of nature j. The computation of the a posteriori probabilities is shown in Exhibit 6.17.

Exhibit 6.17
A Posteriori Probabilities

States of Nature	A Priori Probabilities	Conditional Probabilities P (r/s_i)	Marginal Probabilities P $(s_i)P(r/s_i)$	A Posteriori Probabilities P(s_i/r)	
s_1	.5	.818	.4090	.4090/.5089 =	.804
s_2	.2	.358	.0716	.0716/.5089 =	.141
s_3	.2	.122	.0244	.0244/.5089 =	.048
s_4	.1	.039	.0039	.0039/.5089 =	.0007
	1.0		.5089		1.0000

Exhibit 6.18
A Posteriori Analysis

Decisions	States of Nature				Expected Cost of Each Action	Computation
	$s_1 = .01$ defective	$s_2 = .05$ defective	$s_3 = .10$ defective	$s_4 = .15$ defective		
a_1	$ 4	$ 20	$ 40	$ 60	$ 8.376	(.804x4)+(.141x20)+ (.048x40+(.007x60)
a_2	$ 16	$ 16	$ 16	$ 16	$ 16.000	(.804x16)+(.141x16)+ (.048x16)+(.007x16)
A Posteriori Probabilities	.804	.141	.048	.007		

3. Based on the a posteriori probabilities, compute the expected cost for each action. The results are shown in Exhibit 6.18. Again, the decision should be to investigate the process as being out of control.

CONCLUSION

This chapter has elaborated on various models that can be used as a decision support system by managers deciding which variances to investigate. These models included the traditional solutions with their emphasis on materiality significance, the statistical solutions with their emphasis on statistical significance, the classical statistical solutions with their emphasis on control charts as decision aids, and the decision-theory solutions with their emphasis on Bayesian techniques. Although these techniques could prove useful in practical settings, they do not seem to have been widely adopted yet. The reasons for this lack of enthusiasm need to be determined and researched, but even some academicians express doubts about the models:

> Researchers continue to explore the possibility of finding a mathematical way of stating whether a variance between planned and actual cost is or is not significant. . . . The differences between the data on the overall costs of a department that are measured once a month are so great that a few if any managers believe that statistical techniques in the latter case are worth the effort to calculate them. They prefer either to establish control limits by judgement or to run down the report item by item and determine without any numerical calculation, whether a difference between planned and actual costs is worthy of investigation. . . . Attempts to be even more sophisticated and to apply Bayesian probability theory or dynamic programming to the control chart idea do not strike me as being very promising.[12]

NOTES

1. This material is adapted from an example from J. K. Shank and N. C. Churchill, "Variance Analysis: A Management-Oriented Approach," *Accounting Review* (October 1977), pp. 950–957.

2. Ibid., p. 953.

3. Robert S. Kaplan, *Advanced Management Accounting* (Englewood Cliffs, N.J.: Prentice-Hall, 1982), p. 324.

4. William Hays, *Statistics* (New York: Holt, Rinehart and Winston, 1963), p. 188.

5. Dale H. Besterfield, *Quality Control* (Englewood Cliffs, N.J.: Prentice-Hall, 1979) p. 76.

6. Ibid., p. 77.

7. Ibid., pp. 77–78.

8. Ibid., pp. 78–79.

9. Ibid., p. 79.

10. This is based on the normal approximation to the binomial probability law. It assumes that the probability of Type II error is to be 5 percent and the allowable Type I error is set by a 3 sigma limit.

11. Mohammed Onsi, "Quantitative Models for Accounting Control," *Accounting Review* (April 1967), p. 324.

12. R. N. Anthony, "Some Fruitful Directions for Research in Management Accounting," in N. Dopuch and L. Revsine, eds., *Accounting Research, 1960–1970: A Critical Evaluation* (Champaign, Ill.: Center for International Education and Research in Accounting, University of Illinois, 1973).

REFERENCES

Bierman, Harold Jr., Lawrence E. Fouraker, and Robert K. Jaedicke. "A Use of Probability and Statistics in Performance Evaluation." *Accounting Review* (July 1961), pp. 409–417.

Buzby, Stephen L. "Extending the Applicability of Probabilistic Management Planning and Control Models." *Accounting Review* (January 1974), pp. 42–49.

Cuh, F. "Controlled Cost: An Operational Concept and Statistical Approach to Standard Costing." *Accounting Review* (January 1968), pp. 123–132.

Demski, J. "Optimizing the Search for Cost Deviation Sources." *Management Science* (April 1970), pp. 486–494.

Jacobs, Fredric. "When and How to Use Statistical Cost Variance." *Cost and Management* (January–February 1983), pp. 26–32.

Kaplan, R. S. "Optimal Investigation Strategies with Imperfect Information." *Journal of Accounting Research* (Spring 1969), pp. 32–43.

———. "The Significance of Investigation of Cost Variances: Survey and Extensions." *Journal of Accounting Research* (Autumn 1975), pp. 311–337.

Onsi, Mohammed. "Quantitative Models for Accounting Control." *Accounting Review* (April 1967), pp. 321–330.

Savage, I. Richard. "Probability Inequalities of the Chebyschev Type." *Journal of Research of the National Bureau of Standards—Bureau of Mathematics and Mathematical Physics* (July–September 1961), pp. 211–222.

Zannetos, Zenon S. "Standard Cost as a First Step to Probabilistic Control: A Theoretical Justification." *Accounting Review* (April 1964), pp. 269–304.

APPENDIX—The Significance and Investigation of Cost Variances: Survey and Extensions

ROBERT S. KAPLAN*

1. *Introduction*

Standard cost systems can produce as many variances each period as there are accounts for which standards are set, since actual costs for a period will rarely equal the standard or budgeted cost for any process worth controlling.[1] Nevertheless, no one seriously advocates taking action and investigating every cost variance that occurs each period. Managers recognize that many variances are insignificant and caused by random, noncontrollable factors. Since any investigation will involve a certain expenditure of effort and funds, managers will attempt to take action on only the most significant and correctible variances. An investigation should only be undertaken if the benefits expected from the investigation exceed the costs of searching for and correcting the source of the cost variance.

Many articles have appeared in statistical and accounting journals that directly deal with determining whether a process is in or out of control and, hence, whether it is worthwhile to intervene in the process. Despite the widespread use of quality control techniques in industry, however, the application of these ideas in actual standard cost accounting settings can generously be characterized as minimal. For example, in 1968, Koehler reported that "in some general inquiry from some prominent corporations, I was unable to find a single use of statistical procedures for variance control."[2] He attributes this paucity of applications not to the inherent

* Professor, Carnegie-Mellon University. Many helpful comments on an earlier draft were received from Professors Nicholas Dopuch, Thomas Dyckman, Robert Magee, and Roman Weil. The opinions and interpretations still remaining in this paper are solely the author's responsibility.

[1] I am excluding the budgeting of expirations of accrued costs such as depreciation or prepaid expenses which should equal planned levels in each period. These expenses represent allocations of prior expenditures and, hence, are not interesting to control on an item-by-item basis each period.

[2] Koehler (1968): 35.

inapplicability of such procedures but to "the fact that accountants have not recognized a conceptual distinction between a significant and an insignificant variance."[3] Koehler proceeds to advocate the use of a simple testing procedure which I will consider later in the paper.

In contrast to Koehler's view, that the fault lies with the lack of formal statistical training among practicing accountants, other observers conclude that statistical procedures are rarely used in practice because the procedures themselves are inappropriate for assessing the significance of accounting variances. For example, Anthony, in a review article on management accounting observed that "researchers continue to explore the possibility of finding a mathematical way of stating whether a variance between planned and actual cost is or is not significant."[4] He concludes, though, that

> The differences between the data on a production process that is repeated several times a day and data on the overall costs of a department that are measured once a month are so great that few if any managers believe that statistical techniques in the latter case are worth the effort to calculate them. They prefer either to establish control limits by judgment or to run down the report item by item and determine, without any numerical calculation, whether a difference between planned and actual costs is worth investigation.[5]

He also states that "attempts to be even more sophisticated and to apply Bayesian probability theory or dynamic programming to the control chart idea do not strike me as being very promising."[6]

The final judgment on the appropriateness of formal statistical and mathematical models for cost variance analysis must be based on empirical studies. To date little such evidence is available. There are reasons to believe, however, that some form of screening model would be beneficial to managers by eliminating the need for them to examine extensive variance reports item by item in order to detect a significant variance. A formal screening model could also scan detailed variance reports more efficiently than a manager, thereby permitting a more disaggregate collection of costs. Moreover, there is extensive evidence in the psychological literature[7] that persons consistently underestimate the importance of

---

[3] *Ibid.*, p. 35.

[4] Anthony (1973): 52.

[5] *Ibid.*, p. 52.

[6] *Ibid.*, p. 51.

[7] For surveys of this literature, see Edwards (1968) and Slovic and Lichtenstein (1971). The evidence seems very strong that persons do not process sample evidence very well in complex environments. For example, Slovic and Lichtenstein conclude (p. 714), "[Man as an] intuitive statistician appears to be quite confused by the conceptual demands of probabilistic inference tasks. He seems capable of little more than revising his response in the right direction upon receipt of a new item of information (and the inertia effect is evidence that he is not always successful in doing even this)." Also (p. 724), "We find that judges have a very difficult time weighting and combining information, be it probabilistic or deterministic in nature. To reduce cognitive strain, they resort to simplified decision strategies many of which lead them to ignore or misuse relevant information."

sample evidence in forming probability judgments about events. In other words, a manager with strong prior beliefs that everything is all right with a given process will interpret sizable variances as still being consistent with an in-control situation, whereas a statistical model would clearly signal a low probability that such large deviations could arise from an in-control situation. A statistical model may also indicate that an occasional large variance is consistent with fluctuation that has occurred in the past so that immediate action may not be warranted.

The purpose of this paper is to provide a comprehensive survey of techniques that are potentially useful for assessing the significance of cost variances. A simple taxonomy of various approaches will be described which should help to classify the basic assumptions and purpose of each type of proposed procedure. Important techniques commonly used in industrial quality control will be briefly surveyed and related to proposals made in the accounting literature. Several widely referenced articles in the accounting literature will be reviewed and a number of fundamental errors and hidden assumptions in some of these papers will be noted. Finally, I will suggest extensions and describe a model, new to the accounting literature, that may eventually prove useful for aiding the variance investigation decision.

Before embarking on this survey, it is useful to indicate some aspects of the variance investigation decision I will *not* be considering. First, since I will deal only with a single process and a single variance reported from this process, then models which are designed to identify or isolate the most important variances from a large set [see Lev (1969)] will not be treated. I will not be involved with the actual investigation process [Demski (1970)] and methods for aggregating variances to enhance the reporting and investigation process [Ronen (1974)]. As an aside, Demski (1970), classifies five separate sources of cost deviations and after assuming that we are able to estimate the time to investigate each source as well as the prior probability that the deviation came from each source, describes an algorithm which will minimize the expected time until the source is uncovered. In a more general setting, DeGroot (1970) describes an algorithm when there is a cost, c_i, of investigating each source as well as a probability, α_i, of not detecting the cause even when investigating the true source of the deviation (i.e., imperfect investigation).[8]

I will also deal only briefly with relating the significance of the accounting variance to possible changes in decision models.[9] I am assuming that the significant variances being considered here are, for the most part, correctible and hence should not require changes in the firm's decisions but this point will be mentioned again in Section 6B.

---

[8] DeGroot (1970): 423–29; and Kadane (1971).

[9] This topic is developed in Dopuch, Birnberg, and Demski (1967) and Demski (1967).

2. *A Taxonomy of Variance Investigation Models*

All the papers and models that will be reviewed in this paper can be classified along two dimensions. The first dichotomy is whether the investigation decision is made on the basis of a single observation or whether some past sequence of observations, including the most recent one, is considered in the decision. I refer to this distinction as single-period versus multi-period models. An example of a single-period model is a control chart approach in which a variance is investigated if it falls outside a pre-specified limit, e.g., 2σ or 3σ from the expected value. An example of a multi-period approach occurs if all the most recent observations are used to estimate the current mean of the process to determine whether the process is within its control limits. The second dichotomy is whether or not the model explicitly includes the expected costs and benefits of the investigation in determining when to investigate a variance. A simple control chart or hypothesis test with preset (and arbitrary) levels of a Type I error is an example of a model which does not explicitly include decision relevant costs in the analysis. Economically designed control charts, however, in which control limits are set as a function of the cost of an investigation as well as the cost of making Type I and Type II errors would be an example of a model that included relevant costs in the analysis. Models which use statistical decision theory approaches such as Duvall (1967), Kaplan (1969), and Dyckman (1969) are other examples of this type of model.

Thus, we may classify the papers on the variance investigation decision into a 2×2 table as shown below. An additional sub-classification is useful in the lower right-hand category of multi-period decision theory models.

A Taxonomy of Deviation Investigation Models

	Costs and Benefits of Investigation not Considered	Costs and Benefits of Investigation Considered
Single-Period	Zannetos (1964)	Duncan (1956)
	Juers (1967), Koehler (1968)	Bierman, Fouraker, and
	Luh (1968), Probst (1971)	Jaedicke (1961)
	Buzby (1974)	
Multi-Period	Cumulative-Sum Chart as in Page	Duvall (1967)
	(1954). Also	Kaplan (1969)
	Barnard (1959)	Dyckman (1969)
	Chernoff and Zacks (1964)	Bather (1963)

Some models, such as Kaplan (1969) and Dyckman (1969), assume that the process being controlled can only be in a discrete set of states. Typically, only two states are assumed (in control and out of control) but it is also possible to use a finer classification in which discrete amounts of "out-of-controlness" are allowed. In fact, models such as Duvall (1967) and Bather (1963) allow the mean of the process to vary continuously so that there is an infinite set of states for the process. This leads to slightly different procedures to estimate the current state of the process and, hence, it is useful to introduce this sub-classification of discrete versus continuous process states. In the remainder of the paper, we analyze each compartment in the table, including the sub-classification just described, to indicate the assumptions, strengths, and weaknesses of the proposed models.

3. Decision Models Based on a Single Observation; No Costs of Investigation or Misclassification

In the simplest control formulation, the objective is to determine whether a shift in the probability distribution of the process generating outputs has occurred. Usually, the shift is identified with a change in the location parameter (e.g., the mean) of the distribution though it is, of course, possible to test for any shift in the distribution [see Luh (1968)]. No costs of misclassification are considered and information from previous observations on the process is ignored. The classic example of such a procedure is the simple $\bar{x}$ chart suggested by Shewhart (1931) and widely used in industry. With this procedure, a target mean is established and a standard deviation, σ, is estimated for the process when it is in control. Control limits are typically set so that the probability of an in-control process with normally distributed outcomes producing a signal beyond these limits (a Type I error) is very small (e.g., .01 or .002). In practice, Shewhart charts are modified on an ad hoc basis to detect a run of observations in excess of 1σ or 2σ, but there is no generally accepted modification to the classic Shewhart control chart.

Many articles in the accounting literature are essentially variations of a simple Shewhart chart in which a distribution is assumed under the null hypothesis that the process is in control. An investigation is signaled when the probability that any single observation could have come from this in-control distribution falls below a given level, usually assumed to be .05. For example, the papers by Buzby (1974), Juers (1967), Koehler (1968), Luh (1968), Probst (1971), and Zannetos (1964) are all of this type. Some of these papers [Buzby (1974), Zannetos (1964)] also suggest the use of Chebyschev's inequality to compute the probability of an extreme observation if one does not believe that observations from the in-control distribution are normally distributed (or some other parametric form).

Luh's paper is at a much more disaggregate form of analysis from any of the other papers. Rather than dealing with the total or average cost of a period, he assumes that we will measure the components of actual cost (usage and rate; material and labor) of every item that is produced in a period. The distribution of outcomes from each cost component is then compared with the assumed in-control distribution via a goodness-of-fit test (Kolmogorov-Smirnov or Chi-squared) to see if a significant shift in the distribution has occurred. Thus, Luh is able to detect not only shifts in the mean of the distribution but also shifts in the shape or scale of the distribution. This test will, therefore, signal an investigation much more often than a system which only monitors potential shifts in the mean. In addition, Luh's system requires the collection of far more detailed information than is typically required for traditional control chart-like systems so that the cost of operating this procedure may become a significant factor, especially relative to the incremental benefits the procedure might offer.

To summarize, procedures described in the papers referenced in this section only control for the distribution of outcomes when the process is in control. They test for significant departures from this null distribution based on a single-period's observation. Previous observations are not aggregated together when the statistical test is performed, and no costs of investigation or of failing to correct an out-of-control process are explicitly considered.

4. Decision Models Based on Multiple Observations; No Costs of Investigation or Misclassification

The procedures described in the previous section treat successive observations from the same process as being independent samples. No attempt is made to combine the information from previous observations with the current observation to reach a statistical conclusion as to whether the process is currently in control. These procedures, therefore, ignore a lot of the potentially useful information available from a systematic examination of trends. The use of prior observations should enable a mean shift to be detected much earlier than by successively testing single observations at a low α (probability of Type I error) risk.

The cumulative sum (cusum) procedure, introduced by Page (1954), is the most common procedure that uses previous observations for detecting a shift in the mean of a process. With this procedure, the target mean, μ, is subtracted from the current observation, x_r, and a series of partial sums formed, S_r, where

$$S_r = \sum_{i=1}^{r} (x_i - \mu).$$

Under the null hypothesis, these partial sums should follow a random walk with zero mean. But if a shift in the mean has occurred (away from μ), the partial sums will start to develop a positive or negative drift. While an analytic test to detect a drift is not hard to develop, many writers advocate a graphical approach for the cusum technique. Successive partial sums, $S_r = S_{r-1} + x_r - \mu$, are plotted ($S_r$ on the vertical axis, r along the horizontal axis) and a V-mask applied from the most recent observation (see figure 1). If any previous cumulative sum (S_i, $i = 1, \cdots ,$ $r - 1$) is covered by the V-mask, a significant shift in the mean is deemed to have occurred. Cusum charts can be made sensitive to small changes in the mean of a process since these will cause the trajectory of cumulative

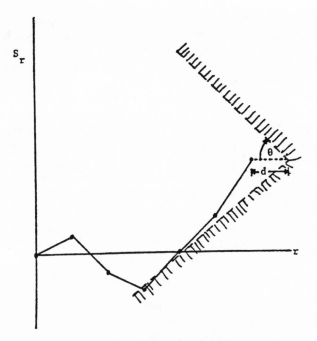

FIG. 1.- Cumulative sum procedure.

sums to drift away from previous observations until one limb of the V-mask cuts across a prior point to signal an out-of-control condition.

The two design parameters of a cusum V-mask are the offset distance, d, and the angle of the mask, θ. These can be set based on (1) an assumed shift in the mean of the process of μ, (2) the average run length in control before a false investigate signal is generated, and (3) the average run length out of control (mean shift of μ) before an investigate signal is given [see Ewan and Kemp (1960) and Goldsmith and Whitfield (1961)]. In practice, these parameters are frequently set by experimenting with different values for d and θ on charts derived from past data from the process being controlled until the right incidence of false and true signals is achieved.

A more formal model of a multi-period nonstationary process is described by Barnard (1959) who formulates the control problem as one of esti-mation rather than hypothesis testing. In order to use all the past data to estimate the current mean of the process, a specific stochastic process of how mean shifts occur needs to be formulated. Barnard assumes that shifts or jumps in the mean occur according to a Poisson process. Con-ditional on a jump occurring, the amount of the jump is assumed to be a normally distributed random variable with a zero mean and known vari-ance. From this process, Barnard derives an expression for a mean likeli-hood estimator (the maximum likelihood estimator would be very difficult to estimate) which is a weighted mean of recent observations with the weights decreasing over time and decreasing if there is a large jump between successive observations. Barnard also suggests an approximate graphical procedure to obtain an estimate of the current mean of the process. Perhaps the most important message from Barnard's paper is to realize that when we wish to aggregate prior observations to estimate or test the current mean of the process, we need to specify a formal stochastic model of how changes in the mean occur. For the nonstationary processes we are considering in this paper, simple unweighted aggregations of past data, such as sample means and variances, will not be good estimates of the current parameters of the process. We will return to this point later when discussing some of the proposals made in the accounting literature.

Other papers in the statistical literature have also dealt with estimating the change in mean of a noisy process. For example, Chernoff and Zacks (1964), Hinich and Farley (1966), and Farley and Hinich (1970) treat a model in which the output of the process is given by

$$x(t) = \theta(t) + n(t)$$

where $n(t)$ is Gaussian distributed noise with zero mean and known covariance function.[10] The mean process, $\theta(t)$, is assumed to undergo discrete shifts according to a Poisson distributed process. These papers assume that the total observation time is less than the mean time between jumps so that the possibility of two or more jumps in the observed interval can be ignored. Efficient estimators of the mean process, $\theta(t)$, are developed as a function of the sequence of observations. These papers and Barnard's can be used to develop an estimator of the current mean of a noisy nonstationary process. Within a standard cost accounting context, such an estimate would correspond to the current level of average cost for the process being controlled. Presumably, if this current level were sufficiently far away from the standard level, an investigation would be signaled. Note, however, that neither the cost of an investigation nor the value of waiting for additional sample information is explicitly included in this analysis.

To date, no article in the accounting literature has advocated the use of the cusum or the other sophisticated statistical techniques described in this section which make use of the entire history of observations to signal an out-of-control situation. Such procedures do represent an improvement over simple control charts and successive hypothesis tests on single observations since they specifically model the stochastic dependence of successive observations. Nevertheless, they are still an incomplete representation of the problem since they do not include the cost and benefit structure of the investigation decision.

---

[10] For the processes discussed in this paper, we have assumed that successive observations are statistically independent so that the covariance matrix would be diagonal.

5. *Decision Models Based on a Single Observation; Cost of Investigation and Misclassification Included*

A third category of papers generalizes the simple hypothesis testing ideas described first to include the cost of investigation and the potential benefit to be achieved from an investigation. In the quality control literature, Duncan (1956) devised a scheme for the economic design of $\bar{x}$ charts. Duncan's model assumed the following types of benefits and costs: (i) Income when the process is in control, (ii) Income when the process is out of control, (iii) Cost of looking for a cause when none exists, (iv) Cost of looking for a cause when one exists, and (v) Cost of charting. With these costs and assuming a specific alternative hypothesis (i.e., a mean shift of known magnitude) Duncan computed control limits that approximately maximized average income per period. Duncan's analysis was subsequently extended by Goel, Jain, and Wu (1968) and Gibra (1971). Note that even though their approaches minimized costs or maximized income over extended periods of time, the decision to investigate is still based on whether the most recent observation falls outside the control limits. Thus, information from previous observations is not used in the investigation decision.

In the accounting literature, Bierman, Fouraker, and Jaedicke (BFJ) (1961) were the first to introduce the costs and benefits of an investigation into the investigation decision. Their paper treated a single-period model and assumed, as did the papers listed in section 3, that management could specify the distribution of outcomes when the process is in control. Given a particular observation, the probability, p, that this observation came from the null (in-control) distribution was computed. With an investigation cost of C and a potential benefit from correcting an out-of-control situation of L, an investigation was signaled if $C < (1 - p)L$. One problem with this formulation is the difficulty of estimating or even interpreting L. BFJ do not devote much discussion to estimating L but in a footnote explain, "In situations where the inefficiency will be repeated, L should be defined as the present value of the costs that will be incurred in the future if an investigation is not made now."[11] Unfortunately, these future cost savings are not easy to estimate. In situations where the inefficiency will be repeated, one would have opportunities in the future to correct the process. Therefore, the discounted future costs assuming no future investigation is an overestimate of L. But L will not equal the one-period costs, assuming an investigation occurs next period, since a good realization may occur next period even when operating somewhat inefficiently so that no investigation would be signaled. Therefore, the benefit, L, depends upon future actions, and models which do not specifically include the consequences of future actions will have a hard time defining, much less estimating, what is the benefit from current actions. BFJ could reply that they are dealing with one-period nonrepetitive situations so

---

[11] Bierman, Fouraker, and Jaedicke (1961), footnote 1, pp. 414–15.

that future costs and actions are not relevant. Such situations do occur in practice. But some of the papers to be discussed in the next section purport to treat multi-period aspects and still fail to deal with this crucial aspect of estimating the incremental benefits from an investigation now rather than in future periods.

Dyckman[12] has criticized the BFJ model for basing the investigation decision on only the most recent observation, thereby ignoring prior information—either sample information from previous periods or subjectively determined priors. To the extent that the outputs from the process are believed to be dependent random variables from a stochastic process, then a reasonable decision should make use of prior observations as well as the most recent one. We turn now to a discussion of such procedures.

6. Discrete State Decision Models with Multiple Observations; Cost of Investigation and Misclassification Included

CONTROL CHARTS

We have already described cusum charts which can signal an investigation based on the relation of the current observation with all prior observations. In a manner analogous to that done by Duncan for $\bar{x}$ charts, Taylor (1968) and Goel and Wu (1973) develop procedures to design cusum charts that minimize long-run average cost. Both papers assume a cost structure similar to Duncan's and a process in which a single shift in the process mean of known magnitude occurs at a random time. Economically determined values of d, the V-mask offset distance, and θ, the angle of the V-mask, are determined based on the magnitude of the shift, the parameters of the distribution of time the process remains in control, the investigation costs, and the costs of operating in or out of control. The optimal design of control charts, however, is optimal in only a special sense. In effect, the form of the optimal policy is predetermined by the characteristics of the control chart, and only the parameters of the control chart are optimized. It is analogous to finding the optimal (s, S) policy in an inventory problem even though an (s, S) policy is not the globally optimal one.

Traditional control charts tend to be non-Bayesian in that no prior information about in- or out-of-control probabilities is combined with sample evidence. An exception is provided by Girshick and Rubin (1952) who considered a two-state model (in and out of control) with a Markov chain describing transitions between the two states in successive periods. Assuming a constant cost of investigation and a constant cost per period for operating out of control, an optimal investigation policy was determined that minimized long-run average cost.

---

[12] See "A Correction," pp. 114–15 in Ozan and Dyckman (1971).

KAPLAN'S MODEL

Kaplan (1969) adapted the Girshick and Rubin procedure for the accounting variance investigation decision. Rather than having to derive a cost from operating out of control, Kaplan used the actual costs when operating in or out of control to derive optimal policies. Thus, a decision to delay investigating for one period incurred the risk of operating one more period out of control, that is, obtaining a cost realization from the higher cost, out-of-control distribution, rather than from lower cost, in-control distribution. Balanced against this risk was the certain cost of an investigation which might find that the system was still in control. Note that the loss function in the accounting variance setting arises directly from the nature of the problem. In the control chart approach, the cost of operating in or out of control must be imputed. In the accounting setting, the incremental costs of operating out of control arise directly from the higher costs that accrue when operating away from standard. Thus the cost variance decision may be more amenable to an economically based decision theory treatment. Dynamic programming was used to compute optimal policies that minimized discounted future costs. Discounted future cost was used as the criterion, rather than long-run average cost as used by Girshick and Rubin, because the time interval between successive accounting reports made the time value of money a relevant consideration. But since the computation of optimal policies in this situation is not very sensitive to the assumed discount rate, the long-run average cost criterion could be achieved simply by using a discount factor of unity (or arbitrarily close to unity) and adopting the policy to which the n-period optimal policy converges.

A key feature of the two-state Markov model used by Girshick and Rubin and by Kaplan is that all the relevant information from the prior observations, since the last investigation was made, could be summarized by a single state variable—the probability that the system is currently operating in control. This variable is updated after each observation via Bayes' theorem to incorporate information from the most recent observation. Assuming a specific form for the transition matrix—in this case geometric distribution for the time until the system goes out of control—provides a tremendous reduction in the amount of information that must be stored about previous realizations of the process. One could even relax the geometric distribution assumption of constant probability of going out of control without a great increase in the complexity of the procedure. Of course, this would require more information about the specific probabilities of going out of control as a function of time. In general, one could define g_k as the probability that, in period k, the system will remain in control given that it was in control at the start of the period. For the geometric distribution, $g_k = g$ for $k = 1, 2, \cdots$, with an arbitrary distribution for going out of control, the discrete state variable k would be appended to the state description and the optimization done with respect to this state variable as well as the one summarizing the current probability that the system is in control. The main difference would be that the operator $\tau_x q^{13}$ which updates the probability, q, of being in control after receiving an observation x would now become a function of k—the number of periods since the last investigation; i.e.,

$$\tau_{x;k} q = g_k[1 + \lambda(x)(1 - q)/q]^{-1}$$

where $\lambda(x) = f_2(x)/f_1(x)$ is the likelihood ratio of the out-of-control distribution to the in-control distribution. The functional equation for $C_n(q)$ then becomes one for $C_n(q; k)$, where $C_n(q; k)$ is the minimum expected discounted cost with present estimate of q of being in control and k periods since the last investigation. The steady state equation for $C_n(q; k)$ is given by

$$C(q; k) = \min \{K + \int [x + \alpha C(\tau_{x;0} g_0; 1)] f_{g_0}(x) \, dx;$$
$$\int [x + \alpha C(\tau_{x;k} q; k + 1)] f_q(x) \, dx\}$$

where K is the cost of the investigation, α is the discount rate and $f_q(x)$ $= q f_1(x) + (1 - q) f_2(x)$, a weighted sum of the in-control and out-of-control density functions.

The first set of terms (before the semi-colon) is the current and expected future costs when an investigation is made now. The second set represents the expected costs when no investigation is made now. The derivation of the functional equation is along the lines developed in Kaplan (1969). Roughly speaking, the density function $f_q(x)$ gives the probability of getting an observation x when q is the probability the observation comes from the in-control density function. After an investigation, the system is reset so that there is a probability g_0 (perhaps equal to 1) that the system will remain in control for one full period after an investigation has taken place. This is why the probability is g_0 that the observation immediately after an investigation comes from the in-control distribution. To solve the equation, some reasonable upper bound on k must be assumed. Perhaps the value such that the a priori probability is .95 or .99 that the system will be out of control after that number of periods is a reasonable upper bound for k.

The infinite period function equation serves as a convenient approximation to a long but unspecified planning horizon. In fact, the infinite period optimal policy is typically very similar to the optimal policy with only 10 or 15 periods remaining. In any case, the infinite period optimal policy is computed as the limit of the finite horizon optimal policies so that one has the information to use the policy optimal for whatever planning horizon one thinks is appropriate.

There are at least two other assumptions that may limit the applicability of this approach. One is the heroic simplification of the process to

---

[13] See pp. 34–35 in Kaplan (1969).

a two-state system, in control and out of control, with sudden transitions between the states. While we have seen that this model is frequently used in the quality control literature, the process by which a controllable cost process suddenly moves from in control to out of control is rather difficult to articulate. Intuitively it is more appealing to consider a process that gradually drifts away from standards through an evolutionary process of neglect and lack of proper supervision. In such a case, the forced dichotomy between in control and out of control may be an unrealistic aggregation of reality. One solution is to expand the number of states to allow for varying degrees of out of controlness. For example we might allow S states ($S = 5$ or 10, say) with state 1 representing perfectly in control, state 2 representing slight deterioration, and state S being well out of control. Each state would be associated with a different distribution of cost outcomes, with the average cost increasing from state 1 to state S. For each state s in S, we would have a density function $f_s(x)$ of outcomes arising from a process while in state s. We could then define an $S \times S$ Markov matrix, P, describing how one-period transitions are made from state to state. If the process is expected to just deteriorate over time, P would be an upper block triangular matrix with no entries below the main diagonal. Unfortunately, the state space would require $S - 1$ states ($q_1, q_2, \cdots,$ q_{S-1}) with q_i being the current probability that the system is in state i.[14] Given an observation, x, the posterior probabilities, $q_i^*(x)$, that the system was in state i when observation x was produced could be computed from

$$q_i^*(x) = \frac{f_i(x)q_i}{\sum_{j=1}^{S} f_j(x)q_j}.$$

These posterior probabilities $\mathbf{q}^* = (q_1^*(x), \cdots, q_S^*(x))$ would then be multiplied by the transition matrix P to yield the q_i's for the system in the next period. While this procedure is not difficult to describe, optimal policies may become difficult to compute for S larger than 4 or 5.

An extended version of such a model was treated by Ross (1971). He assumed that a process could be in a countable number of states i, ($i = 0,$ $1, 2, \cdots$), with quality a function of the state. He assumed that costs of production, inspecting, and revision were all functions of the current state, i. A Markov chain described the movement from state to state of the process for each transition. The state variables of the system consisted of the probability vector $\mathbf{q} = (q_0, q_1, \cdots)$ where q_i is the current probability that the system is in state i. Three actions are possible—produce without inspection, produce with inspection (to learn the current state), and revise the process, to state 0. For this very general formulation, Ross was able

---

[14] Since the q_i's must sum to one, we only need to explicitly consider $S - 1$ probabilities. The omitted probability is determined implicitly by subtracting the sum of the $S - 1$ probabilities from 1.

to obtain only the most general results. He determined that the steady state optimality function $V(\mathbf{q})$ is concave in $\mathbf{q}$ and that the inspection and revision regions are convex. Some more specific results are obtained for a two-state process (good and bad) in which he demonstrated an example for which the "produce without inspection" region could consist of two disjoint regions, a region being defined by those values of q, the probability that the system is in the good state at the start of the period, for which a given action is optimal ($0 \leq q \leq 1$).

In addition to the two-state limitation of Kaplan's model, the model is also limited by the assumption that the process can always be returned to the in-control distribution. The decision model is based on the assumption that if an out-of-control situation is discovered, the process can be corrected so that future costs will likely arise from the in-control cost density function, $f_1(x)$. But, occasionally, fundamental shifts in the process may occur that are not reversible even after discovery. Prices may have risen or operating procedures developed which may be impossible or at best difficult to reverse. Therefore, an investigation undertaken in anticipation of realizing the benefits from a restoration to the historical standard cost may never realize these benefits and, hence, the benefits expected from the investigation will have been overestimated. This feature represents one of the fundamental differences between the traditional quality control setting for which most of the described techniques have been developed and the cost variance setting considered in this paper. The physical processes being monitored in the quality control environment can almost always be reset from an out-of-control situation to the desired setting once such a situation is discovered. The benefits from investigating these processes can, therefore, be measured by the almost certain return to the in-control state.

The feature of the cost variance setting in which the previous standard may no longer be attainable seems difficult to capture in a simple practical model. One could always define a probability that an out-of-control situation is not correctible but then one would have to be concerned with controllable and noncontrollable deviations from the new, but still not completely known, standard and the problem rapidly escalates. About the only ameliorating factor here is that there is some benefit in learning about a fundamental shift in the cost or technology of a process. Such a shift may affect the firm's decision model[15] and thereby effect some savings, though not as much as had been anticipated at the time the investigation decision was made. In a similar vein, the model has difficulty capturing the benefits that may accrue from investigating a below-average cost. If a lower than expected cost performance can be made permanent by resetting the cost standard to adjust to the more efficient process, then a long-term benefit can be achieved. This benefit is ignored in the model which as-

---

[15] See Dopuch, Birnberg, and Demski (1967) and Demski (1967).

sumes that the process is always returned to its original cost standard. Also, the model in its present formulation does not adequately handle problems with below-average costs due to use of lower-quality materials or labor. It always assumes that lower cost is better than higher cost, i.e., it assumes the quality of output remains constant.

The above situations describe one set of reasons why the system may not always be returned to the in-control state after an investigation has occurred. It is also possible to consider the situation in which the investigation fails to detect an out-of-control situation when one exists. This possibility is not considered in Kaplan's model but an extension to allow for imperfect investigations will be discussed shortly. Other extensions to the basic model are discussed in Kaplan (1969). These extensions allow (1) for a delay between the time the investigation decision is made and the time the system is restored to the in-control state, (2) the system to be self-correcting, and (3) the cost of investigation to be a function of the state the system is actually in.

DYCKMAN'S MODEL

Dyckman (1969) dealt with a model very similar to Kaplan's except that the multi-period cost structure was suppressed. The stochastic process with a Markov chain describing transitions between an in-control state and out-of-control state was used with Bayesian updating of the probability of being in either state after each observation from the process. Thus the limitations of the two-state process, just described, apply to this model too.

As in the single-period BFJ model, though, Dyckman assumes a constant saving, L, from investigating an out-of-control situation. Dyckman does not offer much more guidance as to the interpretation or estimation of L. He calls it the "present value of the savings obtainable from an investigation when the activity is out of control," then notes that "where a corrective action is not forever binding, the calculation of L needs to be adjusted to reflect the possibility of future out-of-control periods" and then concludes that "the precise determination of the savings for each future period is not an easy matter."[16]

The difficulty, of course, arises because Dyckman suppresses the sequential decision-making nature of the problem and therefore cannot evaluate the benefits from delaying the investigation for another period when more sample evidence may be obtained. Difficulties with interpreting what L represents, similar to those expressed here, were raised by Li (1970) who observes that "dynamic programming is more appropriate to use under this situation."[17] Dyckman's reply concurs with the logic of this suggestion but claims that "the difficulties attendant on solving large and complex real dynamic programming problems can limit the successful

---

[16] Dyckman (1969): 218.
[17] Li (1970): 283.

application of this technique."[18] It is true that dynamic programs are difficult to solve when there are a large number of state variables. But the model treated by Dyckman can be summarized by a single-state variable [see Kaplan (1969)] and dynamic programs with a single-state variable are quite easy to solve. Therefore, computational costs should not be high relative to the benefits from including the effect of future decisions and actions into the analysis.

Dyckman eventually concludes that L should be measured by the savings over the planning horizon which is taken to be the minimum of the average time until the process goes out of control again and the time until standards need to be revised.[19] This does not settle the issue, however, since some problems inherently remain in his nonsequential decision model. For one thing, L must then be a function of n, the number of periods since the process started. If L is the discounted savings over the planning horizon, then as a number of periods pass, there are fewer periods remaining in the planning horizon so the potential savings last for fewer periods. Hence, L must decrease with increasing n. Dyckman extends in Some Extensions, Section A (pp. 228–30) the traditional two-action space (Investigate, Don't Investigate) model by allowing for an exploratory investigation which costs less than a full investigation but has probability h, with $h < 1$, of detecting an out-of-control situation when one exists. This is certainly a worthwhile extension and can easily be incorporated into the dynamic programming framework already developed. There are two outcomes from the exploratory investigation; either an out-of-control situation is discovered or it is not. If the probability that the system is in control is q, then the probability of finding it out of control with the exploratory investigation is $(1 - q)h$. When the process is found to be out of control, it is reset and a new cycle starts. Conversely, the probability that the system is not found to be out of control by the exploratory investigation is $1 - (1 - q)h$. But in this case, the investigation is not a complete failure since we get some new information about the probability that the system is in control. If q was the probability of the system being in control before the unsuccessful exploratory investigation, the posterior probability of being in control can be obtained via Bayes theorem as $q/[1 - h(1 - q)]$ which is greater than q. Therefore, the decision to undertake an exploratory investigation must include not only the potential benefit from cheaply discovering an out-of-control situation but also the expected future benefits to be achieved by an increase in our estimate of the probability of being in control. Formally, if K' is the cost of the limited investigation, the expected infinite horizon future cost from undertaking an exploratory investigation is given by:

$$K' + (1 - q)h \int [x + \alpha C(\tau_x g)] f_\theta(x)\, dx$$
$$+ [1 - (1 - q)h] \int [x + \alpha C(\tau_x q')] f_{q'}(x)\, dx$$

---

[18] Dyckman's reply, in Li (1970): 283.

[19] *Ibid.*; also in Ozan and Dyckman (1971): 98.

with $q' = q/[1 - h(1 - q)]$ and g = one-period probability of going out of control. Dyckman recognizes that the probabilities of being in or out of control should be revised to reflect the exploratory investigation outcome but advises against this if it will raise one of the probabilities.[20] He incorrectly neglects the value of this anticipated revision (in effect the expected value of sample information) in his decision to conduct the exploratory investigation.

For a more general treatment still, we might let the amount of money spent on an investigation be a continuous variable, z, and define a function $h(z)$ as the probability of detecting an out-of-control situation when one exists. Presumably $h(0) = 0$, $\lim_{z \to \infty} h(z) = 1$ and $h(z)$ is a nondecreasing function of z. The decision then becomes one of not only deciding whether to investigate or not but how much to spend on the investigation. If q is the prior probability that the system is in control, an amount z is spent on an investigation and an out-of-control situation is not found, the posterior probability that the system is in control (after the investigation) is

$$q'(z) = q/[1 - h(z)(1 - q)].$$

Therefore, we may formulate the infinite horizon decision problem as:

$$C(q) = \min_{z \geq 0} \{z + (1 - q)h(z) \int [x + \alpha C(\tau_x g)]f_g(x) \, dx$$

$$+ [1 - (1 - q)h(z)] \int [x + \alpha C(\tau_x q')]f_{q'}(x) \, dx\}$$

where q' is a function of z as defined above and setting $z = 0$ with $h(0) = 0$ and $q'(0) = q$ yields the expected cost when no investigation is undertaken.

Returning to Dyckman (1969), in Some Extensions, Section C (pp. 231–33), n consecutive observations are used to develop posterior probabilities about the states of the process. The sample mean, $\bar{x}$, of these n observations is used as a sufficient statistic to summarize these sample results. But the sample mean of a normal process (with known variance) can only be the sufficient statistic of a *stationary* process. That is, the procedure of combining n sample results into a sufficient statistic, $\bar{x}$, is valid only if one assumes that the process is in a given state at the start of the string of observations and *remains* in that state for all n observations. But since we are dealing with a nonstationary process, the sample mean cannot summarize all the information contained in the first n observations.[21] When drawing statistical conclusions from the observations on a process whose mean can shift over time, the order in which the observations occur provides important information.

A subsequent paper by Ozan and Dyckman (1971) expands on Dyckman's model by defining different types of controllable and noncontrollable variances. Some guidance is offered as to how to estimate some of

---

[20] *Ibid.*, p 230.
[21] A similar error is made by Duvall (1967) and will be discussed in the next section.

the many different probabilities this model requires but the formulation is still in terms of using myopic decision rules which entails the difficulties already discussed. Ozan and Dyckman (1971) eventually derive a reward function similar to that used by Duvall (1967) in a paper discussed in the following section.

In conclusion, attempting to reduce an essentially multi-period problem to a simplified single-period one may produce more difficulties than any potential benefits gained from the simplification. While there are some limitations to the two-state dynamic programming approach, as previously discussed, these still remain under the model with single-period decision rules introduced by Dyckman. Since dynamic programming over a uni-dimensional state space, especially in a two- or three-action space setting, is straightforward and easy to implement, I am skeptical that adopting single-period decision rules will produce a net benefit in situations where the two-state model is a reasonable representation of reality.

7. Continuous State Decision Models with Multiple Observations, Cost of Investigation and Misclassification Included

DUVALL'S MODEL

Duvall (1967) develops an interesting model which allows the state of the system to be the level of controllable costs, a continuous variable. He assumes, as is traditional, that in-control costs are normally distributed with mean μ, equal to standard cost, and variance equal to σ_w^2. An observed deviation away from standard therefore consists of a noncontrollable component, w, (with $w \sim N(0, \sigma_w^2)$) and a controllable component y. The controllable component, y, is also assumed to be normally distributed and statistically independent of the noncontrollable component, w. Duvall develops procedures which allegedly allow the parameters of the distribution of y to be estimated from the observed deviations.

Duvall's reward function from an investigation is a direct function of the continuous variable, y, and I find this an appealing feature of the model. In particular, future savings are assumed to be proportional to the size of the deviation, y. This allows for savings to occur if the deviation is negative, representing the value of resetting standards at lower cost levels. It is intuitively appealing that the savings from an investigation be made a function of the degree of out-of-controlness of the system, and this procedure gets us away from having to impose a simplified discrete state world on an inherently continuous process. There is still a problem as to how to measure the savings from an investigation, since this model does not incorporate the possibility of investigations in the future; e.g., Duvall writes, "Conceptually, it is easy to say that if an investigation revealed that a certain amount could be saved each time period for the life of the project, then the present value of these future savings could be obtained."[22] But this assumes a constrained model in which the current time is the only possible opportunity for an investigation. Nevertheless, there may be circumstances in which this is not an unreasonable assumption.

There are more fundamental problems with Duvall's procedure, however, which raise questions about the validity of his entire procedure. Duvall uses a sequence of 25 observations to compute a sample mean and standard deviation. Just how we know that 25 is the right number of observations to be taken for estimating sample means and standard deviations is never discussed. Nor are we told what to do if some of the early observations indicate an out-of-control situation. Must we still wait until we get the full 25 observations before taking action? These difficulties arise because Duvall has not developed a sequential strategy that, after each observation, compares the value of obtaining additional information with the cost of operating another period at a too high, controllable cost level. But even granting the static nature of the analysis and the heuristic of estimating from an arbitrary number of observations, Duvall's procedure is not even internally consistent. Duvall uses the sample mean and standard deviation of departures from standard, $(\bar{x}, \sigma_x^*)$, computed from these 25 observations to estimate the mean and standard deviation of the distribution of controllable costs, y. Since the mean of noncontrollable costs, w, is assumed to be zero, the mean of y is estimated as the sample mean; i.e., $\mu_y^* = \bar{x}$. Also, with y and w assumed to be statistically independent, the variance of y is estimated from the sample variance as

$$\sigma_y^{*2} = \sigma_x^{*2} - \sigma_w^{*2}$$

where σ_w^{*2} has been previously estimated from an arbitrary period of time during which it was somehow determined that standard conditions prevailed ($y = 0$). This procedure, however, is only valid if the mean, μ_y, of the controllable cost distribution shifted before the first observation was taken. The above procedures treat each observation equally and symmetrically and this can only be done for a stationary process, one in which the parameters do not shift over the course of the observation period. I find this to be an unrealistic assumption. It seems far more likely that a shift in the distribution of y will occur arbitrarily in the interval and it even seems reasonable that multiple jumps could have occurred (recall Barnard's model in Section 4) during the observation period.

After describing the estimation procedure, an inference is done on only the most recent observation, and it is claimed that this inference will enable us to determine whether to investigate or not. While the previous assumption of stationarity might be classified as unrealistic, the procedure of basing an investigation decision on only the most recent observation is obviously inconsistent. For if the process is stationary, then the investi-

---

[22] Duvall (1967): 638.

gation decision should be based on all the observations, not just an isolated one. But if the most recent observation is deemed to be more informative than prior observations, there is a strong presumption of nonstationarity which implies that the procedure to estimate the parameters of the process is incorrect.

Duvall's problems arise because he failed to specify the stochastic process which leads to changes in the distribution of y. As previously noted, when we deal with noisy nonstationary processes it is vital that we identify the source of the nonstationarity before we estimate the parameters of the process. Otherwise we will be unable to separate out the effects of normal fluctuations (noise) from changes in the level of the process.

BATHER'S MODEL

In fact, a model which overcomes the previously described difficulties in Duvall's procedure had already appeared in the statistics literature. Bather (1963) describes a process which, like Duvall's, has a state described by a single continuous variable which represents the performance level of the process. Costs are similarly assumed to be a function of this continuous variable. Let y_t be the unknown performance level of the system at time t (assume that $y_t = 0$ is the state representing no deviation from standard) and let x_t be the observation at time t. As before, we assume that $x_t \sim N(y_t, \sigma^2)$.[23] Bather, however, postulates a process by which the performance level changes from period to period:

$$y_t = y_{t-1} + z_t,$$

where $z_t \sim N(0, \rho^2)$; i.e., the process mean undergoes a random walk without drift over time. Successive changes in the process mean are independent and identically distributed with zero mean and constant standard deviation, ρ. This process is the limit of the Barnard Poisson jump process as the Poisson parameter, λ, goes to infinity to yield a continuous string of infinitesimal changes.

Assume, initially, that the process is reset with some error to the standard level of performance so that $y_0 \sim N(0, v_0)$ where v_0 is the initial level of uncertainty in the current mean of the process. Then, since y_t is the sum of independent normally distributed random variables, $y_t \sim N(u_t, v_t)$, with u_t and v_t to be determined from $(x_1, \cdots, x_t)$, the observed values. The conditional distribution of y_{t+1} given just $(x_1, \cdots, x_t)$ is

$$y_{t+1} \mid (x_1, \cdots, x_t) \sim N(u_t, v_t + \rho^2)$$

and the distribution of x_{t+1} given y_{t+1} is

$$x_{t+1} \mid y_{t+1} \sim N(y_{t+1}, \sigma^2).$$

-----

[23] This notation denotes that x_t is normally distributed with mean y_t and variance σ^2.

Therefore, by Bayes theorem,

$$y_{t+1} \mid (x_1, \cdots, x_{t+1}) \sim N(u_{t+1}, v_{t+1})$$

where

$$\frac{1}{v_{t+1}} = \frac{1}{v_t + \rho^2} + \frac{1}{\sigma^2}$$

and

$$\frac{u_{t+1}}{v_{t+1}} = \frac{u_t}{v_t + \rho^2} + \frac{x_{t+1}}{\sigma^2}.^{24}$$

Since the sequence $v_0, v_1, \cdots, v_t$ is deterministic (not affected by sample outcomes, x_t), u_t by itself is a sufficient statistic for this process. Note that u_t is *not* the sample mean. Even though the process outcomes are normally distributed, the nonstationarity of the process causes the sample mean to be an uninteresting characterization of the process. The posterior variance v_t converges (geometrically) to v, with

$$v = \frac{1}{2} \rho^2 \left[\sqrt{1 + \frac{4\sigma^2}{\rho^2}} - 1 \right]$$

which represents the long-run tracking variance of the process. In effect, it represents a minimal level of uncertainty of the current mean of the process which cannot be reduced even by taking longer sequences of observations. If we make the simplifying and not unreasonable assumption that the process is reset with an uncertainty equal to this tracking variance (i.e., that $v_0 = v$), then we have the convenient result:

$$v_t = v \qquad \text{for all } t$$

and

$$u_t = \frac{v}{v + \rho^2} u_{t-1} + \frac{v}{\sigma^2} x_t.$$

Defining $\gamma = v/(v + \rho^2)$, so that $1 - \gamma = v/\sigma^2$, we have

$$u_t = (1 - \gamma)(x_t + \gamma x_{t-1} + \cdots + \gamma^{t-1} x_1),$$

an exponential moving average of prior observations.

Define $k(y)$ to be the cost of investigation and subsequent repair when the true process mean is y. This is a more general treatment than previous cost investigation papers which assumed this function to be a constant [but see Ross (1971)]. Let $g(y)$ be the cost of continuing to operate, for one period only, when the present state is y. We will assume the following sequence of events for the Bather model: A cost report is received, followed

---

[24] This development is analogous to the Bayesian analysis on the mean of a stationary normal process; see DeGroot (1970): 167. A more detailed derivation appears in the Appendix.

by an immediate decision whether to investigate the process or allow it to operate for another period. If the process is investigated, it is assumed that the process can always be reset back to the desired initial state in which $y_0 \sim N(0, v)$. Thus the previously mentioned difficulties of modeling situations for which it is impossible to reset the standard back to the desired level and for which it is possible to reset the standard to a lower cost level for the future are still not captured by the Bather model.

If u is the best estimate of the current mean of the process, the expected investigation cost is

$$K(u) \equiv \int k(y) f_N(y \mid u, v) \, dy$$

where $f_N(\cdot \mid u, v)$ is the density function of a normally distributed random variable with mean u and variance v. The expected one-period cost of operating when the best estimate of the current mean of the process is u will be denoted $G(u)$ with

$$G(u) \equiv \int g(y) \, f_N(y \mid u, v) \, dy.$$

The only remaining term needed for the dynamic programming equation is the prediction of the next period's state variable given the current period's state variable. We know that

$$u_{t+1} = \gamma u_t + (1 - \gamma) x_{t+1}$$

and we can write x_{t+1} as

$$x_{t+1} = y_t + (y_{t+1} - y_t) + (x_{t+1} - y_{t+1}).$$

Each of the three terms on the right is, by assumption, normally and independently distributed with means and variances given, respectively, by: (u_t, v); $(0, \rho^2)$; and $(0, \sigma^2)$. Therefore $x_{t+1} \sim N(u_t, v + \rho^2 + \sigma^2)$ and

$$E(u_{t+1} \mid u_t) = u_t.$$

Also,

$$\begin{aligned} \mathrm{Var}\,(u_{t+1} \mid u_t) &= (1 - \gamma)^2 \, \mathrm{Var}\,(x_{t+1}) \\ &= (1 - \gamma)^2 (v + \rho^2 + \sigma^2) \\ &= \rho^2 \end{aligned}$$

where the last equality follows from the definition of γ.[25] We therefore

---

[25] Since $1 - \gamma = \dfrac{v}{\sigma^2} = \dfrac{\rho^2}{v + \rho^2}$, we have that

$$\begin{aligned} (1 - \gamma)^2 \, (v + \rho^2 + \sigma^2) &= \frac{v}{\sigma^2} \frac{\rho^2}{v + \rho^2} (v + \rho^2 + \sigma^2) \\ &= v\rho^2 \left[\frac{1}{\sigma^2} + \frac{1}{v + \rho^2} \right] \\ &= \rho^2[(1 - \gamma) + \gamma] \\ &= \rho^2. \end{aligned}$$

have that

$$u_{t+1} = u_t + z \quad \text{with} \quad z \sim N(0, \rho^2).$$

While Bather computes optimal policies to minimize expected (undiscounted) costs per unit time I will reformulate the problem to minimize total expected discounted costs in the future. For convenience in notation, I assume an infinite horizon problem with a discount factor, α, less than one. Some mild regularity conditions on the cost functions $k(\cdot)$ and $c(\cdot)$ will ensure the geometric convergence of the finite period optimality functions to a unique steady state minimum expected cost function, $C(u)$. We can write $C(u)$ as

$$C(u) = \min \{K(u) + C(0); G(u) + \alpha E[C(u + z)]\}.$$

The first term in the minimization is the expected investigation cost, $K(u)$, and the effect of immediately resetting the process to its desired mean, 0. The second term consists of the expected costs of operating for one period at the current level plus the discounted expected future costs, one period in the future. The expectation of this latter term is taken with respect to the random variable z defined above ($z \sim N(0, \rho^2)$). Of course, the actual state variable, u', for the next period will become known after the next period's cost report, x, is received:

$$u' = \gamma u + (1 - \gamma)x.$$

The solution to the above functional equation can be easily obtained by taking the limit of the optimal policies of the finite horizon optimality equation:

$$C_n(u) = \min \{K(u) + C_n(0); G(u) + \alpha E[C_{n-1}(u + z)]\}.$$

The preceding formulation could represent only the starting point for more elaborate models. Additional features such as adding a third action alternative of an exploratory investigation could be included as we have already discussed. Also, if one wanted to assume a gradual increase in controllable costs over time, the distribution of z could have a small positive mean. In a private communication, Dyckman has suggested the possibility that y_t be modeled as a mean reverting process, rather than a random walk, due to corrective actions undertaken by subordinates. A particularly interesting possibility to pursue would involve attempting to model the reduction in future cost due to investigating a process whose mean has drifted below the previously set standard. If such a procedure could be developed, we might similarly be able to model those situations for which a higher current level of costs would become the new standard because of our inability to reset the process back to its original standard. These extensions represent opportunities for further research. Carter

(1972) has already extended Bather's model to allow for assignable causes to occur at exponentially distributed inter-arrival times rather than continuously.

8. *Summary and Conclusions*

This paper has surveyed papers in the accounting, statistics and management science literature dealing with the significance and investigation of realizations from a process which deviate from preset standards. A simple 2 x 2 classification scheme was developed which distinguished (i) models using only the most recent observation for decisions from those that used all observations since the last action time, and (ii) models which were mainly concerned with estimation or hypothesis testing from those whose actions were imbedded in a decision model which attempted to assess the costs and benefits from alternative actions. A number of questions were raised with respect to some models that have been proposed for the accounting cost variance decision and, it is hoped that, at the very least, the key assumptions and limitations behind all these models have been identified.

To gain some closure on this issue, suppose a hypothetical situation in which I must design a system that would track cost variances. Given the large number of alternative models surveyed in this paper and their limitations and assumptions, which would I choose to implement in a real-life ongoing situation? My short-range solution would probably be to install a cusum chart to track the accounting variances. This procedure is already widely used in quality control and would likely be reasonably robust with respect to the causes of nonstationary behavior. Initially, I would set the parameters of the cusum chart using prior data from the processes to establish the right tradeoff between false alarms and failures to detect changes quickly. With more time, I would try to estimate the cost and benefits from an investigation and use these to design "economic optimal" cusum charts [Taylor (1968), Goel and Wu (1973)]. In the long run, I would attempt to develop a continuous state model (e.g., along the lines of Bather) by attempting to directly model the source of nonstationary behavior and build this into the decision model.

My bias therefore is to first implement a procedure that systematically and sensibly processes the current data with all prior observations (i.e., the cusum chart). With this as a benchmark, I would then attempt to develop models that are closer to being "right" from a cost-benefit analysis. As more experience and data develop from such a process, I would then feel more comfortable about directly modeling the underlying stochastic process and implementing procedures which are optimal for that particular stochastic process. For the present, our most pressing need is for empirical research to uncover a set of plausible stochastic processes to describe the accounting cost variance environment.

APPENDIX

Derivation of Sufficient Statistics (u_t, v_t) in Bather's Model

Assume that $y_t \mid x_t \sim N(u_t, v_t)$, with u_t, v_t to be determined from $x_t = (x_1, x_2, \cdots, x_t)$. Since $y_{t+1} = y_t + z_{t+1}$ with $z_t \sim N(0, \rho^2)$ and with y_t and z_{t+1} independently distributed, we have that

$$y_{t+1} \mid x_t \sim N(u_t, v_t + \rho^2).$$

Also, $x_{t+1} \mid y_{t+1} \sim N(y_{t+1}, \sigma^2)$ by definition. Therefore, the likelihood function for y_{t+1} given $(x_1, x_2, \cdots, x_{t+1}) \equiv x_{t+1}$ (denoted by $\Lambda(y_{t+1} \mid x_{t+1})$) can be written (using the rule of conditional probability and Bayes Theorem) as

$$\Lambda(y_{t+1} \mid x_{t+1}) = k_1 \Lambda(y_{t+1}, x_{t+1} \mid x_t)$$

$$= k_2 \Lambda(x_{t+1} \mid y_{t+1}) \Lambda(y_{t+1} \mid x_t)$$

(where k_1 and k_2 are known constants). We write the two likelihood functions on the right-hand side of the above equation as:

$$\exp -\frac{1}{2}\left[\frac{1}{\sigma^2}(x_{t+1} - y_{t+1})^2\right] \exp -\frac{1}{2}\left[\frac{1}{v_t + \rho^2}(y_{t+1} - u_t)^2\right]$$

$$= \exp -\frac{1}{2}\frac{1}{\sigma^2(v_t + \rho^2)}\left[(v_t + \rho^2)(x_{t+1} - y_{t+1})^2 + \sigma^2(y_{t+1} - u_t)^2\right]$$

$$= \exp -\frac{1}{2}\left[\frac{1}{\sigma^2} + \frac{1}{v_t + \rho^2}\right]\left[y_{t+1} - \frac{(v_t + \rho^2)x_{t+1} + \sigma^2 u_t}{v_t + \rho^2 + \sigma^2}\right]^2 + k_3$$

where the last expression is obtained by completing the square and rearranging terms, and k_3 is a complicated expression involving terms such as v_t, ρ, x_{t+1}, etc., but *not* y_{t+1}.

Therefore if we identify u_{t+1} as

$$u_{t+1} = \frac{(v_t + \rho^2)x_{t+1} + \sigma^2 u_t}{v_t + \rho^2 + \sigma^2} \quad \text{and} \quad \frac{1}{v_{t+1}} = \frac{1}{\sigma^2} + \frac{1}{v_t + \rho^2}$$

we may write

$$\Lambda(y_{t+1} \mid x_{t+1}) = k_4 \exp -\frac{1}{2}\left[\frac{1}{v_{t+1}}(y_{t+1} - u_{t+1})^2\right]$$

so that $y_{t+1} \mid x_{t+1} \sim N(u_{t+1}, v_{t+1})$ with u_{t+1} and v_{t+1} defined above. Thus, the posterior distribution of y_{t+1} conditional on the previous realizations $(x_1, x_2, \cdots, x_{t+1})$ is a normal distribution with mean u_{t+1} and variance v_{t+1}.

REFERENCES

ANTHONY, R. N. "Some Fruitful Directions for Research in Management Accounting." In N. Dopuch and L. Revsine (Eds.), *Accounting Research 1960–1970: A Critical Evaluation* (Center for International Education and Research in Accounting: University of Illinois), 1973.

BARNARD, G. A. "Control Charts and Stochastic Processes." *Journal of the Royal Statistical Society, Series B* XXI (1959): 239–57.

BATHER, G. A. "Control Charts and the Minimization of Costs." *Journal of the Royal Statistical Society, Series B* XXV (1963): 49–70.

BIERMAN, H. AND T. DYCKMAN. *Managerial Cost Accounting* (New York: Macmillan). 1971.

——, L. E. FOURAKER, AND R. K. JAEDICKE. "A Use of Probability and Statistics in Performance Evaluation." *The Accounting Review* XXXVI (July 1961): 409–17.

BUZBY, S. L. "Extending the Applicability of Probabilistic Management Planning and Control Systems." *The Accounting Review* XLIX (January 1974): 42–49.

CARTER, P. "A Bayesian Approach to Quality Control." *Management Science* XVIII (July 1972): 647–55.

CHERNOFF, H. AND S. ZACKS. "Estimating the Current Mean of a Normal Distribution Which Is Subjected to Changes in Time." *Annals of Math. Statistics* XXXV (December 1964): 999–1018.

DEGROOT, M. H. *Optimal Statistical Decisions* (New York: McGraw-Hill), 1970.

DEMSKI, J. "An Accounting System Structured on a Linear Programming Model." *The Accounting Review* XLII (October 1967): 701–12.

——. "Optimizing the Search for Cost Deviation Sources." *Management Science* (April 1970): 486–94.

DOPUCH, N., J. G. BIRNBERG, AND J. DEMSKI. "An Extension of Standard Cost Variance Analysis." *The Accounting Review* XLII (July 1967): 526–36.

DUNCAN, A. "The Economic Design of $\bar{x}$ Charts Used to Maintain Current Control of a Process." *Journal of the American Statistical Association* LI (June 1956): 228–42.

DUVALL, R. M. "Rules for Investigating Cost Variances." *Management Science* XIII (June 1967): 631–41.

DYCKMAN, T. R. "The Investigation of Cost Variances." *Journal of Accounting Research*, Vol. 7 (1969): 215–44.

EDWARDS, W. "Conservatism in Human Information Processing." *Formal Representation of Human Judgment*, B. Kleinmuntz, Ed. (New York: Wiley), 1968.

EWAN, W. D. AND K. W. KEMP. "Sampling Inspection of Continuous Processes with No Autocorrelation Between Successive Results." *Biometrika* XLVII (1960): 363–80.

FARLEY, J. AND M. HINICH. "Detecting 'Small' Mean Shifts in Time Series." *Management Science* XVII (November 1970): 189–99.

GIBRA, I. N. "Economically Optimal Determination of the Parameters of $\bar{X}$-Control Charts." *Management Science* XVII (May 1971): 635–46.

GIRSHICK, M. A. AND H. RUBIN. "A Bayes Approach to a Quality Control Model." *Annals of Math. Statistics* XXIII (1952): 114–25.

GOEL, A. L., S. C. JAIN AND S. M. WU. "An Algorithm for the Determination of the Economic Design of $\bar{X}$-Charts Based on Duncan's Model." *Journal of the American Statistical Association* LXIII (1968).

—— AND S. M. WU. "Economically Optimum Design of Cusum Charts." *Management Science* XIX (July 1973): 1271–82.

GOLDSMITH, P. L. AND H. WHITFIELD. "Average Run Lengths in Cumulative Chart Quality Control Schemes." *Technometrics* III (February 1961): 11–20.

HINICH, M. AND J. FARLEY. "Theory and Application of an Estimation Model for Time Series with Nonstationary Means." *Management Science* XII (May 1966): 648–58.

JUERS, D. A. "Statistical Significance of Accounting Variances." *Management Accounting* XLIX (October 1967): 20–25.

KADANE, J. "Optimal Whereabouts Search." *Operations Research* XIX (July–August 1971): 894–904.

KAPLAN, R. S. "Optimal Investigation Strategies with Imperfect Information." *Journal of Accounting Research*, Vol. 7 (1969): 32–43.

KOEHLER, R. W. "The Relevance of Probability Statistics to Accounting Variance Control." *Management Accounting* L (October 1968): 35–41.

LEV, B. "An Information Theory Analysis of Budget Variances." *The Accounting Review* XLIV (October 1969): 704–10.

LI, Y. "A Note on 'The Investigation of Cost Variances'." *Journal of Accounting Research*, Vol. 8 (1970): 282–83.

LUH, F. "Controlled Cost: An Operational Concept and Statistical Approach to Standard Costing." *The Accounting Review* XLIII (January 1968): 123–32.

OZAN, T. AND T. DYCKMAN. "A Normative Model for Investigation Decisions Involving Multi-Origin Cost Variances." *Journal of Accounting Research*, Vol. 9 (1971): 88–115.

PAGE, E. S. "Continuous Inspection Schemes." *Biometrika* XLI (1954): 100–15.

PROBST, F. R. "Probabilistic Cost Controls: A Behavioral Dimension." *The Accounting Review* XLVI (January 1971): 113–18.

RONEN, J. "Nonaggregation Versus Disaggregation of Variances." *The Accounting Review* XLIX (January 1974): 50–60.

ROSS, S. "Quality Control Under Markov Deterioration." *Management Science* XVII (May 1971): 587–96.

SHEWHART, W. A. *The Economic Control of the Quality of Manufactured Profit* (New York: Macmillan), 1931.

SLOVIC, P. AND S. LICHTENSTEIN. "Comparison of Bayesian and Regression Approaches to the Study of Information Processing in Judgment." *Organizational Behavior and Human Performance* VI (November 1971): 649–744.

TAYLOR, H. M. "The Economic Design of Cumulative Sum Control Charts for Variables." *Technometrics* X (August 1968): 479–88.

ZANNETOS, Z. A. "Standard Cost as a First Step to Probabilistic Control: A Theoretical Justification, An Extension and Implications." *The Accounting Review* XXXIX (April 1964): 296–304.

INDEX

About the Author

AHMED RIAHI-BELKAOUI is Professor of Accounting at the College of Business Administration, The University of Illinois at Chicago, and Chairman of the Cultural Studies and Accounting Research Committee, American Accounting Association (Internal Accounting Section). Riahi-Belkaoui is also a member of the editorial board of several professional journals and is the author of 23 previous Quorum books and co-author of 3 more.